THE PHILOSOPHIC MIND

THE

PHILOSOPHIC MIND

A STUDY OF WORDSWORTH'S

POETRY AND THOUGHT

1797–1805

BY ALAN GROB

OHIO STATE UNIVERSITY PRESS : COLUMBUS

Library of Congress Cataloging in Publication Data
Grob, Alan.
The philosophic mind.
1. Wordsworth, William, 1770–1850—Philosophy.
I. Title
PR5892.P5G7 1973   821.'7   72-13783
ISBN 0-8142-0178-4

Manufactured in the United States of America

TO SHIRLEY

Contents

Preface

Most of the interests and allegiances expressed in the following chapters derive from the writings of those we may justly speak of as "the Wordsworthians," borrowing that celebrated term of Arnold's to describe those students and critics of Wordsworth who, whatever their differences, share a common philosophic orientation and a common faith in the pertinence of that orientation to the poet. What Arnold intended as both an admonition and a warning to Wordsworthians of his own time has fortunately gone largely unheeded by the Wordsworthians of ours, so that through the investigations of Arthur Beatty, Melvin Rader, R. D. Havens, Newton Stallknecht, W. H. Piper, and others who have brought to the poetry an explicitly philosophic point of view, we have learned how well Wordsworth merited the claims made for him as philosophic poet by Wordsworthians of the nineteenth century from Coleridge to Leslie Stephen. More important, from our recent scholarship, we have also learned that we need not bind ourselves to Arnold's choice: neither the poetry nor the philosophy are in themselves the reality or the illusion; rather, the two are so interwoven, so mutually dependent, that they stand or fall together as a single vision, poetic and philosophical, whose elements are ultimately inseparable.

In writing an avowedly philosophic study of Wordsworth,

I have had as my primary aim accommodation rather than innovation, the reconciliation of competing critical-philosophical approaches already enunciated rather than their supplanting by some alternative interpretative premises. In large measure, this is because the Wordsworthians, though having done much to demonstrate the originality and depth of Wordsworth's philosophy, have been less successful in proving its coherence and consistency. The rival claims of empiricism and transcendentalism, first set forth in detail almost fifty years ago by Arthur Beatty and Melvin Rader, each apparently possessing its own kind of plausibility and yet each ultimately excluding the other, have produced an impasse in Wordsworth studies beyond which, as often as we have tried, we have never seemed able to advance. Having assumed the apparent necessity of choice, we find that selecting one philosophic alternative inevitably precludes giving the other what we sense to be its due emphasis, so that even as resourceful and formidable a critic as Geoffrey Hartman, by asserting the primacy of mind for Wordsworth, leaves us troubled in our final assessment of Wordsworth as a poet of largely unfulfilled intentions, celebrating nature in poems and passages that are in actuality, according to Hartman, records of defeated yearnings for apocalypse, the thwarting of consciousness in its aspirations. The continuing question of empiricism or transcendentalism, nature or consciousness, is the major concern of the present study too, but hopefully the chronological approach to the poetry adopted here will show that we need not view these two rival philosophies as evidence of confusion or contradiction but as elements in an unfolding pattern of intellectual change in which each competing system serves as the basis of a relatively self-contained and independent phase.

If I have given more attention than is customary in recent years to Wordsworth's empiricism, perhaps it is because the direction of my scholarship was set some fifteen years ago at the University of Wisconsin where the study of Wordsworth's thought had its modern beginnings in the seminal work of Professor Arthur Beatty, to whose valuable notes and papers I was given access while a graduate student there. But my deepest obligations are to the Wordsworthians who succeeded Professor Beatty at Wisconsin, my own teachers, Carl Woodring, generous with both learning and counsel, and Alvin Whitley, who, as adviser, guided me through my earliest attempt at a full-scale interpretation of Wordsworth's poetry and thought, the basis for much in the present study.

My debts to other Wordsworthians are far too many to enumerate in full, but some cannot be omitted. Like all students of Wordsworth, I owe so much to the great editorial labors of Ernest de Selincourt and Helen Darbishire that it seems almost superfluous to acknowledge that all quotations from the poetry of Wordsworth are from *The Poetical Works of William Wordsworth,* ed. Ernest de Selincourt and Helen Darbishire, 5 vols. (Oxford, 1940–49, Vol. II, 2nd ed. 1952), cited as *PW,* and from *The Prelude,* ed. Ernest de Selincourt, 2nd ed. rev. by Helen Darbishire (Oxford, 1959). Because my argument deals almost exclusively with the poetry written between 1797 and 1805 and with the changes that occur within that period I have used the 1805 text throughout except where reference to the 1850 text is specifically noted. I have made extensive use of the wealth of manuscript information in the de Selincourt and Darbishire editions and have conformed to their practices in identifying manuscript material. Michael Jaye, whose unpublished New York University dissertation, "The Growth of a Poem," a study and edition of the early versions of *The Prelude,* proved to be a valuable supplement to the work of de Selincourt and Darbishire, kindly answered a number of textual queries I had and later, at Grasmere, guided me through the intricacies of the manuscripts of *The Prelude.*

A shorter version of chapter two was read at the Rydal

Mount Summer School, where I benefited from conversations with Russell Noyes and Marilyn Gaul, and from the attentions of the kindest of hosts, Richard Wordsworth.

I also wish to thank the following journals for granting me permission to reprint materials that first appeared in their pages: *JEGP* for "Wordsworth's *Nutting*" (1962), now a portion of chapter four; *Studies in Romanticism* for "Wordsworth and Godwin: A Reassessment" (1967), a part of which appears in chapter five; and *ELH* for those sections of chapters six and seven that were published in that journal as "Process and Permanence in *Resolution and Independence*" (1961) and "Wordsworth's *Immortality Ode* and the Quest for Identity" (1965). To my colleagues at Rice University, Will Dowden, Walter Isle, and David Minter, I owe many obligations of many different kinds. To Jack Ward, I must express my thanks with special pleasure. My final and foremost acknowledgement is to my wife, to whom this book is lovingly dedicated.

THE PHILOSOPHIC MIND

Introduction

In the half century since Professor Arthur Beatty declared Wordsworth to be an associationist in the tradition of David Hartley and thereby initiated an intensive and truly systematic study of Wordsworth's thought, one repeated motive to such study has been the continuing desire to affix labels, whether Professor Beatty's or some other, and to identify the single tradition or theory or belief underlying the major poetry. Not all of those who have written on Wordsworth's thought, but certainly most of them, have concerned themselves with unity rather than with variety, seeking to delineate for us, from whatever special perspective may have been chosen, the figure of the one Wordsworth, a poet faithful to his deepest beliefs, perhaps not for the whole of his long career, but certainly during the major portion of its most satisfying decade. Such singleness of purpose has not been maintained, however, without frequent displays of critical uncertainty and discomfort. For we know that poems as familiar to us as *Tintern Abbey* and the *Immortality Ode, My heart leaps up* and *Ode to Duty,* seem to express very different philosophic orientations, to rest upon very different philosophic premises, and to arrive at correspondingly different philosophic conclusions. The apparent presence of differences so pronounced is not often or easily denied openly, but given the unitary intentions that have dominated the criticism of Wordsworth, we find that points of philosophic divergence within the poetry are invariably minimized, elements of conflict and even instances of contradiction being either ignored completely or else admitted into discussion as material that can be somehow subsumed by the larger controlling generalization. But, where conflict and contradiction are minimized for the sake of unity, they invariably emerge in some other form, most often at the level of generalization itself. Unsurprisingly, then, each of the several philosophic positions that the poetry seems to suggest has, at one time or another, been put forward as the distinguishing attribute that identifies the one Wordsworth, the unifying conception that supplies the habits, attitudes, and dogmas of the major poetry. As a consequence, criticism's course has been marked less by cumulative progress than by dialectical swings, each representation produced for us of the one Wordsworth having somewhere its antithesis, the contrasting figure of contrasting traits—the strict empiricist and the transcendental visionary; the announced lover and champion of man and his covert adversary temperamentally hostile to all significant human enterprise; the priest of harmony between man and a divinized nature and the prophet of an apocalyptic fulfillment that banishes nature entirely so that imagination may achieve finally a wholly autonomous condition of being. It would be naïve to assume that such irreconcilable critical disagreement about the character of the one Wordsworth is in itself sufficient to refute the notion that such a unitary conception may be true, for any one theory or set of theories may be correct and the others mistaken; or even if all of the theories thus far propounded can be proven to be in error, the truth may, nonetheless, reside in some generalization as yet unannounced or undiscovered. But it would be no less naïve to neglect altogether the possibility that critical controversy, so deep and so persistent, may have its basis in intellectual differences and divisions within the poetry itself.

It is from this second possibility that the present study proceeds, its working hypothesis being that the philosophic disagreements within the poetry indicate not confusion but change—change, moreover, that can be observed to occur within a relatively orderly and fixed chronological pattern. The golden decade (a convenient fiction, here as elsewhere, for those years that in a more exact reckoning would cover the period from 1797 to 1805) is taken to be not an event but a process, a span of time distinguished more by the sustained level of excellence that Wordsworth achieves during these years than by any constant adherence to some single belief or set of beliefs. To insist that due recognition be given to the dynamics of his career, recognizing that the beliefs of 1802 are not those of 1798 and that those of 1804 depart even further from those held in earlier years, is not to slight, however, traditional claims for Wordsworth's philosophic seriousness or his philosophic accomplishments; nor must we deny that there is a uniquely distinctive Wordsworthian philosophy, speculatively bold, coherent, and original. Indeed, in the pages that follow, system is to receive as much attention as change; the metaphysics, epistemology, and ethics of a specifically Wordsworthian scheme will be delineated as fully as the intellectual processes by which it was relinquished. What the argument of the present study does seek to establish, and where it differs from most other accounts of Wordsworth's thought, is that, without minimizing the scope or power of that philosophy or the success with which he employed it for poetic ends, it must be recognized as a comparatively localized phenomenon, its tenets maintained only briefly, even when measured solely by the chronology of the golden decade. Only in the years between 1797 and 1800 do we find that philosophy firmly held and consistently elaborated, a period that includes the first two books of *The Prelude, The Ruined Cottage, Home at Grasmere,* and *Lyrical Ballads* of 1798 and 1800: a body of poetry whose considerable achievement is made possible by the special philosophic vision that informs it. But if that vision did give rise to the remarkable accomplishments of the years between 1797 and 1800, there still remains another group of poems of comparable significance and achievement: the splendid lyrics of the spring of 1802, such major meditations as *Resolution and Independence* and the *Immortality Ode,* and, most important, almost all of *The Prelude's* last twelve books—a body of work that, if the present chronology is valid, is not to be explained by those prior conceptions that philosophically served as the initiating impulse to the poetry of the golden decade.

The chapters that follow attempt to deal with system and change by approaching Wordsworth's career, or at least that portion of it treated here, as a sequence of stages, each possessing a separate and identifiable philosophic character and each falling within reasonably well-defined chronological boundaries. If the years from 1797 to 1800 receive a seemingly disproportionate share of attention, five of seven chapters being devoted to this first stage, whatever justification such organization requires rests not upon some assumed aesthetic superiority of the poetry of these years but upon the systematic comprehensiveness which that poetry exhibits and the greater philosophic complexity and creativity that such comprehensiveness allows. Building upon the foundations of an empirical tradition, Wordsworth develops a conceptual design authentically his own, one that in its metaphysical and epistemological assertions goes well beyond the restrictive limits set by those writers who had been most influential in formulating that tradition. To be sure, Wordsworth begins with the fundamental Lockian premise that knowledge originates largely in sense-experience, in the effects of external and material objects working through the senses to register upon the passive and receptive tablet of the mind. But to the essential materiality of the external world, Wordsworth adds moral and spiritual attributes and moral and spiritual purposes inadmissible by the criteria of a more orthodox empiricism; and transmitted to the mind in the same way as all other sense-phenomena, these special qualities of the objective world, working slowly and cumulatively, must induce in man modes of thought and habits of action that are equivalent in character—insofar as the mind and the world may possess such characteristics in common—with the external agency that fostered them. From the effects of the external world (endowed with the additional properties Wordsworth attributes to it) upon the mind, he formulates a concept of development, the moral and spiritual formation of man by a morally and spiritually determining environment, that serves as the shaping principle of the autobiographic and semiautobiographic poetry of this first phase. This concept of development not only explains Wordsworth's own personal history, recounted in these years as a chronicle of progress from the morally self-centered concerns of childhood to the pure and lofty benevolence of his present maturity, but also justifies the deep impulse in the poetry of these years to social prophecy that expresses itself in Wordsworth's confident prediction that mankind in general, by submitting itself to these same environmental influences, must on this larger social scale reenact the poet's own exemplary history and move, like him, from selfishness to virtue. Utopian and pragmatic, the poetry written between 1797 and 1800 bases its faith in the eventual transformation that can and will take place in the community of man upon the concrete and personal illustration, Wordsworth's sensed conviction of his own attainments, not as a poet but as a man, his consciousness of having had moral endowments bestowed upon him by nature as part of its larger purpose of bringing man into conformity with nature's ends.

Whatever the reasons for change, whether the inward assurances of personal moral progress that had substantiated his general philosophic argument were no longer forthcoming or whether that argument itself, in its systematic entirety, was no longer deemed an adequate or accurate explanation of the workings of nature or of the behavior of man, it is evident that from 1802 onward Wordsworth was to reject virtually every important detail in this first and fullest exposition of philosophic belief. The attribution of overtly ethical intentions to the external world, the empirical premise that the self is essentially compounded from its sensory experience, and the developmental hypothesis that is the logical corollary of the two preceding propositions are concepts that were central to Wordsworth's formulation of his poetic world between 1797 and 1800: at this later time they are subjected to a new and unsympathetic critical scrutiny and are either silently discarded or expressly repudiated. But the poetry that Wordsworth writes in the years of change that begin in 1802 is considerably more than a record of his quarrels with earlier beliefs; there is also a staking out of new positions, the development of a set of alternative philosophic proposals that, if less fully detailed and perhaps less deeply held, attempt, nonetheless, to explain the self and the world as he at these later times perceived them.

The poetry of the spring of 1802, a season of remarkable lyric activity by Wordsworth, provides us with the first of these alternative proposals, a philosophic argument that, from the larger perspective of the years from 1797 to 1805, may be considered essentially transitional, setting the poetry of 1802 apart as a kind of middle phase. The order of nature still provides the ontological basis for philosophic explanation, but within that order relations between the self and the external world and between man's past and present being have been drastically revised. The self, granted far greater autonomy in this new Wordsworthian presentation of it, still acts in conjunction with nature, with man's most satisfying moments based now upon his responses to the stimuli of external events, the appearance of a rainbow or the song of the cuckoo; but nowhere in the lyrics of 1802 is there any suggestion that the external world has actually determined the character of the self that responds to it. And in the poetry of 1802, the personal goals that Wordsworth establishes for himself are for the first time unreservedly regressive. No longer is self-judgment determined by the developmental criteria applied between 1797 and 1800, the ways in which he has outgrown the self-interested passions of his childhood waywardness for a later moral maturity. In 1802 Wordsworth's characterization of childhood is drastically revised; its passions are perceived now as possessing an intrinsic value and providing an ultimate source of spiritual and, perhaps, even moral authority for the conduct of the whole of life. Recollection, thus, becomes a means not of measuring growth but of seeking continuity, since it is upon the power to preserve contact with his earliest past and to renew the emotions he had known in childhood's most intensely felt moments that the adult Wordsworth now believes his happiness and well-being to depend.

Compared to the work that comes before and that which comes after it, the poetry of this middle phase appears troubled and uncertain, with Wordsworth deeply divided in his expectations of maintaining the contact with the past so essential to his present happiness, and nature itself, represented in the spring of 1802 largely by its most evanescent particulars, seems no longer sufficiently stable to serve as the foundation for any of the poet's larger human hopes. With *Resolution and Independence* and, to a larger degree, the *Immortality Ode* supplying important transitional arguments, Wordsworth in 1804 turns away from the philosophic naturalism that had fixed both faith and doctrine until this time and enters a new phase based mainly upon metaphysical and epistemological principles of transcendence. The autonomy of the self that the lyrics of 1802 had suggested becomes in 1804 simply an expression of man's essential separateness from nature. The self is now seen to be determined by other forces, its character derived from that transcendent realm in which before birth the self originated and to which after death it will return and with which, even during this period of apparent removal from transcendence it still retains vital connections, the self's continuing contact with the transcendent informing all other significant knowledge acquired and all other significant action undertaken during the course of our natural existence. For the purposes of our present study, we need only consider the implications that this thoroughgoing shift to transcendence has for the third and final phase of the period between 1797 and 1805, and these are clearly immediate and far-reaching; but when we look upon Wordsworth's career in its entirety, we find that adoption of this transcendental principle has even more extensive effects. Readily assimilated into the tenets of orthodox Christianity, the concept of transcendence employed in 1804 becomes the philosophic vehicle by which Wordsworth passes from an essentially secular apprehension of man and the world to that conventionally religious interpretation of them that determines his poetry and thought during that long remainder of his career following the golden decade.

However convenient and useful the chronological divisions set forth here may be, at some points they may seem inexact or confusing. For example, the great lyrics written at Goslar, the "Matthew" poems and the "Lucy" poems, strongly indicate that even in the earliest phase, those years when Wordsworth spoke most confidently of the Utopian possibilities held out to man by nature, his optimism was tempered by at least momentary misgivings, recognition that there are areas of human experience, vital to our individual happiness, in which man is invariably beset by difficulties and sorrows for which nature could furnish no comforts and surely no solution. Furthermore, because major sections of *The Prelude* are composed at widely separated intervals, that poem, the longest single work of the period under discussion, must necessarily pose problems for any such chronological interpretation as this. With much of it written before 1798 and 1800 and still more written during 1804 and 1805, there seems to me little question that *The Prelude,* considered as a single work, exhibits any number of inner contradictions reflecting clearly those philosophic differences that set these phases apart. Yet a simple aesthetic necessity dictates that there be some overlapping of earlier beliefs into later sections of the poem: those original philosophic intentions that provided motive for, and lent shape to, Wordsworth's plan for an extended poetic autobiography and that, moreover, gave substance to those parts of it written between 1798 and 1800 could not be altogether dispensed with in 1804, except at the prohibitively high price of divesting *The Prelude* of any form of intellectual unity whatsoever. As a consequence, although some of the philosophic assumptions of the first phase are challenged, others do carry over as reiterated argument in sections of the poem written much later, and particularly in that part of it specifically designated as retrospective summary.

Important as these exceptions are, they should not obscure for us the general consistency with which the chronological pattern is maintained and the way in which Wordsworth's work, through that pattern, illustrates both system and change. For it is by our recognizing both of these tendencies in Wordsworth that he is most truthfully revealed to us as a poet whose powerful metaphysical impulse—the distinctly modern need to construct from one's own essentially secularized experience a complete, coherent, and, if possible, spiritually satisfying interpretation of the reality in which man now finds himself—is matched by the strength and energy of the critical temper, a countervailing openness to all of life's data that allows no system, either sacred or secular, to go un-challenged in its claims to render faithfully the meaning of our existence. And through the success of his poetry in expressing both system and change, the metaphysical impulse and the critical temper, Wordsworth provides us with an especially instructive instance (one potentially far more useful to us than the example of final failure with which too often we find ourselves morbidly obsessed) of the poet for our time, of his power and his predicament as these have emerged since his entrance at the beginning of the nineteenth century into the spiritual conditions of the modern world.

1

The Empirical Phase:
Tintern Abbey

Of the poems of the initial phase, none seems more truly paradigmatic than *Tintern Abbey*. In its presentation of mind and nature and the interaction between them, *Tintern Abbey* details what, in one sense or another, are the views of almost every work of substance written between 1797 and 1800. It is not a transitional episode as the later meditations, *Resolution and Independence* and the *Immortality Ode,* are: there are no abrupt shifts in mood or feeling, no unexpected challenges that test and then nullify an assured faith, no dramatic reversals that within the course of the poem carry the mind's allegiance from one set of metaphysical suppositions to another. Wordsworth organizes *Tintern Abbey*'s structure not by a play of dialectic but by elaboration of the hidden premises contained in its opening presentation of landscape.[1] His method is essentially one of expansion, widening the concerns to which he applies these premises and at the same time preserving the logic of their internal relation, so that the poem possesses a speculative range and logical coherence that we might expect to find only in a much longer poem of sustained philosophic exposition.

In effect, *Tintern Abbey* exemplifies—with an orderliness comparatively rare in Wordsworth—what Earl Wasserman has so well described as the fundamental task of the poet since the end of the eighteenth century: the need to "conceive his own structure of order, his own more-than-linguistic syntax, and so to engage that structure that the poetic act is creative both of a cosmic system and of the poem made possible by that system." [2] As a vehicle for symbolic discourse, the landscape of *Tintern Abbey* possesses a latent multiplicity of reference so that almost every ethical, epistemological, and metaphysical judgment rendered later in the poem seems latent in its initial image. Through a careful, compositional grouping of the elements around that point of juncture at which "these steep and lofty cliffs . . . connect / The landscape with the quiet of the sky" (5–8), Wordsworth defines the most important properties of that ultimate reality which underlies and informs the visual scene. These properties are, as critics have frequently noted,[3] a deep and abiding calm and a coalescence of particulars into a single, interlocking and indivisible pattern of harmony. But the qualities of harmony and calm that supply the key to nature's inner being function within the poem not only as metaphysically descriptive but as ethically normative as well. For the idealized prospect that Wordsworth observes—though initially defined in terms of nature's larger and more impersonal scenic effects—is quickly shown to include within it products of human agency that unite readily into an almost uniform composition, harmonious and silent, with their purely natural surroundings. What he sees amidst "a wild secluded scene" are

> These plots of cottage-ground, these orchard-tufts,
> Which at this season, with their unripe fruits,
> Are clad in one green hue, and lose themselves
> 'Mid groves and copses.

> (11–14)

And the hedge-rows, another instance of human cultivation, seem to the eye of Wordsworth equally indistinguishable from the nonhuman aspects of the setting—"hardly hedge-rows, little lines / Of sportive wood run wild" (15–16). Indeed, to a surprising degree Wordsworth incorporates even the most distinctively human features of the scene within its general atmosphere and texture. The place of man's lodging is "pastoral" and "Green to the very door," and the smoke, evidence of his labor, rises in "wreaths" that are "Sent up, in silence, from among the trees" (18).

In his essential character, man too, therefore, is, or at least should be, a creature of the calm, one who is also linked in that harmonious interchange that unites all being. But man possesses special attributes of reflection and volition, and he must transpose those qualities expressed by nature as silence and unity into their equivalent forms as aspects of human consciousness. He experiences silence as tranquillity, the sense of "tranquil restoration" that secures man from threats posed to his true welfare by "the din / Of towns and cities" (25–26)—a phrase that contrasts conspicuously with the landscape calm of the preceding verse paragraph; and he experiences unity as sympathy, a feeling of shared participation in the being of a life outside oneself, that issues in the moral concern and moral will that make up

> that best portion of a good man's life,
> His little, nameless, unremembered, acts
> Of kindness and of love.
>
> (33–35)

Finally, rarer moments of deeper illumination, when man becomes introspectively aware of the true nature of the self and at the same time penetrates into and spiritually apprehends the vital core of the objects he perceives, confirm the common identity all things share. These virtually atemporal points of ultimate disclosure in which—impediments to true self-realization removed—we "become a living soul" (46) and thereby gain power to "see into the life of things" (49) are defined by Wordsworth in quietistic language much like that of the opening landscape. So tranquil and quiescent is this "serene and blessed mood" in which weights and burdens are lightened and knowledge of the self achieved, that physiological process nearly ceases:

> the breath of this corporeal frame
> And even the motion of our human blood
> Almost suspended, we are laid asleep
> In body, and become a living soul.
>
> (43–46)

Similarly, the means by which "We see into the life of things" is "an eye made quiet" (47), in this case "by the power / Of harmony" (47–48), another phrase that carries with it symbolic resonance from the previous stanza.

Such moments of absolute knowledge and of total participation in the calm and harmony that nature seems perpetually to express possess a questionable authority, as Wordsworth quickly acknowledges in lines that follow; and even if we do achieve such transfiguring moments they are soon lost, receding from us as we move once more within the uncertain flow of time. Man can be a creature of the calm, but he does not dwell there in unchanging repose as the objects of nature do. Nature is inherently stable, the narrator of *Tintern Abbey* observes upon returning there after an absence of five years and finding the river, the cliffs, the general landscape, and even the individual hedge-rows unchanged in their individual forms or in the relations they bear to each other. Each verb of perception (to hear, to behold, to view, to see) taken in combination with the repeated modifier "again" implies a perfect renewal of earlier impressions, an exact restoration of the sounds, colors, shapes, and proportions that had been present there at the time of his earlier visit. It almost necessarily follows that during the intervening passage of time, the objects before him have presumably stood as they do now, a body of permanent forms held together within a structure

of permanent relationships. Within this span, the only alteration among these relationships we can speak of with any certainty is that between observer and landscape, for we do know
that before his return he had passed from this quiet site to
"the din / Of towns and cities" (25–26), that he had left the
pleasures of repose on the banks of the Wye for "hours of
weariness" in a far different environment.

To say that the individual, who must live in time and experience time as change, cannot remain an integral part of
an unvarying order of nature does not mean that man in
some ominous sense is alienated from nature. The landscape
symbolism that blends the works of man with those of nonhuman nature does not really misrepresent the actual situation of man as the poem goes on to describe it. The changed
perceptual relationship between the observer and the objects
he perceives is not as radical a change as their physical separation might seem to imply. "These beauteous forms,"
Wordsworth also tells us, "Through a long absence, have not
been to me / As is a landscape to a blind man's eye" (22–24).
The scenes he has viewed, if not continually present to perception, can return before the mind's eye through memory,
which for Wordsworth is highly pictorial and very nearly
photographically duplicates earlier experience, and can exercise their tranquilizing and unifying influence during activities that call him away from such places as the prospect a few
miles above *Tintern Abbey.* Man can know no such perfect
stability as the objects of nature display; but because the objects of his past experience of nature are always at least potentially available through memory, he can acquire a general
disposition to calm and harmony that for the time-bound
individual constitutes, for all practical purposes, a life lived
in accordance with the ways of nature. The "tranquil restoration" that relieves "hours of weariness"; those acts of gener-
osity that form only a portion but that the "best portion of a
good man's life" (33); that "gift, / Of aspect more sublime"

(36–37) when through the apprehension of perfect peace and perfect unity we find momentarily removed from us "the heavy and the weary weight / Of all this unintelligible world" (39–40)—all of these indicate, in one sense, the necessarily unstable and irregular character of human life, the comparative infrequency of these most satisfying moments revealing to us that man, his life bound to time's changing order, can never maintain that changeless perfection which nature everywhere in *Tintern Abbey* continually exhibits. But, considered in another sense, that he has such moments demonstrates that he does possess dispositions that, periodically fulfilling themselves in thought and action, must be taken into account as essential attributes of man in any reasoned attempt by him at self-definition.

Such praiseworthy acts and occasions, Wordsworth implies in *Tintern Abbey,* are ultimately external in origin, that is, environmentally determined; and the dispositions they express, one must assume, are also acquired rather than inherent. To landscape as recollected image, he owes (a term that clearly denotes external causality) [4] these best and most rewarding of moments. For nature, though it is itself permanent, can use time to transmit nature's own essential properties to man, so that he is finally able to enter into that relationship with it which the earlier symbolism of landscape figuratively intimates to exist ideally between them. The potential breach between man and nature, the one temporal and the other immutable, never actually takes place because time itself is goal-oriented, the instrumental medium by which the permanent achieves its ends. Structurally the movement of *Tintern Abbey* is governed by an order of logical sequence. It begins by setting forth its metaphysical premises—premises that simultaneously point to both the real and the ideal—by means of a landscape symbolism joining man and nature in unity and peace and offering, in its apparent changelessness, a Wordsworthian approximation of eternity. Since the state of individual man, however, can never be one wholly free of change, any account of human life as it is actually lived must interpret the absolutes of this idealized landscape in terms of practical equivalents to them that exist within the context of time. Here, of course, these equivalents are the acquired dispositions to pleasure, virtue, and knowledge, whose origins Wordsworth traces back to the beauteous forms of the preceding stanza. In terming these dispositions acquired, we are saying that at some point in time man did not possess these externally formed qualities of mind that correspond so closely to the essential properties of landscape. The next step in the poem's logical sequence, therefore, is to determine how these qualities were developed by the formative agency of nature as it works in and through time. It is to this end that Wordsworth in the fourth stanza presents an account of his own development with its threefold classification of childhood, youth, and maturity as a descriptive summary of the essential pattern of individual growth, the way in which the life of man is purposefully arranged in time to move forwards toward assimilation into the modes and processes of the eternal.

Perhaps the most accurate structural image for *Tintern Abbey* is that of the individual life moving upon the teleologically directed currents of time into the repose of eternity. Yet it should be noted that the direction of flow and journey's end are, for the individual, not inevitable but contingent. For *Tintern Abbey* presents two possible movements of time: one is teleological (and it is this with which we are most concerned here), but the other is disorganized and directionless, a random succession of movements that we experience as "the fretful stir / Unprofitable, and the fever of the world" (52–53). This second manifestation of time, though excluded from any connection, either potential or actual, with the poem's abiding reality, is unfortunately the form of time in which ordinary human activities are most often conducted;

and it is the pervasiveness of flux in the lives of so many others that gives Wordsworth's account of his own personal history the programmatic character and much of the emotional urgency and intensity that it possesses. In fact, it is because these two opposing modes of human time exist and two conflicting schemes of human behavior follow from them that Wordsworth chooses autobiography in *Tintern Abbey*'s fourth stanza as his principal vehicle for effecting the reformation of man. However subjective that fourth stanza may be, we cannot explain its subjectivity by appealing to any of those habits of mind we now judge to be modern. Wordsworth looks backward not because retrospection serves some deep and compelling need or because he believes his character to be irrevocably fixed to its earliest psychological crises.[5] Neither does he examine his inner life to savor a self-taste—a unique self-conscious awareness—exclusively his own, never to be transferred or duplicated, that sets him apart from all other men. Instead, *Tintern Abbey*'s principal psychological assumptions are far more elementary and unsophisticated, those of Lockian empiricism with its uniformitarian postulates. Wordsworth makes public his own private history not to assert the autonomy and inviolability of the self but to exhibit the workings and effects of a process of environmental shaping that can be adequately presented in no other way. The proper function of this retrospective survey for Wordsworth is to explain how others by subjecting themselves to the formative agencies that determined his own growth can acquire what he has acquired, how they too can move from time's random to its ordered flow.

The principal devices that Wordsworth uses in stanza four to measure his personal evolution come directly from the poem's opening and determining figure: for internal growth is interpreted essentially as the mind's increasing awareness of tranquillity (the human equivalent of the calm of landscape) and as a growing consciousness of the depth and extensiveness of one's relational ties with man and nature (the human equivalent of the harmony of landscape). Both of these characeristics have their counterparts, of course, in the poem's symbolically expressed metaphysics, indicating that in *Tintern Abbey*, at least, Wordsworth conceives of the mind's growth as primarily a matter of its correspondence to, or perhaps identity with, nature and hence with the metaphysically real. The first of these defining traits of growth, tranquillity, is set forth in predominantly negative terms. As Wordsworth outlines it, the recollected course of his life has the stages of its development most notably marked by a constantly diminishing intensity of feeling. Childhood is a time of "coarser pleasures" and "glad animal movements"; in youth feeling remains foremost, and there are "aching joys" and "dizzy raptures," but these are less coarse, that is, less physiological and corporeal in their intensity of effect; or to appropriate to our own purposes the Humeian distinction between impressions and ideas, these later feelings are less vivid in their perceived character.[6] Youth, in its turn, must give way to maturity; and, correspondingly, the passions and appetites of youth must disappear to be replaced by meditative pleasures, "the joy / Of elevated thoughts" (94–95), that perhaps are more fruitful, but again undoubtedly are less intense. Feeling, thus, during the course of life undergoes a process of virtual disembodiment, a conversion from sensory into psychological phenomena. Yet Wordsworth knows that such conversion plays upon the pulses as a difference in degree as well as in kind; intensity of feeling seems to diminish so as virtually to cease altogether. At a later date a similar decline in intensity will be understood as a numbing of spirit under a "weight" of "custom" that is "Heavy as frost, and deep almost as life" (*Immortality Ode,* 129), but in *Tintern Abbey*'s general atmosphere of confidence and self-satisfaction Wordsworth finds in his awareness of decline offsetting virtues. For such loss there is in *Tintern Abbey*'s famous formula "Abundant recompense." Stilled passion signals an achieved calm; the ear no longer dominated by "The sounding cataract" becomes attuned to the finer and more morally elevating tones of "The still, sad music of humanity" (91). And any explanation that would interpret this reduction in intensity primarily as loss seriously misjudges the poem's true placement of emphasis.

The second major theme, Wordsworth's treatment of relations in stanza four, again is characterized by a line of progressive development from childhood's "glad animal movements" to the later condition of adult thoughtfulness. The area of our first concerns is naturally bounded by the force of immediate sensations, and since the child who "feels its life in every limb" (*We Are Seven,* 3) is most fully aware of his own animal being as it registers its vital and overpowering presence on the senses, it inevitably follows that the state of childhood is virtually devoid of significant relational involvement, that interests then are, for the most part, self-generated. The child, as a later manuscript account of his behavior explains, finds "his own person, senses, faculties, / Centre and soul of all." [7] As children we come to experience and to know ourselves not as participants in a scheme of relationship but almost as autonomous and self-contained beings. With youth these self-restricting limits are breached by the potency of the external world, and consciousness enters into that engagement with the natural world that shall eventually transform it. "Then," as Wordsworth expresses it in this same manuscript,

> will come
> Another soul, spring, centre of his being,
> And that is Nature.[8]

Or in language propounding much the same concept in *Tintern Abbey,* then nature "was all in all" (75). By the force of his attachment to nature, the youth thus secures release from his earlier and too exclusive bondage to the self. But this single strand of relationship, this equally exclusive concentration on nature, does not as yet adequately fulfill the metaphoric or metaphysical conditions set forth at the outset of the poem. The initial landscape of *Tintern Abbey* has blended within it the works of man as well as the objects of nature, and involvement with both is necessary to reach any full and abiding relationship with what the poem designates as reality. Youth is, of course, but the midpoint in Wordsworth's developmental history, and love of nature is not an end in itself but leads instead to love of man. Only with maturity does Wordsworth truly complete this necessary pattern of relationships by becoming sympathetically responsive to the sounds of man as they mingle with the silences of nature. He finally hears in

> The still, sad music of humanity,
> Nor harsh nor grating, though of ample power
> To chasten and subdue
>
> (91–93)

a message of pain and suffering that is to be the basis of future moral concern, a sound, moreover, that, like the stream's "soft inland murmur" heard earlier, seems in its stillness to reinforce rather than to disturb the essential calm of his setting.

The function of the fourth stanza then is to reconstitute in his own person the externalized qualities of the poem's opening landscape. Since "thought" is plainly the key term in Wordsworth's description of what he has finally become, it is primarily by his evolution to thoughtfulness that we must understand this task of internally reconstituting the landscape to be brought about. Wordsworth here certainly proposes no absolute antithesis between thought and feeling, for, unlike the abstracting processes of the "meddling intellect," these operations of the mind create their own emotional states, "the joy / Of elevated thoughts" (94–95) as *Tintern Abbey*

describes them. When compared, on the other hand, to the
emotional peaks or even to the emotional plateaus of childhood and youth, the workings of his mature thoughtfulness
are clearly experienced by Wordsworth as a predominantly
quiescent mode. It is this state of meditative tranquillity that
brings Wordsworth's life into conformity with nature and
that also furnishes the defining characteristics of his best self:
"The calm existence that is mine when I / Am worthy of myself" (*Prelude,* I, 360–61). But thought is by no means simply
a state of static repose. Thought is the cognitive agency
through which we apprehend more widely and understand
more deeply the relational complex to which feeling originally introduces us. Not until he passes beyond the stage of
"thoughtless youth" does Wordsworth recognize the incom-
pleteness of nature when man is excluded from it. Of greater
consequence is the disclosure that concludes this condensed
history of the mind of a poet, the discovery that the ultimate
ground of the harmony he has so lately discerned resides in

> something far more deeply interfused,
> Whose dwelling is the light of setting suns,
> And the round ocean and the living air,
> And the blue sky, and in the mind of man:
> A motion and a spirit, that impels
> All thinking things, all objects of all thought,
> And rolls through all things.
>
> (96–102)

This passage, usually extracted as a textbook citation of Romantic pantheism, serves in context to demonstrate that the
relational system he originally presented had nothing fortuitous about it. The harmonious grouping of particulars assembled by the poem's visual surface arises because earth and
sky, hedge and wood, man and nature have lodged within
them as the impelling fact of their being a single presence

whose goal is to overcome their individuated separateness and to fuse them together into a single, unified structure.

From the point of view of Wordsworth's own development, the most important of these separations that the power which "rolls through all things" dissolves is that between perceiver and perceived, between "all thinking things" and "all objects of all thought." But we should not take this statement that both thought and its objects contain and express the same ultimate reality as a veiled suggestion that in their epistemological relationship they function in the same way, with each an equally active participant in the mind's acquisition of knowledge. It is not here that Wordsworth speaks of imagination, in a Kantian or Coleridgean sense, projecting its creative powers outward upon the materials that the external world has given it so that it may shape these materials in accordance with the mind's own needs and ends. In the lines that follow this chronological account of his personal development, Wordsworth makes clear that it is to nature, and to nature alone as the major force that directed his development, that he must direct his thanks in the important statement that concludes this autobiographical section. Only now, Wordsworth says, having completed the developmental process and realized his own best and truest self, is he

> well pleased to recognise
> In nature and language of the sense
> The anchor of my purest thoughts, the nurse,
> The guide, the guardian of my heart, and soul
> Of all my moral being.
>
> (107–11)

Custom has done much to temper the force of these familiar lines and to minimize the radically empirical character of their key phrases of praise and obligation.[9] Wordsworth's description of "nature and the language of the sense" as "The

anchor of my purest thoughts" forestalls any interpretation of
the inner life that would explain it either in terms of transcendental origins or of transcendental ends. At its best—its
purest—the activities of thought remain grounded in the
world as we experience it, and whatever dualistic perplexities we encounter in the mind-body relationship must be resolved within the poem's naturalistic framework and not by
appeal to any alien realm of spirit. But nature here is much
more than a fixed and potent force that anchors the human
spirit to the world. In lines that bring the abstractions of *Tintern Abbey* into momentary correspondence with the great
animistic episodes of Book I of *The Prelude* and *Nutting,*
"nature and the language of the sense" undergo metamor-
phosis into a far more humanized form as "the nurse, / The
guide, the guardian of my heart." Wordsworth's development
has succeeded as well as it has because the order of nature, in
a way that is personal and intimate, has made him the object
of its solicitous regard. It has tutored and protected him,
reached out to him "With gentlest visitation" (*Prelude,* I,
367) and "Severer interventions" (*Prelude,* I, 370). It has led
him into temptation, whether it be the attractions of an un-
attended boat or the enticements of a virgin grove of hazels,
so that it might unloose its corrective powers and thereby
foster in him a just regard for the property of man and of
nature.

Since nature has shown such sympathetic concern for him,
Wordsworth may plausibly address it as the "soul / Of all my
moral being." But the phrase also implies an epistemological
content that is radically empirical. To speak of "nature and
the language of the sense" as the "soul / Of all my moral
being" is to consider the element in the self that we judge
responsible for our most truly human behavior to derive totally from inanimate nature. Our moral being exists because
nature transfers its properties—at least those possessing ethical attributes—to us; and we can therefore comprehend man's

moral aptitudes as easily, or perhaps more easily, by observing external nature as by attending to human conduct, either our own or that of others. Carried to its proper conclusions, what Wordsworth here puts into a single phrase is but a condensed variant of the familiar claim of *The Tables Turned:*

> One impulse from a vernal wood
> May teach you more of man,
> Of moral evil and of good,
> Than all the sages can.
>
> (21–24)

Of course, it is always possible that Wordsworth means nothing more by such statements than what we have been taught to impute to the hyperbolic vagueness of Romantic nature-worship. But this is to disregard substantial evidence for taking such statements as literal renderings of Wordsworthian beliefs. In a number of passages written at approximately the same time as *Tintern Abbey,* Wordsworth indicates how he arrives at true self-knowledge not by self-reflection, by introspectively peering into some autonomous and vital core of the interior life, but by observing impressions transmitted externally to the senses. In the first and most troublesome of these passages, a fragment from the Alfoxden notebook, he describes a curious state that fluctuates between a profound consciousness of life when contemplating the untransformed impressions of nature and a lapse into utter forgetfulness and vacancy induced when these images are withdrawn from the mind.

> To gaze
> On that green hill and on those scattered trees
> And feel a pleasant consciousness of life
> In the impression of that loveliness
> Until the sweet sensation called the mind
> Into itself, by image from without

> Unvisited, and all her reflex powers
> Wrapped in a still dream [of] forgetfulness.
>
> I lived without the knowledge that I lived
> Then by those beauteous forms brought back again
> To lose myself again as if my life
> Did ebb and flow with a strange mystery.[10]

One can hardly speak with assurance about a passage describing so extraordinary a phenomenon in a form that is little more perhaps than a random and unrevised jotting, probably never intended for the public. But clearly whatever Wordsworth learns of life on this occasion depends upon the "pleasant consciousness" that accompanies his visual sensations, while introspection can yield no knowledge of life's character when it delves into pure mind, that is, a mind devoid of images.

Similarly another fragment from 1798–99, this one from the *Christabel* notebook, leads us to roughly comparable conclusions:

> In many a walk
> At evening or by moonlight, or reclined
> At midday upon beds of forest moss,
> Have we to Nature and her impulses
> Of our whole being made free gift, and when
> Our trance had left us, oft have we, by aid
> Of the impressions which it left behind,
> Looked inward on ourselves, and learned, perhaps,
> Something of what we are.[11]

Once more Wordsworth offers in a fragmentary passage only the unanalyzed data of an unusual psychological event. But the theory of mind underlying that event is unambiguous and familiar. Its origin is the interaction between the human mind, essentially receptive, and the productive workings of nature's active powers. What would seem to take place here is that the impressions of nature, by their sheer force and vivacity, compel the mind to suspend its normal self-conscious activities and to enter into that state of pure receptivity in which the inward being becomes virtually indistinguishable from the external image it beholds. This experience is not very different from other moments of self-forgetfulness induced by the apparent pressure of nature's images, such as the youthful boating expedition described in *The Prelude* where Wordsworth tells how

> the calm
> And dead still water lay upon my mind
> Even with a weight of pleasure, and the sky
> Never before so beautiful, sank down
> Into my heart, and held me like a dream.
> (II, 176–80)

When these immediate pressures cease and the trance to which consciousness had submitted itself lifts, the mind will, of course, revert to its usual cognitive activities. Even then, however, the impressions of nature remain engraved upon consciousness (perhaps as after-images),[12] and it is to these impressions—that is, to nature itself—that Wordsworth paradoxically turns to comprehend his true self, to learn "Something of what we are" in the act of introspective appraisal that follows nature's deep impregnation of the mind.

Another episode similar in character and structure to those described in the Alfoxden and *Christabel* notebooks figures prominently in the autobiographic section of *The Ruined Cottage*. Again the occasion of self-discovery, recognition that the true basis of identity is the external world, is a moment when the forms of nature inundate consciousness and displace all of its other activities. Here it is a sunrise of visionary splendor experienced by the Pedlar during childhood that discloses to him the true origins of his essential self:

                          Sound needed none
          Nor any voice of joy: his spirit drank the
          Spectacle. Sensation, soul and form
          All melted into him. They swallowed up
          His animal being; in them did he live
          And by them did he live. They were his life.[13]

Though such moments of revelation in which the impressions
of nature swallow up the "animal being" are of too great an
intensity to sustain themselves as a continuing presence in
the child's consciousness, they are not at all rare occurrences
for the child brought up amidst the grandeur of nature's
forms, as the narrator's further account of the Pedlar's childhood reveals:

          A shepherd on the lonely mountain tops
          Such intercourse was his, and in this sort
          Was his existence oftentimes possessed.[14]

Moreover, these occasions produce not only an immediate
revelation of the true relationship of nature to the most significant portion of the inner life but also, through their cumulative effect, more distant benefits to be reaped in maturity.
For in a passage originally written as one of several projected
conclusions to *The Ruined Cottage,* Wordsworth, using language much like that with which he had described the Pedlar's childhood raptures when nature had seized his being,
expresses the conviction (less as logical inference than as
creed) of what the necessary consequences for adult life of
such influence by nature must be: "Thus deeply drinking in
the soul of things / We shall be wise perforce." [15] It should
be evident with these examples before us that in identifying
"nature and the language of the sense" as the "soul / Of all
my moral being," Wordsworth is being not rhetorically ex-
travagant but philosophically consistent, that in these fa-

miliar lines from *Tintern Abbey* he is doing no more than reformulating and compressing the illustrations and arguments he had drawn upon elsewhere to explain how our richest experiences, our wisest thoughts, and our most generous acts are in origin and essence creations of the external world.

Like so many other works that assume environment to be determining, *Tintern Abbey* is implicitly a gesture of protest directed toward the existing social order. As an alternative to that order, the poem offers us the life pattern of its hero, a developmental process that is presented as both exemplary and, given the surroundings and circumstances in which it takes place, as necessary. According to the poem's empirical premises, such a process is, of course, universally accessible and universally beneficial, available to any and all who would submit themselves to the circumstances and surroundings that had determined the life and behavior of its hero and who would thereby participate in bringing about a true reformation of man and society. The progressive—indeed, virtually millenial—suppositions that *Tintern Abbey,* like most of Wordsworth's autobiographic poetry of this period, indirectly sets forth are suppositions common to most of those who, in the eighteenth century, advocated an empiricism that traced all human knowledge back to sensory and hence external origins. Indeed, when in *The Recluse* Wordsworth seeks to justify the "lowly matter" upon which this poem of epic intention rests, its extensive recounting of the affairs of "The transitory Being that beheld / This vision" and "all his little realities of life," he openly voices the hope that his personal history may "Express the image of a better time / More wise desires and simple manners," [16] a prophetic expectation based on principles little different from those of David Hartley who, observing the tendency of associational psychology "to make us all ultimately similar," concludes "that if one be happy, all must." [17]

There is danger, however, that such expectation may be

misconceived. Wordsworth submits the history of his personal development to his readers as an exemplary instance, a pattern to recur universally once man learns to substitute nature for his present environment; but what Wordsworth proposes as the typical instance is possibly the exceptional case. His education by nature may well be a gift uniquely bestowed upon him but withheld from the remainder of men and, therefore, of no practical relevance to them. In *Tintern Abbey* Wordsworth takes measures to insulate his poem against this potential criticism by providing a second exemplary and necessary instance in the developmental process exhibited by his own sister. Elsewhere in his writings Dorothy performs different functions and appears in a variety of guises: she acts in some cases simply as domestic and spiritual partner; in others she is offered to us as an acute and accurate observer of nature's forms; and on a number of occasions she appears as a tutor to the poet in the gentler passions and milder pleasures, a role in which her conduct and character are usually introduced for the sake of their pointed contrast with the conduct and character of her brother. But *Tintern Abbey* deals in no such intrinsic contrasts. The moral intention of the poem, instead, dictates a common psychological history for the two, and Dorothy, thus, reenacts the course of the poet's own development with such exactness that she supplies living confirmation of the deterministic axiom that similarity of circumstance produces similarity of character, "that if one be happy, all must." Whatever differences exist between brother and sister are explained not by reference to a uniquely constituted and essentially autonomous personality but by the general laws of human development that Wordsworth earlier in the poem had already abstracted from the analysis of his own growth. Since Dorothy, though conditioned by the same surroundings as the poet, is as yet a chronological stage behind him, the two differ, according to the poem's empirical formulations, as the stages of Wordsworth's own life have been shown to differ from one another, as his current maturity differs from his turbulent youth. In Dorothy, Wordsworth finds his own former self—a lost being from a past recently discarded—fully reconstituted with an insistent and astonishing literalness:

> in thy voice I catch
> The language of my former heart, and read
> My former pleasures in the shooting lights
> Of thy wild eyes.
>
> (116–19)

In effect, she has assumed his identity; and it is from personal nostalgia for the self he has put behind him that, as he tells his sister, he yet lingers to "behold in thee what I was once" (120).

To be sure, remembrance in the autobiographic section of *Tintern Abbey* yields its own intrinsic pleasures, and the youthful self he introduces there is portrayed with obvious affection, an affection openly acknowledged and intensified when that earlier self is rediscovered in the voice and eyes of the sister he loves. Just as the poet of *The Prelude* finds himself

> loth to quit
> Those recollected hours that have the charm
> Of visionary things
>
> (I, 658–60)

so here, too, Wordsworth interrupts the onward progress of his poem with a gesture of nostalgic tenderness that clearly reveals the depth of his attachment to the past. We may, of course, see such confessional moments as containing within themselves the seeds of destruction of the developmental assumptions that govern *Tintern Abbey* and *The Prelude,* an admission of the inescapable need to repossess and preserve the past and thereby satisfy the regressive hunger that, even as early as 1798, provides the true impulse to Wordsworth's retrospective habits. By 1802 retrospection does, for the most part, serve regressive purposes, but the yearning to remain fixed to the past is neither the dominant nor the authentic note of *Tintern Abbey*. What is most striking in Wordsworth's treatment of his sister here is the ease with which he incorporates her presence into the established intellectual framework of the poem, how briefly he actually lingers over contemplation of the remembered self she has re-created for him despite his genuinely professed attachment to it, and how quickly he turns from nostalgia to prayer, prayer expressed not as anxious supplication but as assured prophecy.

The empirical belief that the individual identity is externally constituted still remains the poem's governing conception, so that Wordsworth, turning again to the epistemological transaction between the world and the self in the final verse paragraph of *Tintern Abbey*, continues to define their relationship as one of cause and consequence by employing a vocabulary that is uncompromisingly sensationalistic. In this transaction Wordsworth ascribes to nature all active agency: nature's role is to "inform / The mind that is within us" (125–26), to "impress" it "With quietness and beauty" (126–27)—the faintly metaphoric coloring of both verbs suggesting that the resultant self is the imprint left by the stamp upon the wax. Mind and its functions are also conceived of in rigorously empirical terms as nature's passive complement in the epistemological relation. Mind is described to us not as a dynamic cluster of activities but as "a mansion for all lovely forms" (140), and memory, correspondingly, is depicted not as a faculty that under the direction of the will acts to re-create the past but merely as a location, a Lockian storehouse that serves "as a dwelling-place / For all sweet sounds and harmonies" (141–42). Indeed, if it is the function of nature to "feed" the mind "With lofty thoughts" (127–28), thought itself would seem to be nothing more than the matter of the world reduplicated as the content of consciousness, a substance indistinguishable from its material origins except for possession of those mysterious properties that enable it to occupy the interior space that is the mind instead of that exterior space that constitutes the world.

Because of the emphasis that Wordsworth's empirical orientation places on the determining causality of nature, the parallels he has already observed between his sister's development and his own have an obvious predictive value. If Dorothy is what William was, eventually she too must become what he is now. The tranquilizing forces of nature that had subdued Wordsworth's youthful intensity of emotion and produced his mature calm are plainly formative influences upon Dorothy's character as well. Since it is nature's designated task to "impress" the mind "With quietness and beauty," we can safely anticipate for Dorothy, on the strength of her brother's example, some moment

> in after years,
> When these wild ecstasies shall be matured
> Into a sober pleasure.
>> (137–39)

The future that Wordsworth here foresees for his sister has application to the collective destiny of man in a way that escapes the attention of those who would reduce the reasons for Dorothy's presence in the closing section to the pleasures of retrospection or to the pressures of nostalgia.[18] For *Tintern Abbey* is not a poem hobbled by memory but Wordsworth's most forward-looking and most optimistic work. By exhibiting in himself and in his sister a repeated process of personal growth, Wordsworth indicates the universal possibility of moral betterment and spiritual salvation open to all under the auspices of a benevolent nature. To be sure, human life remains exposed to the threats of "solitude, or fear, or pain, or grief" (143), conditions that, as Wordsworth demonstrates in such works as the "Lucy" poems, the "Matthew" poems, *Resolution and Independence,* and the *Immortality Ode,* impinge deeply upon our hopes for happiness. In *Tintern Abbey,* however, Wordsworth treats these threats less as potential sources of tension than as obstacles inevitably to be overcome in that triumphant processional in which nature asserts

> her privilege,
> Through all the years of this our life, to lead
> From joy to joy.
>
> (123–25)

But the faith that Wordsworth here advances is not limited in its application to the poet and his coterie of followers. For Wordsworth it forms the assured basis for what are ultimately Utopian hopes: the means by which mankind shall prevail against "all / The dreary intercourse of daily life" (130–31) and transform its daily existence into a developmental process that carries us "From joy to joy."

Nowhere else during the years from 1797 to 1800 does Wordsworth elaborate the major concepts of *Tintern Abbey* with such fullness or coherence, and, consequently, nowhere else during these years does he achieve such sustained grandeur of exposition. But if all of *Tintern Abbey*'s major parts do not appear elsewhere with the same amplification or in the same proportions, the poem's major and controlling premise —that nature reduces our inward turbulence to a state of relative calm in the course of our development in order to bring our lives into conformity with nature's own essential being— exerts what is, nonetheless, a determining influence upon every other major autobiographic and semiautobiographic work of the period. In *The Ruined Cottage* this premise binds together what might otherwise seem to be two tenuously connected, if not, in fact, altogether disparate halves: the poem's biographic and narrative segments. The restraint and calm with which the Pedlar relates the story of Margaret, itself

> a common tale
> By moving accidents uncharactered
> A tale of silent suffering, hardly clothed
> In bodily form, and to the grosser sense
> But ill adapted,[19]

are qualities induced in the narrator by those purposeful workings of nature described in the poem's introductory section. The meditative pathos, the characteristic tone of Wordsworthian narrative, that the Pedlar achieves is made possible because nature has managed to allay "the fever of his heart" [20] and to bring "His mind" to "a just equipoise of love," [21] thus reproducing in the Pedlar and bringing to consciousness and expression the tranquillity and relational sympathy that originally were nature's own. Biography and narrative come together in *The Ruined Cottage* as two interrelated aspects of a single concern, the poetical character, its formation and its proper expression. Behind the grave dignity of the subject matter that the Pedlar chooses, the austere diction in which he clothes it, and even the cadenced blank verse with which he relates it, stand—as initiating causes—the mountains, the crags, and the sunlit and starlit heavens of his boyhood.

In *Home at Grasmere* Wordsworth speaks even more explicitly of nature's subjugation of childhood's "wild appetites and blind desires" [22] and its displacement of these by a peace and mildness that fix the direction of the poetic vocation he is to follow. Once, he tells us, were "Motions of savage instinct my delight / And exaltation," [23] but now "me hath Nature tamed"; [24] then using the frequently to be repeated simile of the stream, Wordsworth goes on to summarize the progress of his life as one in which nature

> Hath dealt with me as with a turbulent Stream,
> Some nursling of the mountains, whom she leads

Through quiet meadows, after he has learnt
His strength, and had his triumph and his joy,
His desperate course of tumult and of glee.[25]

The use to which Wordsworth puts this figure contrasts instructively with its use in a better-known but later instance, the metaphoric account of imagination's progress in the last book of *The Prelude*. In *Home at Grasmere* he develops the figure in accordance with his major beliefs, employing it as a vehicle expressing his benevolently necessitarian doctrine of change and growth; and he therefore emphasizes the alterations in character that the symbolic stream of self undergoes in its journey over the terrain through which nature conducts it. But by the time he reached the end of *The Prelude,* Wordsworth's principal article of faith had unmistakably shifted from the teleology of change to the self's essential and unbreachable unity, so that the metaphorical stream of this somewhat later period was to be defined not by its rate or direction of flow or by the shaping contours of the banks that contained it but by the internal composition of its basic material: material whose essential substance remains unaffected by the accidents of diversion or concealment that befall it during life's course and whose internal being remains unalterably the same during its self-contained progress from "the very place of birth / In its blind cavern" (XIII, 173–74) to its final destination, the implied sea to which it flows to unite with "life endless, the great thought / By which we live, Infinity and God" (XIII, 183–84).

If *Home at Grasmere* specifically repudiates any view of the self closely linked with the Romantic conception of a creative and autonomous faculty of imagination, the view of the self that it does provide does much to help explain Wordsworth's own conception of the poetic enterprise. For corresponding to the course of his personal development is a parallel development in poetic interests. As a child who

"breathed" then "Among wild appetites and blind desires,"
he delighted to hear "of danger, met / Or sought with cour-
age," tales of "one" or of "a resolute few who for the sake /
Of glory, fronted multitudes in arms." [26] In brief, his interests
were heroic projects and martial exploits, those actions and
events that had traditionally comprised the matter of epic
poetry; but the nature that had tamed his early passions was
also responsible for redirecting his poetic interests and ultimately for redefining his poetic aims. Her injunction to him
was " 'Be mild and cleave to gentle things, / Thy glory and
thy happiness be there.' " [27] The best measure of how well
Wordsworth carried out nature's instruction is to be found in
Home at Grasmere, as in *The Ruined Cottage,* in those ties
that connect tale to teller, the way in which the events of *The
Recluse* are to embody the design and desires of a mind whose
habits have been shaped by the informing calm of nature.
Wordsworth's stated ambitions in *The Recluse* are clearly
epic, but compared with the epic materials of the past, his
radically untraditional choice of themes indicates how closely
he heeded nature's counsel. In addition to his implied rejection of Miltonic subjects in the familiar lines he later selected
as a preface to *The Excursion,* Wordsworth in the passage
immediately preceding the first appearance of these lines in
Home at Grasmere tells of his rejection of a still earlier epic
tradition that posed a far greater personal temptation for
him: the exploits of arms and the man, "That other hope,
long mine, the hope to fill / The heroic trumpet with the
Muse's breath." [28] Instead of martial exploit his own epic
argument was to be that of one trained by nature to " 'Be
mild and cleave to gentle things' ":

> On Man on Nature and on human life
> Thinking in solitude, from time to time
> I feel sweet passions traversing my soul
> Like Music, unto these, where'er I may
> I would give utterance in numerous verse.[29]

In a more literal sense than Arnold would probably have understood, Wordsworth both in theory and in practice would doubtlessly have assented to the Arnoldian judgment—certainly for each of the narrators of *The Ruined Cottage* and *Home at Grasmere*—"that Nature not only gave him the matter for his poem, but wrote his poem for him." [30]

Because *The Prelude* does have a complex chronology and because it does mirror the philosophic changes Wordsworth underwent even during the eight-year period of composition of the poem's first full version, a philosophically consistent exposition of his developmental views can scarcely be expected from this major work. Indeed, as the passage I cited earlier from the final book suggests, Wordsworth, by the time he had completed the poem, understood its subject to be imagination, a faculty that is autonomous, continuous, and self-sustaining. But at the outset, in the very earliest lines of the earliest manuscripts, he clearly assumes that *The Prelude* will record another instance of the subjugation of human passions to nature's calm and anticipates conclusions there that the poem in its finished form, of course, never realizes. Unable to commence a work of any magnitude, Wordsworth understandably raises the question of how one so carefully trained by nature—through whom nature in a very real sense speaks—can apparently have failed in his destined vocation:

> Was it for this
> That one, the fairest of all Rivers, lov'd
> To blend his murmurs with my Nurse's song,
> And from his alder shades and rocky falls,
> And from his fords and shallows, sent a voice
> That flow'd along my dreams? For this, didst Thou,
> O Derwent! travelling over the green Plains
> Near my 'sweet Birthplace,' didst thou, beauteous Stream,
> Make ceaseless music through the night and day
> Which with its steady cadence, tempering
> Our human waywardness, compos'd my thoughts

To more than infant softness, giving me,
Among the fretful dwellings of mankind,
A knowledge, a dim earnest, of the calm
That Nature breathes among the hills and groves.

(I, 271–85)

Implicit here in the interrogative form, surely rhetorical in intention, is further confirmation of Wordsworth's belief that his poetic powers are finally dependent upon the influence of natural objects. But in more significant ways the passage reflects, in a considerably condensed form, the structural arrangements and attendant values that we observed earlier in *Tintern Abbey*. Again Wordsworth mingles the natural and the human in the blending of the river's "murmurs with my Nurse's song," joining the two here however to indicate the generous intentions that nature possesses in common with those we ordinarily consider responsible for our protection and welfare. Nature's songs, too, are born from motives of love; and nature, no less than the human figure the passage alludes to, serves as a nurse superintending the child's growth —"the nurse / The guide, the guardian of my heart" as *Tintern Abbey* reminds us. Moreover, the passage also expresses, though in a somewhat truncated form, *Tintern Abbey*'s threefold classification of time: time as the seemingly changeless and hence symbolically eternal order of nature; time as a teleologically directed sequence in which human life follows nature's determinations; and time as a random and purposeless flow, the human condition when man lives apart from nature. Although the sounds of the Derwent suggest the temporal process far more readily than the great visual appearances of *Tintern Abbey*'s landscape, Wordsworth tends to minimize the presence of time in the Derwent's movements by emphasizing the stream's unvarying rhythms: its "ceaseless music" (an intimation of eternity given even more positive force in earlier manuscripts, JJ and the *Christabel* notebook, as a "Murmur perpetual") and "steady cadence." And these sounds that by their regularity come to signify the eternity of nature, by the same means, functioning just at the threshold of consciousness as an apparently permanent and changeless background against which the infant's shifting experience occurs, come also to signify nature's essential repose, one far deeper than any that man by his own design is capable of achieving. The effect of the river's cadences is to introduce the child to time in its teleological orderings. In a phrase that strikingly expresses the profundity of nature's calm, even by comparison with infancy's most tranquil and innocent moments, Wordsworth tells how the Derwent's song "compos'd my thoughts / To more than infant softness," not as a permanent condition of being but as a premature and partial revelation of that consciousness of nature's repose which through nature's continuing ministry later experience was to grant him in full: "A knowledge, a dim earnest of the calm / That Nature breathes among the hills and groves." It is primarily by means of these later experiences that Wordsworth finds himself irreversibly caught up in those teleological currents whose final goal is the harmonious unity of man and nature. Less important here perhaps than the details of infant life are the passage's anticipations of what is to come: the shaping of conduct and character in accordance with nature's most fundamental attribute, an indwelling calm that in the poet's maturity shall be matched by an equivalent sense of inward repose, the feeling described in what are probably the most informative lines of the earliest books of *The Prelude* as "The calm existence that is mine when I / Am worthy of myself" (I, 360–61).

More remarkable than the powers attributed here to nature is the passage's characterization of man, since it states that even in the earliest of man's rememberable days, in the seeming innocence of infancy, the charge entrusted to nature is "tempering / Our human waywardness." In one sense,

Wordsworth is still dealing with the question of time, using "waywardness" to suggest its random flux—how man experiences time when he departs from the ordered, sequential pattern through which nature seeks to guide him. But in a more obvious sense, the term "human waywardness" points toward ethical considerations, the behavior to be expected of man when he fails to enact or deviates from the role of moral agent that nature has chosen for him. Looked at in isolation, uninfluenced by nature's moral direction, man, Wordsworth seems here to indicate, can only be spoken of as intrinsically wayward; and the human community itself, untempered by nature's ethical design, seems to be composed of nothing other than "the fretful dwellings of mankind." The ultimate source of this waywardness is a quality that Wordsworth suggests we possess from life's very beginning, a passionate self-regard that nature alone can diminish and transform, but this is a matter that will receive fuller attention in a later chapter. For the present, it is enough to recognize that the part played by nature in Wordsworth's poetry, at least between 1797 and 1800, is not to act during his most crucial spiritual moments as a stimulus to a self-liberating act of imagination, as Hartman would have it, one that gives us a *"consciousness of self raised to apocalyptic pitch"* [31] and that thereby effaces nature from the inner life. At such moments, nature may instead be seen as the self's truest constituent element, so ineffaceable that it emerges as the vital core of every significant moral or poetic impulse.

1. To be sure, the poem's expansive pattern does not go altogether unchecked. Cautionary expressions of tentativeness and qualification follow in the wake of the boldest and most unorthodox cosmic speculations. But Albert S. Gérard seems to me to overemphasize these relatively few expressions of diffidence (ll. 49–50, 111–13, 146–49) in his structural analysis of *Tintern Abbey* in *English Romantic Poetry* (Berkeley, Calif., 1968), pp. 89–117. As a result, Gérard views the poem as far less assured than Wordsworth's professed attitude of confidence would lead us to believe. " 'Perplexity,' " Gérard writes, "is probably the key word to the total meaning of the poem" (p. 107).

2. *The Subtler Language* (Baltimore, 1959), p. 172.

3. See especially James Benziger, "*Tintern Abbey* Revisited," *PMLA* 65 (1950): 154–62; and Florence Marsh, *Wordsworth's Imagery* (New Haven, Conn., 1952), pp. 39–42.

4. Gérard, p. 104.

5. Richard J. Onorato, in his interesting psychoanalytic study of Wordsworth, *The Character of the Poet: Wordsworth in "The Prelude"* (Princeton, N.J., 1971), offers an exceptionally comprehensive interpretation of *Tintern Abbey* in these terms. Even Onorato, though compelled by methodology to seek out those insecurities latent beneath the poem's surface of assertion, "to see the man who needs order beneath the artist who attempts to impose it" (p. 87), must nonetheless concede an authenticity of confidence and optimism in the poem that sets it apart from Wordsworth's later work. " 'Tintern Abbey,' " Onorato writes, "is a young man's poem in exactly the way that 'The Immortality Ode,' written only a few years later, but after a few significant events in his life, is not."

6. Two lines in *Tintern Abbey* that contain the single comparative "coarser" may seem a slender basis for the distinction I make here between the feelings of childhood and those of youth. I find this distinction confirmed elsewhere, however, in the writing of this period, particularly in the opening books of *The Prelude* where the child's pleasure, his "vulgar joy" (I, 609) and "giddy bliss / Which, like a tempest, works along the blood" (I, 611–12) so often has physiological or implicitly physiological effects as its measure of intensity.

7. *The Prelude*, ed. Ernest de Selincourt, 2d ed. rev. by Helen Darbishire (Oxford, 1959), p. 574, ll. 133–34 (MS.Y, VIII, 159–72).

8. Ibid., p. 575, ll. 137–39 (MS.Y, VIII, 159–72).

9. H. W. Garrod found a "pure sensationalism" the inescapable inference to be drawn from these lines (*Wordsworth: Lectures and Essays* [Oxford, 1923], pp. 105–9), but few later critics will acknowledge this. Bennet Weaver, to be sure, reads these lines as sensism; but Weaver, in his dogmatic advocacy of a transcendental Wordsworth, then dismisses them as an *ignis fatuus* that misdirects Wordsworth away from the clearly marked avenues of truth (*Wordsworth: Poet of the Unconquerable Mind* [Ann Arbor, Mich., 1965], p. 42). Probably the majority view is best represented by Melvin Rader, who admits the empirical basis of this passage but then so hedges it with transcendental qualifications that he virtually divests it of any genuine philosophical significance for Wordsworth (*Wordsworth: A Philosophical Approach* [Oxford, 1967], pp. 154–58).

10. *The Poetical Works of William Wordsworth*, ed. Ernest de Selincourt and Helen Darbishire, 5 vols. (Oxford, 1940–49; vol. II, 2d. ed. 1952) (hereafter cited as *PW*), V, 341 (Appendix B, II, iv).

11. Ibid., pp. 343–44 (Appendix B, IV, vi, 8–16).

12. I use the term in its traditional sense. For a discussion of the afterimage as part of Wordsworth's structure of consciousness, see Geoffrey H. Hartman's phenomenological analysis of it in *Wordsworth's Poetry: 1787–1814* (New Haven, Conn., 1964), pp. 269–72.

13. *PW*, V, 382 (*The Ruined Cottage*, ll. 128–33).

14. Ibid., p. 382 (*The Ruined Cottage*, ll. 142–44).

15. Ibid., p. 402 (*The Ruined Cottage* [Addendum to MS.B], ll. 92–93).

16. Ibid., p. 339.

17. David Hartley, *Observations on Man, His Frame, His Duty, and His Expectations*, 2 vols. (Gainesville, Fla., 1966), I:84.

18. Among those who take this passage as evidence of Wordsworth's attachment to memory, either as a means of reviving the past or of feeling regret for its loss are Harold Bloom, *The Visionary Company* (Garden City, N.Y., 1963), p. 147; David Ferry, *The Limits of Mortality* (Middletown, Conn., 1959), p. 110; Herbert Lindenberger, *On Wordsworth's "Prelude"* (Princeton, N.J., 1963), p. 160; Christopher Salvesen, *The Landscape of Memory* (Lincoln, Neb., 1965), p. 39; and Onorato, p. 85.

19. *PW*, V, 393 (*The Ruined Cottage*, ll. 486–90).

20. Ibid., p. 385 (*The Ruined Cottage*, l. 237).

21. Ibid., p. 386.

22. Ibid., p. 336 (*Home at Grasmere*, l. 706).

23. Ibid. (*Home at Grasmere*, ll. 707–8).

24. Ibid., p. 337 (*Home at Grasmere*, l. 726).

25. Ibid. (*Home at Grasmere*, ll. 728–32).

26. Ibid., pp. 336–37 (*Home at Grasmere*, ll. 716–20).

27. Ibid., p. 337 (*Home at Grasmere*, ll. 735–36).

28. Ibid. (*Home at Grasmere*, ll. 749–50).

29. Ibid., p. 338.

30. *Poetry and Criticism of Matthew Arnold*, ed. A. Dwight Culler (Boston, 1961), p. 343.

31. Hartman, p. 17.

2

The Empirical Phase:
Theory of Mind

Like the term *nature,* the word *growth* may seem to be too
broadly connotative to enable us to describe Wordsworth's
thought between 1797 and 1800 with any philosophic exactness. Presumably the recurrent figure of the stream, his summarizing metaphor for the life process at the conclusion of
both *Home at Grasmere* and *The Prelude,* would indicate
that he continued to subscribe to a developmental hypothesis
throughout the golden decade. But it is questionable whether
the beliefs of any period of his career other than this first and
most empirical phase can be convincingly characterized as developmental. For in *The Prelude,* as I indicated earlier,
Wordsworth manipulates this key figure to stress the mind's
self-enclosed unity and internal consistency rather than, as in
the earlier instance, its receptivity to change and capacity for
expansion. Moreover, in accordance with this later view of
the mind, Wordsworth speaks of that change which does occur as taking place in conformity with those preexisting laws
that regulate the self's inner dynamics. "Imagination," he
tells us in a statement that is used as the conceptual basis for
the figure of the stream that appears in *The Prelude,* "hath
been the moving soul / Of our long labour" (XIII, 171–72),
a statement that makes apparent the organic assumptions that
underlie his conception of growth in the closing years of the
golden decade. Change or growth, he tells us here, emerges

from the centrifugal urgings of some animating and vital principle that seeks through development to actualize and fulfill a potentiality latently present within us from life's beginnings. But the laws of organic form do not yield a concept of mental growth that would satisfy the requirements of an empiricist epistemology. Growth, in the organic sense, entails the creation of nothing truly new and original, nothing that does not exist, at least latently, prior to its actualization—a view of growth as intrinsic changelessness, which Coleridge neatly epitomizes by the proposition that in "whatever is truly organic and living, the whole is prior to the parts." [1]

Between 1797 and 1800, Wordsworth required a conception of growth unrestricted by organicism's qualifying conditions. Without giving a traditional philosophic label to his alternative to the organic, Wordsworth, in a variety of sources from this period, leaves little doubt that he views growth empirically, that mind can undergo radical change and that mental change is a consequence of external determination. More indicative, perhaps, than any discursive statement of the depth of Wordsworth's commitment to the empirical are the recurrent metaphors of mind and its development that appear in the writings of this period either as extended analogy or as figurative coloration. For in these metaphors, mind is plainly conceived of not as an organism fulfilling latent potentialities but as something molded from without, an art form, or artifact, or, in even more commonplace terms, a piece of masonry put together from what Coleridge contemptuously called the "brick and mortar" of sensation. The most familiar and most detailed of these analogies, one using the work of art as the basis of comparison, occurs in *The Prelude* with the meditative simile that follows the incident of the plundered nest:

> The mind of man is fram'd even like the breath
> And harmony of music. There is a dark
> Invisible workmanship that reconciles

> Discordant elements, and makes them move
> In one society.
>
> (I, 351–55)

Within this metaphor, Wordsworth manages to incorporate most of the essential features of his sensationalist philosophy of mind. Experience he views as fundamentally atomistic, composed of elements that, taken in isolation, seem essentially discordant in their relation to one another. But when brought together and unified, these elements enter into a new whole that is something far more than the sum of its parts, just as a chord of music is a new creation, differing in essence from what might have been anticipated as the collective effect of its separate notes if they could form no more than a purely aggregate whole. Furthermore, this unity is not a chance unity but an imposed unity, achieved by means of a preconceived controlling design: the formation of the self being like the formation of any artifact, an idea that exists as the conception of its maker even before he brings it to its material execution. Behind this final harmony, the mind's composer, to continue the analogy, is, of course, nature, which has used its shaping powers of beauty and fear to mold its materials in accordance with its desired ends.

Musical harmony, however, carries with it an inevitable suggestion of simultaneity, whereas growth that is empirically determined must necessarily view the reconciliation of the mind's disparate experiences as a temporal ordering brought about through the mind's growing accumulation of sense-data. Thus, the most common metaphors for human development in these years are those that involve a process of building or fashioning or framing:

> But I believe
> That Nature, oftentimes, when she would frame
> A favor'd Being;
>
> (*Prelude*, I, 362–64)

and, addressing nature in the first book of *The Prelude,* Wordsworth tells how she did "intertwine for me / The passions that build up our human Soul" (I, 433–34) and "how the heart was fram'd / Of him thou lovest" (I, 656–67). The same kind of constructive metaphors also appear in references to development in *The Ruined Cottage:* the Pedlar's early history summed up by the phrase "So was he framed," [2] and a more general account of the laws of man's growth concluded with the proposition, "So build we up / The being that we are." [3] Indeed, even in that passage where the harmony of music serves as descriptive vehicle for the mind's growth, Wordsworth in the earliest manuscript version incorporates into that metaphor the relatively alien concept of temporal construction, emphasizing the sequential rather than the simultaneous as he tells how "The soul of man is fashioned & built up / Just like a strain of music." [4]

These mind metaphors, which are essentially compressed renderings of Wordsworth's most deeply rooted epistemological assumptions, are perhaps our most reliable guides in assessing the shifting pattern of Wordsworth's developmental beliefs. We might note that from 1802 onward, figures from biology come to replace constructive metaphors, and their frequent appearance provides a useful index to Wordsworth's growing reliance upon organic explanations of the mind's processes. Wordsworth did, of course, eventually adopt the Romantic notion of the organic, and the thoroughness with which he assimilated this idea is perhaps most clearly shown in one of the most successful of his later sonnets. In *"A Poet! —He hath put his heart to school"* Wordsworth, who at a much earlier time had characterized the poetic process as being "altogether slavish and mechanical," [5] describes it, instead, in this later sonnet as a vital growth impelled from within and determined by principles common to all organic development. To understand what Wordsworth in this later sonnet considers the poet's most important attributes—freedom and grandeur—he suggests we turn to the blooming flower "Because the lovely little flower is free / Down to its roots, and in that freedom, bold" (10–11), or to "the grandeur of the Forest-tree" (12), the final product of "its *own* divine vitality" (14). But this later habit of presenting the mind's development in terms of biological analogues is noticeably absent from the poetry written between 1797 and 1800. How free the writing of this period was of organic implications is perhaps most tellingly illustrated by a negative instance. Nowhere in the early manuscripts of Book I of *The Prelude*—those written no later than 1800—do we find that crucial organic metaphor with which all later versions begin their chronological recounting of the poet's spiritual history: "Fair seed-time had my soul" (I, 305). However hazardous any guess at motive may be, it seems probable that Wordsworth's decision to preface his account of childhood with a distinctively organic metaphor when he began to incorporate these earliest manuscripts with their emphasis on external determination into the full A text of *The Prelude,* can be explained by those practices of revision that reveal themselves still more strikingly in the textual changes to be found in *The Prelude* after the A text was completed. Just as Wordsworth in these later instances turned to revision as a means of disguising beliefs once firmly held but later discarded by introducing, for example, conventional forms and phrases of piety into passages that as originally written expressed convictions of the boldest unorthodoxy; so, too, here the insertion of an organic metaphor, it may be assumed, is intended to neutralize the effect of an empirical argument to which Wordsworth after 1800 no longer subscribed.

Another revealing aspect of the conflict between empiricism and organicism as to whether the mind's growth should be characterized mechanically or biologically appears in Wordsworth's treatment of the problem of personal identity. Philosophers before Locke, particularly those in the Christian tradition, had generally dealt with personal identity within the context of belief in a substantial soul that was simple, unitary, and continuous in time, even persisting through bodily death unaffected—or, at least, unaltered in basic structure—by the fluctuating appearances of the external world. But by his polemic against innate ideas, Locke had philosophically discredited the notion of a fully formed self given us at birth, providing in its place a new concept of the self, empirically grounded, that was to become the dominant theory for the eighteenth century. The once continuous ego had become the momentary "I" compounded from the ever-changing ideas of sensation and reflection; and personal identity in Locke came to be lodged "not in the identity of substance, but . . . in the identity of consciousness," [6] the result being that personality, as Ernest Tuveson characterizes its Lockian version, "exists, not throughout a lifetime as an essence, but hardly from hour to hour." [7] By the middle of the eighteenth century, David Hume had reduced the fixed element in personal identity still more, denying that any discernible consciousness of self is given us with our internal perceptions and attributing the unverifiable belief of man in his own continuing identity to the processes of memory alone. Finally Joseph Priestley, the most noted exponent of Hartley's radical empiricism at the close of the century, brings the debate of the empiricists to what would seem to be its logical close by denying that empirical reality can ever resolve the mystery of the origins of this belief. Although acknowledging as incontrovertible psychological fact that the awareness of identity has been a universal phenomenon, Priestley nonetheless contends that it would be as difficult to explain why we feel a sense of self-identity as to explain why we speak of the waters of the river Thames, which are "continually and visibly changing," as "the *same river* that it was a thousand years ago." [8] This was not, of course, to be the end of the larger philosophic controversy. Organicism later reintroduced the concept of a continuing, substantial self into philosophy, but in a much more sophisticated form. Within this new framework, the mind is no longer held to be completely formed from its first beginnings and provided at birth with a battery of self-evident propositions, as the most naïve proponents of innate ideas had argued before the appearance of Locke's *Essay.* Instead, the essential components of the self, according to these later proponents of organic development, are merely present in embryo, in beginnings that are, however, ultimately determining, so that the whole, even when materially unrealized, is understood always to exist, and subsequent growth is a process in which, as one critic who seeks to interpret Wordsworth from a purely organic point of view, E. D. Hirsch, writes, "The essence is the same, only the stage is different." [9]

For the empirically oriented writer, then, the principal measure of growth is substantive change; and though some mental content may persist in consciousness through memory, the fundamental habits and attitudes that constitute mind will undergo considerable variation during life's course. Conversely, the writer who accepts organic assumptions commits himself to seek that which is continuous and binding in the mind's evolution, those ways in which the child remains father of the man. This last phrase, and the poem whose argument it so succinctly expresses, provide a striking resumé of organicism's interpretation of human behavior in terms of a permanent core of the self that withstands change and produces an unbroken identity of response throughout life to a common sensible stimulus. But the fact that Wordsworth in 1802 was so deeply attuned to a nonempirical conception of human identity does not mean we can transfer this conception back to the poetry of earlier years when Wordsworth held a far different theory of mind, one requiring far different epistemological corollaries. Nonetheless, the views on identity expressed in the lyric on the rainbow are given an excessive centrality in studies of Wordsworth, and the majority of his critics have concluded with Hirsch that Wordsworth consistently conceived of mind as developing in accordance with a "pattern of organic, nonradical development." [10]

Despite Wordsworth's profession of faith in *My heart leaps up* that a sustaining thread of "natural piety" (the offspring of life's affective unity) runs through all our experience in defiance of external change and thus enables us to recognize the governing traits of later life even in our earliest childhood responses, the retrospective poetry written prior to 1800 offers no comparable basis for believing that either in an actualized or even latent form is there present in the child those traits that will later constitute the adult personality, as it is to be ideally realized. Such a statement must, of course, seem paradoxical, since Wordsworth's fullest and most memorable accounts of his childhood appear in the opening books of *The Prelude*. But when in an effort to fix his vacillating spirit and to carry out his poetic vocation, he searches among the events of childhood for new impetus, he does not refer to some continuing emotional impulse, primal intuition, or to any other quality of the interior life in the self-reproachful series of rhetorical questions that establish the structure of these opening books. Instead, these questions are addressed to the world of external nature that had endowed and transformed him, a transformation altering his character from what it had been in childhood and thereby making it possible for him now to be a poet; and in his failure to fulfill that vocation, it is the ministering agency of nature rather than the childhood self Wordsworth considers himself to have failed. About the value of these remembrances as an aid to self-analysis or to comprehension of his present lethargy, he is highly skeptical, asking doubtfully, in the digressive lines that conclude Book I, whether he can at all "be taught / To understand" (I, 654–55) himself or Coleridge learn "how the heart was fram'd / Of him thou lovest" (I, 656–57) through recollections of early childhood. The tone of the en-

tire digression is confessional, and at times even apologetic,
ascribing the poet's interest in his beginnings to "The weak-
ness of a human love, for days / Disown'd by memory" (I,
642–43), and admitting that those days may have little current
relevance to a study of the growth of a poet's mind. Even
the possibility that recollections of his early years will furnish
him with a necessary corrective to his present indolence,

> meet reproaches, too, whose power
> May spur me on, in manhood now mature,
> To honorable toil,
>
> (I, 651–53)

must be voiced tentatively, since "these hopes" (I, 653),
Wordsworth quickly and diffidently adds, might well "Be
vain" (I, 654). In the end, he rests his case for so extended
an account of his childhood years not upon any justifying
grounds of present utility but upon grounds of momentary
delight, the tempting pleasures held out to him by memory.
Thus, when he asks Coleridge for sympathy and tolerance
toward the prolonged act of self-indulgence that constitutes
Book I, it is because, Wordsworth tells us, he is

> loth to quit
> Those recollected hours that have the charm
> Of visionary things, and lovely forms
> And sweet sensations that throw back our life
> And almost make our Infancy itself
> A visible scene, on which the sun is shining.
>
> (I, 658–63)

Wordsworth does not suggest that the pleasurable acts of
memory carry with them some tangible mark that conveys to
us a sense of personal identity; they are not reverberations
that literally re-create emotions once felt by us but long since
suppressed. The pleasures of memory, instead, involve an

aesthetic responsiveness to an experience defined pictorially, the renewal by consciousness not of its earlier states of being but of its earlier contents. And though these recollected contents of consciousness "have the charm / Of visionary things," our perception of them remains relatively detached. Unlike the "visionary hours" of *To the Cuckoo,* the childhood past described in the opening book of *The Prelude* cannot be effectively reclaimed and born anew; it can be present to us as all recollected fact is present, but by no stimulus, such as that of the cuckoo, does Wordsworth here expect, as he later does in 1802, to "beget / That golden time again" (*To the Cuckoo,* 27–28). Indeed, the earliest manuscript (JJ) of this important meditation on the uses of memory closes on a deeply elegiac note, speaking to us of the essential pastness of the past, which may perhaps be contemplated but can never again be felt on the pulses as we move beyond it in our forward progress impelled by life's irreversible flow: "Those recollect[ed] hours that have the charm / Of visionary things" are finally pronounced to be irretrievable, "islands in the unnavigable depth / Of our departed time." [11] But once again Wordsworth tends to obscure the unmistakably empirical drift of this important passage and to disguise its controlling premise that the mind is essentially discontinuous by his additions to the passage in the A text. Having adopted a basically organic position by the time he came to revise, Wordsworth adds a second statement of desire to lines that had originally done no more than express a hope that from reminiscence he might fetch reproaches powerful enough to spur lagging poetic energies, a statement phrased in clearly vitalistic terms expressing the wish that through memory he also "might fetch / Invigorating thoughts from former years" (I, 648–49). With this, he raises hopes unvoiced prior to revision that the past can live in and, in fact, give life to the present, a fusion of the two that Wordsworth would have deemed impossible in 1798 or 1799.

Virtually every epistemologically significant revision of the A manuscript operates in this way, introducing into the text either a pointedly organic concept or some judgment that follows quite naturally from an organic point of view. Besides those already noted, one further manuscript addition merits discussion, since in it Wordsworth comes closest to claiming that past and present selves are indistinguishable, that an inseparable bond of self-identity might be assumed from the fact that childhood states of feeling can be reproduced with a remarkable degree of exactness in the later adult consciousness. To the description of his boyhood episodes of kite-flying, Wordsworth adds a brief but important reference to the emotional pleasures induced by recollection:

> Unfading recollections! at this hour
> The heart is almost mine with which I felt
> From some hill-top, on sunny afternoons
> The Kite high up among the fleecy clouds
> Pull at its rein, like an impatient Courser.
>
> (I, 517–21)

Since Wordsworth could hardly have anticipated the painstaking collection and analysis of manuscripts by de Selincourt, it seems reasonable to conclude that this addition, like the others, was consciously intended as a means of covering earlier traces and of bringing these important early books into seeming harmony with, or at least to diminish their dissonance from, the organically conceived sections that make up the great remainder of the poem.

But awareness of this consistent pattern of revision tends in the end to make us even more sensitive to the ineradicable fact of dissonance between early and late beliefs. Not only are Wordsworth's views on identity between 1797 and 1800 empirical, but they are radically empirical. It is not that he hesitates to admit the presence of organic connections between life's several stages but that he sees these areas as set apart by divisions that no attempt at retrospective scrutiny can ever bridge. The most important distinguishing traits of the past cannot persist in the present. The more nearly our lives approach the quiescent goals prescribed for them by nature and the more closely we move toward the state of being a fully perfected moral agent, the greater becomes our awareness of the permanent inaccessibility to us of the best of our childhood attributes. Thus he who becomes "the wisest and the best / Of all mankind" (*Prelude,* II, 22–23) can, Wordsworth complains, never again give "to duty and to truth / The eagerness of infantine desire" (*Prelude,* II, 25–26). What Wordsworth records in these early books is a personal experience of sensed disparity between present and past so intense and so vivid that it extends well beyond purely mental phenomena to affect, in a very literal sense, the physiological pulse of our being. It is not just the turbulent emotions of childhood that, overflowing their apparent psychic boundaries, carry with them "that giddy bliss / Which, like a tempest, works along the blood" (*Prelude,* I, 611–12), for the spiritual calm of maturity works in the same way, reaching out beyond mind to body, so that even as the poet reflects upon the passionate season of childhood, he is made aware of the positive change that the present has brought him, a new consciousness of the self experienced physiologically, "A tranquillizing spirit" that "presses now / On my corporeal frame" (*Prelude,* II, 27–28).

So great actually is the gulf between the child and the man, so alien are the feelings and conduct of early years to the poet's later temperament, that when Wordsworth enters into his longest sustained discussion of the mysteries of identity, he can contemplate them finally only in a mood of wonder:

> Ah me! that all
> The terrors, all the early miseries
> Regrets, vexations, lassitudes, that all

> The thoughts and feeling which had been infus'd
> Into my mind, should ever have made up
> The calm existence that is mine when I
> Am worthy of myself! [12]
>
> > *(Prelude,* I, 355–61)

Even here the binding force that draws these seemingly dis-connected elements into a new whole, one that bears little apparent resemblance to its contributing parts, is, as Words-worth makes clear in the lines that follow, the agency of ex-ternal nature. For when Wordsworth offers "Praise to the end" (I, 361) and "Thanks likewise to the means" (I, 362), he addresses himself to "Nature" (or in the animistic phrases of JJ and V to the "genii" or "spirits" of nature) who sought him out "With gentlest visitation" or "Severer interventions" in her efforts to "frame / A favor'd Being" (I, 363–64). No-where, however, does he point to any internal basis for the incontestable psychological fact of personal identity, that knowledge universally attested to which assures us that our past experience is our own. At times, instead, so distant in modes of apprehension and feeling do our present and past selves seem, that introspection seems to repudiate the neces-sary fact of identity, the inward consciousness seemingly un-able to locate those notations of memory that convey to us the knowledge that what we recollect we have actually ex-perienced. Thus, looking back upon the boyhood days he describes in *The Prelude,* Wordsworth writes:

> That, sometimes, when I think of them, I seem
> Two consciousnesses, conscious of myself
> And of some other Being.
>
> > (II, 31–33)

But a more systematic exposition of Wordsworth's views on identity than the occasional glimpses of discontinuity re-ported in *The Prelude* is found once more in the fully elaborated scheme of *Tintern Abbey*. In setting forth his doctrine of the three stages of human life, Wordsworth treats each of them as wholly discrete. There is, he seems to say, continuity of mental content through retention and storing of mental images, but there is little else, except perhaps memory, upon which to base the identity and continuity of the receptive self. Human growth proceeds according to a series of essentially distinct stages: as each stage is abandoned, its defining characteristics are not assimilated into a subsequent stage but are finally and irretrievably lost. The "glad animal movements" and "coarser pleasures" of childhood and the "appetite," the "feeling," and the "love" that characterized youth have, for Wordsworth, literally vanished, those earliest feelings "all gone by," and the "dizzy raptures" that followed "now no more." Of course, despite its radical discontinuity, the process of development remains purposeful. The consciousness of lost vitality, when understood properly, is to be borne not as a burden but as a banner, testifying to the possession of an inward calm mirroring nature's and to the acquisition of that compensatory moral and spiritual awareness by which Wordsworth defines maturity.

Wordsworth's handling of such topics as personal growth and personal identity between 1797 and 1800 further corroborates the deeply empirical orientation of these years. And with such an orientation, it is not surprising that mind stands to the external world in an essentially passive relationship. To speak of mind as essentially passive in its relation to the principal source of its experience does not mean, however, that it is altogether passive, that in every instance our perceived experience is received by us completely independent of our own acts and choices. Any empirical theory must, to some extent, make allowances for a limited number of internal controls over what materials finally present themselves to consciousness and even over the form these materials will take. That is, there is an indisputable element of willed activity in such mental processes as choosing to attend to the external world or, oftentimes, even in selecting an object from that world on which to concentrate. Recollection, too, seems in some cases to involve processes of selection inexplicable solely on the basis of associationism's automatic shuffling of stored images. Finally, it is difficult to ignore the fact that when the individual perceives the world about him, his given perceptions must always occur within a frame of reference created by the characteristics and activities of human consciousness. Man perceives not as a blank tablet but as a psychological being; and feeling tones, pleasures and pains, and aesthetic responses (though many of these forms of response may be themselves complex derivatives of earlier impressions), all contribute qualities of their own to the objects impressed upon us.[13]

We may concede the difficulty of a pure empiricism in which mind is absolutely passive, particularly its difficulty for a poet who must concern himself more closely with the a posteriori truths of his own personal experience than with the a priori necessities of philosophy's methodological rigor. Wordsworth's occasional allusion to activities of mind that seem self-determined does not, however, mean that we must therefore withdraw the case for Wordsworth's fundamental empiricism, as some critics—arguing that such occasions express his profoundest intuitions, intuitions projected in opposition to the age's profoundest beliefs—would have us do.[14] Such a denial seems warranted by neither the bulk nor the spirit of Wordsworth's philosophical opinions; and, more important, even those occasions that present instances of the mind's active powers do not upon closer inspection seem themselves to be greatly at odds with his more commonly expressed philosophic opinions. For he either so hedges these instances in qualifications or so clearly frames them within an empiricist context that he substantially mutes any suggestion of deviation from his more frequently stated views on the nature of mind. At one place, for example, he tells how the Pedlar

> attained
> An *active* power to fasten images
> Upon his brain, and on their pictured lines
> Intensely brooded, even till they acquired
> The liveliness of dreams.[15]

This *"active* power," though deemed by Wordsworth as sufficiently important to be underscored in his reference to it, is, despite this mark of emphasis, very clearly a power to select rather than to synthesize. Even with so limited a function, the mind's activity, a "precious gift," is not a power implanted from the first in the Pedlar but one he acquired through the cumulative effects of prior experience. Its genesis, as Wordsworth details it, is in a combination of earlier factors mutually and beneficially interacting: an extraordinary sensibility governed by "deep feelings," receiving and retaining images with an astonishing clarity and solidity, in interaction with the productive source of these images, nature, whose grandeur leaves the mind dissatisfied with anything less than the beauty and power of natural impressions. It is through this empirical union of internal sensibility (wisely passive) and external grandeur that the Pedlar had

> had impressed
> Great objects on his mind, with portraiture
> And colour so distinct [that on his mind]
> They lay like substances, and almost seemed
> To haunt the bodily sense.[16]

Such receptivity and the images that result from it for the Pedlar constitute "A precious gift"; for it is from images thus implanted and preserved virtually intact by memory, Wordsworth explains, that the Pedlar attains even this narrowly conceived form of *"active* power."

At times, of course, even in these years, Wordsworth does undeniably speak of the mind as contributing something of its own to experience. Such instances appear most frequently in Wordsworth's accounts of youth, his own or others, the stage in which he first became alerted to the intrinsic qualities and values of nature, but when he still responded to these in a spirit of passion rather than with the maturer habits of receptivity of "a heart / That watches and receives." The epistemological consequences of these youthful passions are most fully described in a well-known passage from *The Prelude:*

> A plastic power
> Abode with me, a forming hand, at times
> Rebellious, acting in a devious mood,
> A local spirit of its own, at war
> With general tendency, but for the most
> Subservient strictly to the external things
> With which it commun'd. An auxiliar light
> Came from my mind which on the setting sun
> Bestow'd new splendor, the melodious birds,
> The gentle breezes, fountains that ran on,
> Murmuring so sweetly in themselves, obey'd
> A like dominion; and the midnight storm
> Grew darker in the presence of my eye.
>   (II, 381–93)

Again one must cautiously assess these lines, bearing in mind the broader epistemological context in which they occur. In the majority of cases, the process Wordsworth describes here does little more than deepen the primary characteristics of objects of perception, investing these characteristics with a kind of luminous aura that greatly heightens their vividness without in any way altering their appearance or design. What the passionate mind of youth thus contributes to experience are its own moods rather than, in any Kantian sense, its own categories. Furthermore, when this "plastic power" acts otherwise and, in opposition to the customary appearances of "external things," "dissolves, diffuses, dissipates, in order to recreate," the result, as Wordsworth interprets it, is not a new and higher creation justified on the grounds of imaginative truth, the laws of which preempt all others, but a distortion of the world as it in reality exists. Later in *The Prelude,* that is, in the books composed in 1804 and after, Wordsworth does return to this plastic power and distorting tendency and makes it the basis for his theory of the fancy and, therefore, the basis, in part, for his important distinction between fancy and imagination. But at the time Book II was written, Wordsworth was clearly disinclined to ascribe any such positive virtues—even those of being a minor adjunct to the poetic process—to a power that is so willfully distorting. His language when he speaks of its "war / With general tendency" is, in a comparative sense, unfailingly critical: here in *The Prelude* he speaks of it as "Rebellious, acting in a devious mood"; and when, in the semiautobiographic section of *The Ruined Cottage,* he tells how at a similar stage the Pedlar was moved by similar feelings, those moments when the youthful Pedlar "wished the winds might rage / When they were silent" [17] are characterized as moods in which "his mind became disturbed" [18] and in which he was driven by "the fever of his heart." [19]

At the risk of overqualifying my argument, I have said that Wordsworth was critical only in a comparative sense, since the mind's active power, whether it actually distorts the appearances of nature or merely intensifies them, is in this case of instrumental value, one of the tendencies of man that nature must play upon in guiding him to maturity. Because we begin childhood as creatures of passionate intensity and because in youth this state of feeling is only slightly reduced, nature must generate vivid splendors and excitements of its own as fuel for our passions, if it wishes to capture our attention and direct our destinies toward its larger and more tranquil ends. Nevertheless, what is epistemologically significant about this passage is the temporary duration that Wordsworth implicitly assigns to this plastic power, apparently limiting its span of activity only to the period of youth. For this operation of mind is clearly not a foretaste of some greater power of imaginative synthesis that we acquire and use in maturity. Instead, maturity requires as its necessary precondition a quelling of the mind's disturbances and of "the fever in the heart," a stilling of passion so that mind, which in its obtained tranquillity becomes increasingly passive and receptive, can view things not through the distorting medium projected by youth's fevered vision but in ways that more nearly approximate the "general tendency" of things as they are.

Perhaps the statement of the mind's creativity that for many critics has served as the test case of how consistently and how genuinely empirical Wordsworth actually was during these early years are those lines from *Tintern Abbey* (intentionally set aside in my earlier analysis of that poem) that describe his love for

> all that we behold
> From this green earth; of all the mighty world
> Of eye and ear,—both what they half create,
> And what perceive.

>   (104–7)

Since these lines seem to stand free of the restrictive conditions attached to other statements of the mind's activity written at this time, the passage is often treated as a transcendental protest lodged by Wordsworth's deeper nature against the general sensationalism expressed in *Tintern Abbey* and as a transcendental anticipation of the belief in the mind's creative mastery over the senses that he elaborates later.[20] But it is also possible, as Professor Abrams cautions, that in this passage Wordsworth does not really contradict the poem's otherwise uniformly sensationalistic argument, since "the elements created in the act of perception may well be nothing more than Locke's secondary sense-qualities." [21] Abrams bases his conjecture on Wordsworth's own annotation of these lines that cites as their source a passage of unmistakably Lockian character from Young's *Night Thoughts*.[22] In that passage, Young describes the formation of secondary qualities by a kind of sensory creativity (or perhaps we may reverse our terms and use Wordsworth's phrase "creative sensibility") in which the senses "Give taste to fruits; and harmony to groves; / Their radiant beams to gold, and gold's bright fire." From this Young concludes that the senses can, in an important sense, be said to "half create the wondrous world they see," and it is to this line that Wordsworth's note on *Tintern Abbey* alludes. And in a still more surprising turn, Young adds that so important is this form of sensory creativity that, without overstepping the empirical limits prescribed by Locke, it may be said that

> Our senses, as our reason, are divine.
> But for the magic organ's powerful charm,
> Earth were a rude, uncolour'd chaos still.[23]

These parallels between *Tintern Abbey* and *Night Thoughts* strikingly confirm Abrams's conjectures and do much to justify his cautionary warnings. But it is in a number of notebook entries from 1798–99 that we are made most aware of just how similar Wordsworth's view of man's creative role in the epistemological process is to that of Young, a poet, who, Marjorie Nicolson tells us, "in theory expressed, and in practice carried to its ultimate extreme, the implications . . . inherent in the scientific philosophy of the late seventeenth century." [24] Indeed, in one particular, at least, Wordsworth goes beyond Young in the lengths to which he seems willing to carry the empirical argument. To anyone still adhering to the age-old Platonic-Christian belief that man's likeness to God is most evident in the purely intellectual and rational faculties that distinguish men from beasts, the elevation of the senses above reason in the scale of divinity is a notion obviously tinged with heresy. Young, therefore, is careful in exalting the senses not to dethrone reason from its former place of authority. Wordsworth, however, at least in the privacy of his notebooks, makes no such concessions to tradition or orthodoxy. In one of these passages, he writes:

> the godlike senses gave
> Short impulses of life that seemed to tell
> Of our existence, and then passed away.[25]

In another unpublished notebook entry (of obvious relevance to *Tintern Abbey*'s "mighty world / Of eye and ear") [26] Wordsworth presents an exceptionally detailed explanation of the part played by the senses in the perceptual process. Wordsworth here speaks again of the mind's activity, but in a way that is so uncompromisingly sensationalistic that it should, I think, convincingly dispel any possibility that Wordsworth at this time either held transcendental beliefs about the nature of the mind or, as some critics maintain, found himself attracted at a deeper and more intuitive level of feeling to such beliefs while maintaining a kind of public loyalty to the more conventional position of Locke and Hartley:

> There is creation in the eye,
> Nor less in all the other senses; powers
> They are that colour, model, and combine
> The things perceived with such an absolute
> Essential energy that we may say
> That those most godlike faculties of ours

At one and the same moment are the mind
And the mind's minister. In many a walk
At evening or by moonlight, or reclined
At midday upon beds of forest moss,
Have we to Nature and her impulses
Of our whole being made free gift, and when
Our trance had left us, oft have we, by aid
Of the impressions which it left behind,
Looked inward on ourselves, and learned, perhaps,
Something of what we are.[27]

In this account of the derivation of our knowledge through
the senses Wordsworth plainly follows Locke's theory of representative perception quite closely. "Nature," the world of
material substance, transmits "impulses," "singly imperceptible bodies" that emanate from external objects, to the senses
"and thereby convey to the brain some motion which produces these ideas which we have of them in us." [28] Moreover,
Wordsworth apparently agrees with Locke that the world as
we perceive it is not an exact copy of the material world but
only a partial representation of it, since such secondary qualities as color do not exist in the substantial object but only in
the representation of that object given us in sense perception.
But Wordsworth, in fact, seems to place even greater restrictive limits than Locke upon what we can know of the external
world. For in addition to coloring the things perceived, the
senses also "model" them, according to Wordsworth. By suggesting that figure too has no existence apart from the mind,
Wordsworth would seem to leave the material world even
stranger and vaguer than the colorless, odorless, but geomet-
rically figured, universe conceived of by Locke. Within the
circumscribed limits of empiricism, Wordsworth does then
allow the individual a form of activity in the act of perception, but it is an activity that paradoxically involves the conversion not of appearance to reality but of reality to appearance.

What emerges from this important passage then is basic

agreement with Locke's general account of perception, but points of variance from it where Wordsworth seems allied with the even more radical versions of sensationalism that had evolved from Locke. The astonishing hold Locke's new way of ideas had upon the eighteenth century can be attributed largely to its willingness to accommodate the methods and findings of the new science to our common-sense view of perception with its sharply polarized distinction between the stuff of the world and the contents of consciousness. But the price paid by Locke for his advocacy of a common-sense epistemology was an acquiescence, conceded with obvious reluctance, in the Cartesian dualism of mind and body with all its attendant difficulties. During the next century, followers of Locke almost invariably sought to rid his philosophy of its dualistic perplexities and to recast it in the form of a more logically intelligible monism. From the long perspective of the history of philosophy, the true line of descent—at least for us—is basically idealistic and phenomenalistic and runs from Locke to Berkeley to Hume. Of comparable interest to the eighteenth century—certainly to the radical circles in which the young Wordsworth moved—were the attempts at a materialistic reformulation of Locke undertaken tentatively at first by Hartley and then more boldly by Joseph Priestley. Locke himself had, to a certain extent, left the way open to a materialistic reformulation of his doctrine by admitting that it was no more difficult "to conceive that God can, if he pleases, superadd to matter a faculty of thinking, than that he should superadd to it another substance with a faculty of thinking." [29] Judiciously applying to Locke's speculative aside the philosophic prohibition against needless multiplication of entities, Priestley found in Locke's epistemology—particularly when viewed from the perspective offered by Hartley's mechanistic modifications of it—sufficient authority to argue materialistically that "man does not consist of two principles so essentially different from one another as *matter* and *spirit*" but is of "some *uniform composition,* and that the property of *perception,* as well as the other powers that are termed *mental,* is the result (whether necessary or not) of such an organical structure as that of the brain." [30]

Though Wordsworth must certainly have known of Priestley's opinions and would probably at some time have read the work of a contemporary radical, politically and philosophically so eminent,[31] I am in no way trying to suggest that Wordsworth was covertly either a follower of Priestley or a committed materialist. Most of the poetry of the period under discussion treats matters concerned with perception or the knowledge based upon perception within the framework of a conventional mind-body dualism. Again this is so, not, I think, because Wordsworth was unable to escape the influence of Locke, but because this is the way men, when they do not have to concern themselves with the challenges of philosophic disputation, have habitually characterized their experience of mind and the world. But though, in the majority of cases, Wordsworth as poet, "a man speaking to men," expresses such a dualism, passages like those from the *Christabel* notebook reveal a deep yearning for monism, a desire to understand wherein the unity of man and nature consists and to learn from that "Something of what we are." What is clear, however, is that Wordsworth's resolution of the most basic of epistemological problems does not lead him to transcendentalism; he does not try to bridge the gulf between mind and matter by reading nature as spirit. Alert as he probably was to the materialistic philosophies that in France and England had attached themselves to the cause of political liberty, Wordsworth tended in his less-guarded speculations to reduce the status of the mind in the hierarchy of man's faculties and to elevate to its place those human powers which resemble most closely the productive powers of nature. In the most striking illustration of this, Wordsworth, unlike Young, characterizes the senses—and the senses alone—as "godlike."

Furthermore, Wordsworth expands the activities of the senses, delegating to them the important function of "combining," which in Locke's *Essay* had been one of the primary operations of the mind, the means whereby "all complex ideas are made." [32] To exalt the senses, Wordsworth not only dispossesses the mind of what in the Lockian scheme are its normal creative functions, but he also divests it of the grandeur or intensity customarily attributed to mind in its creative aspects. Indeed, what causes Wordsworth to praise the senses as "godlike" is the "absolute / Essential energy" with which they "colour, model, and combine" the things perceived. And this conception of the divine creativity of the senses, although paradoxically anticipating the language later used by the Romantics to describe the transcendental imagination, draws Wordsworth as close as he is ever to come to a materialistic interpretation of man. By so shifting man's necessary creative functions from mind to the senses, Wordsworth is led to conclude

> that we may say
> That those most godlike faculties of ours
> At one and the same moment are the mind
> And the mind's minister.

Even here his views are scarcely doctrinaire, since to speak of the senses as being simultaneously "the mind / And the mind's minister" is to leave this complicated epistemological relationship still ambiguous and unresolved. Yet by reducing his options to these two possible relations between mind and the senses, Wordsworth makes perfectly evident—Coleridge's later suppositions notwithstanding—that at the time the plans for *The Recluse* were first contemplated its author was as yet hardly ready to lay "a solid and immovable foundation for the edifice by removing the sandy sophisms of Locke, and the mechanic dogmatists." [33] In truth, it would seem that the author of *The Recluse* was far more inclined in 1798 to the belief that the mind was a product of the senses than to the conviction held by Coleridge—and more than likely by Wordsworth at that later time as well—that "the senses were living growths and developments of the mind and spirit." [34]

Exactly what authority these passages have in any exposition of Wordsworth's thought is, of course, difficult to assess, since Wordsworth saw fit neither to develop nor to publish them. They may be nothing more than poetic jottings, random speculations and conjectures of sufficient interest to him to be entered in a notebook, but not of sufficient merit to win his full assent. But I do not think that this is the case. Considering what is already known of Wordsworth's habits of composition, I think it far more probable that he withheld these passages, like others of equally questionable orthodoxy, from publication out of fear that they would divert attention from the undeniable strengths of his poetry and jeopardize its chances of public acceptance. If in the end, the notebook entries do not establish a hard and fast position for Wordsworth, one that would meet the test of the academic philosopher, they do, nonetheless, indicate a general tendency and drift of mind of sufficient strength and consistency to allow us to place Wordsworth, for all practical purposes, securely in the empirical tradition.

1. Samuel Taylor Coleridge, *The Philosophical Lectures,* ed. Kathleen Coburn (New York, 1946), p. 196.

2. *PW,* V, 388 (*The Ruined Cottage,* l. 301).

3. Ibid., p. 402 (*The Ruined Cottage* [Addendum to MS.B, ll. 57–58]).

4. *Prelude,* p. 640 (a passage from MS. JJ).

5. *PW,* II, 394, n. 2.

6. John Locke, *An Essay Concerning Human Understanding,* ed. A. S. Pringle-Pattison (Oxford, 1924), p. 195.

7. Ernest Lee Tuveson, *The Imagination as a Means of Grace* (Berkeley, Calif., 1960), p. 29.

8. Joseph Priestley, *Disquisitions on Matter and Spirit,* in *Works* (Hackney, n. d.), III: 330.

9. E. D. Hirsch, *Wordsworth and Schelling: A Typological Study in Romanticism*, Yale Studies in English, vol. 145 (New Haven, Conn., 1960), p. 78.

10. Ibid.

11. *Prelude*, p. 641 (a passage from MS. JJ).

12. There is some confusion in the de Selincourt-Darbishire edition as to whether these lines first appear in MS.V or MS.A. They are not to be found in the variant reading from V, which the edition cites, but the notes to I, 351–72 do refer to another unspecified manuscript version that would seem to contain this passage on identity. I am very grateful to Mr. Michael Jaye for making the results of his own research on the early manuscripts of *The Prelude* available to me. Mr. Jaye informs me that these lines do appear in a corrected passage from V in a form that differs slightly but not, I think, substantively from the lines printed by de Selincourt in A. Mr. Jaye thinks that the most probable date for this addition to V is 1801, that is, a year prior to the time when Wordsworth's views on identity underwent a major change.

13. M. H. Abrams discusses this in *The Mirrror and the Lamp* (New York, 1958), pp. 62–64.

14. In its extreme form, this is the position held by Weaver. But others who seek to transcendentalize Wordsworth argue in essentially this way.

15. *PW*, V, 381 *(The Ruined Cottage*, ll. 90–94).

16. Ibid. *(The Ruined Cottage*, ll. 81–85).

17. Ibid., p. 384 *(The Ruined Cottage*, ll. 225–26).

18. Ibid. *(The Ruined Cottage*, l. 224).

19. Ibid., p. 385 *(The Ruined Cottage*, l. 237).

20. For a transcendental interpretation of these lines, see, among others, Weaver (p. 41), Rader (p. 156), and Hirsch (p. 124).

21. Abrams, p. 62.

22. Wordsworth writes, "This line has a close resemblance to an admirable line of Young's, the exact expression of which I do not recollect." *PW*, II, 262.

23. Edward Young, *Night Thoughts*, in *Poetical Works* (London, 1913), I: 124.

24. Marjorie Hope Nicolson, *Newton Demands the Muse* (Princeton, N.J., 1946), p. 149.

25. *PW*, V, 344 (Appendix B, IV, vii, 12–14).

26. Hartman notes the three-way resemblance between this entry and the lines from *Night Thoughts* and from *Tintern Abbey*, but he fails to explore their relationship more thoroughly, largely, I suspect, because of the transcendental presuppositions that underlie his own argument. James A. W. Heffernan in *Wordsworth's Theory of Poetry* (Ithaca, N.Y., 1969) also notes the resemblance of these passages. Similarly committed to an approach that assumes the transforming powers of imagination, he cites the fragment from the *Christabel* notebook as evidence of "the continuity between sense perception and imaginative transformation" so that "creation begins, not in the psyche, but in the eyes and ears" (p. 70). But neither in *Tintern Abbey* nor

in this fragment (with its suggestion that the senses alone may constitute mind) does Wordsworth mention any autonomous faculty of imagination that concludes the work of creativity begun by the senses.

27. *PW*, V, 343–44 (Appendix B, IV, vi, 1–16).

28. Locke, p. 68.

29. Ibid., pp. 269–70.

30. Joseph Priestley, *Introductory Essays to Hartley's Theory of the Human Mind*, in *Works*, III:181–82.

31. "No name appears so frequently as his [Priestley's] among the book reviews of the *Gentleman's Magazine* and *The Monthly Review* between 1789 and 1796." George McLean Harper, *William Wordsworth* (London, 1929), p. 197. It is worth noting too that Joseph Johnson, who served as publisher to Priestley, also published Wordsworth's earliest work.

32. Locke, p. 92.

33. Samuel Taylor Coleridge, *Letters*, ed. Ernest Hartley Coleridge (London, 1895), II:648.

34. Ibid.

3

The Empirical Phase:
Theory of Nature

In his valuable study of Shelley's *Prometheus Unbound,* Earl Wasserman maintains that the true stimulus to Shelley's thought came from a complex cultural situation in which the poet found himself necessarily placed by historical circumstance rather than from the writings of any single philosopher, however eminent and however congenial. Arguing against those who would uncritically superimpose upon the pattern of Shelley's own philosophic scheme the essentially alien doctrines of a historically distant Plato, Wasserman writes, "Shelley's thought must be understood as generically derived from British empiricism and its eighteenth-century developments, which more than ever had made the problems of ontology crucial. The direction his thinking took was determined by his efforts to settle in his own way the kinds of questions raised by the British empiricists, whose heirs the Romantics were, not by his conviction of the truth of any one philosopher's system." [1] As a result, the thought of Shelley evolves into a highly idiosyncratic form of idealism that "in many of its features," as Wasserman observes, "closely resembles that of the German post-Kantians, precisely because the historical situation presented them with approximately the same questions in approximately the same philosophic context." [2]

What Wasserman says of Shelley can be applied—with appropriate modification—to Wordsworth on much the same grounds. Writing two decades earlier than Shelley in a climate of still fervent political expectation more conducive to Lockian sensationalism than to Humeian skepticism or Kantian or post-Kantian idealism, Wordsworth obviously found the materialistic offshoots of empiricism more suited to his personal objectives than its idealistic derivatives. The result in Wordsworth's case—at least during the years from 1797 to 1800—is an idiosyncratic form of sensationalism based essentially on Locke that, nonetheless, resembles the theories of Hartley and Priestley "because the historical situation presented them with approximately the same questions in approximately the same philosophic context." By approaching Wordsworth in this way, we avoid many of the problems of an older historical method that, with its excessive emphasis on causation through source and influence, demanded a one-to-one equivalence between poetic statement and philosophic antecedent. We still preserve a significant historical context, while granting the poet sufficient imaginative freedom to assemble his own philosophic structures in accordance with the incentives and checks of lived experience.

Something of this sort appears (as we have already learned from the notebook entries) in the adjustments Wordsworth makes in his basically Lockian theory of the mind in response to certain highly charged moments of personal revelation, adjustments that almost always move him in the direction of a stricter and more radical sensationalism. But Wordsworth's departures from the Lockian scheme are even more pronounced and idiosyncratic in his presentation of the external world than in his presentation of mind. First, the external world is value-oriented, and not merely in the traditional sense of being an emblem of values beyond itself, illustrating by the working of a great chain of being or by *concordia discors* the will of that benevolent but hidden power whose pur-

poses underlie the entire natural order. Instead, for Wordsworth the external world—at least that part of it which makes
up Wordsworthian nature—possesses as part of its own internal constitution intrinsic moral and aesthetic qualities
that it transmits directly and palpably to us by sensation. In
founding knowledge upon experience, Locke had introduced
into philosophic discourse a dangerous split between knowledge and value. Wordsworth sought to heal this split (inevitable perhaps with empiricism's scientific orientation) not
by reestablishing the origins of knowledge in their former
home, the mind, but by implanting value in the world itself.
The second major departure from Locke by Wordsworth is
in his willingness to ascribe to the ontological reality that
generates all phenomenal appearances attributes that on strict
Lockian principles should have remained forever unknowable.

Even these changes take place within a relatively stable
Lockian framework, for the world view implied by the representative theory of perception is the model presupposed in
all of Wordsworth's metaphysical speculations. The implied
presence of such a model is most apparent in those places
where Wordsworth describes perception in terms of impulse:
when he tells, for example, of those occasions in which we
have "to nature and her impulses / Of our whole being made
free gift," or when he celebrates the moral benefits conferred
by "One impulse from a vernal wood." A more detailed de-
piction of this view of reality occurs in a passage in *A Poet's
Epitaph*, a passage significant for our purposes not because it
possesses the abstract and formalized qualities of Wordsworth's lengthier passages of philosophic exposition but because its very concreteness and unobtrusiveness disclose how
habitual a basis for thinking about the world this model had
become in 1799:

> The outward shows of sky and earth,
> Of hill and valley, he has viewed;

And impulses of deeper birth
Have come to him in solitude.
(45–48)

Natural objects according to these lines manifest themselves in three forms, each of them taking its place in a kind of hierarchy of values, a hierarchy determined by the ontological status Wordsworth assigns to each of its three components. The first of these manifestations is as phenomenal appearance, "outward shows," the form in which we commonly experience the world as visually perceived images; the second manifestation is as impulse, unperceived particles produced by objects to impinge upon the senses and, thus, to mediate between the self and the world; finally, there is a form of existence of things that can properly be spoken of as objective, in which things truly exist in a world external to consciousness as real objects, serving there as the deep birthplace of mediating impulse and hence acting as the initiating cause of our sensible impressions. This description of metaphysical nature, whatever special features Wordsworth himself contributes to it, derives its basic outlines from those versions of the corpuscular theory prevalent in the eighteenth century, a theory whose best-known prototype and source was Locke's representative theory of perception with its similar tripartite division of the external world into idea, impulse, and substance.[3]

Between "outward shows" and image, and between Wordsworthian and Lockian impulse, there is sufficient correspondence to demonstrate at least a loose indebtedness and a common tradition. It is in the third element, Wordsworth's object and Locke's substance—in both schemes, the ontological ground of all else—that differences become marked enough to indicate how dissimilar the speculative intention of each writer truly is. For Locke's *Essay*, though not categorically repudiating all metaphysical inferences like some later empiricisms, proposes what is, in large measure, a critical philosophy aimed at scholastic excesses and designed to establish epistemological limits beyond which speculation becomes unprofitable. To be sure, Locke does attribute to objects themselves the primary qualities of "solidity, extension, figure, and mobility," [4] a conclusion indefensible on purely empirical grounds, as Berkeley readily understood, but one that Locke probably thought unavoidable if the integrity of the mathematically measurable findings of science was to be preserved. More often though, Locke's observations about the external world were cautious and critical of those whose observations were freely speculative. We give credence, Locke suggests, to the idea of substance because we believe that qualities "cannot subsist *sine re substante,* without something to support them"; [5] but substance in itself exists for us only as a vague substratum, what Locke in a famous confession of metaphysical uncertainty speaks of as an "uncertain supposition of we know not what." [6] For Wordsworth, on the other hand, the proper end of speculation, certainly poetically inspired speculation, is not the contraction but the expansion of our metaphysical horizons. And in this respect, Wordsworth concurs, and most significantly, with the majority of his Romantic contemporaries and successors, who with their fundamentally idealistic orientation believed that the primary task of those who lived in the aftermath of a skeptically and scientifically inclined empiricism's analytical dismemberment of the traditional classical-Christian world view was metaphysical reconstruction. The external world at the level of the ontologically substantial was for Wordsworth a real object of knowledge. The unity and calm of *Tintern Abbey*'s visual landscape could, without misgivings, be transferred as qualities—descriptive attributes—to the underlying reality which that perceived landscape represents. But the attribution of unity and calm to the substances of nature does not depend solely upon inference, hypothetical judgments reached about the unknown from our experience of the empirically known.

Above all, for Wordsworth, real essences are knowable by direct perception; in a phrase whose full importance to him should not be underestimated, "We see into the life of things."

In a curious way, there seems to exist a very rough correlation between the threefold division of the external world into idea, impulse, and object and Wordsworth's three-stage explanation of human development in terms of childhood, youth, and maturity. This, of course, does not mean that during youth or maturity we no longer find it necessary to perceive the world through sensible ideas or that we are any less dependent upon visual, auditory, or other sensible faculties for the bulk of our ordinary—but though ordinary, nonetheless, indispensable—knowledge. As in each stage the mind seems to acquire new comprehensive powers, powers of perceiving and understanding an expanding and increasingly complex structure of relations, so also in each stage does the mind seem to acquire new penetrative powers, powers that seem to reach beyond the barriers of phenomenal knowledge and to carry us to deeper contact with, and more extended knowledge of, the real essences that comprise the external world.

The dominant mode through which nature speaks to us in the course of our lives is "the language of the sense." [7] In childhood, however, that language comes to us with an extraordinary vividness and a remarkable directness of address, so that whether its tones be inciting or admonitory, whether it moves us to pleasure or pain, it provides a crucial source of feeling and, ultimately, a persuasive guide for much of our conduct. At that time, Wordsworth writes, the epistemologically distant though animistically characterized "Presences of Nature," operating through sense phenomena,

> On caves and trees, upon the woods and hills,
> Impress'd upon all forms the characters

> Of danger or desire, and thus did make
> The surface of the universal earth
> With triumph, and delight, and hope, and fear,
> Work like a sea.
>
> (Prelude, I, 496–501)

In several other instances in *The Prelude* in which Wordsworth alludes generally to the part visual images played in his
early development, he is also careful to preserve this fundamental distinction between objects as they actually exist in
the external world and as they appear to consciousness, treating their relationship, moreover, as one of cause to effect. Nature is never the image itself but the causal agent that
"Peopled my mind with beauteous forms or grand" (I, 573).
Even the "changeful earth" is thought of—probably from
force of habit—as a body of objects located beyond consciousness whose operations, consequently, "on my mind had
stamp'd / The faces of the moving year" (I, 586–88).

Experience in childhood is almost without exception an
experience of sense phenomena, of "outward shows." Not
even in those rarest and most memorable of intervals isolated
from the ordinary round of daily activities, the childhood
spots of time, does the light of sense go out so that we are able
to set aside phenomenal appearance and spiritually intuit the
invisible world. Instead, these moments are themselves occasioned by sense-experience; sensory images or events that
take on exceptional overtones of depth and strangeness, or
that clash sharply with their surrounding context or with ensuing events, or that arise because the senses in a moment of
stress perceptually distort the normal state or configuration
of objects. The sight of "the naked Pool, / The Beacon on
the lonely Eminence" (*Prelude,* XI, 313–14) and "A Girl who
bore a Pitcher on her head" (*Prelude,* XI, 306), a spectacle
attended with "visionary dreariness" (*Prelude,* XI, 311); the
grotesque surfacing of a drowned man from the untroubled

waters of Esthwaite; the shattering of a child's expectations of homecoming by the disruptive and guilt-tinged shock of a father's death, a sequence of emotions somehow permanently incorporated into the gloomy landscape images of "The single sheep, and the one blasted tree, / And the bleak music of that old stone wall" (*Prelude,* XI, 378–79); and the apparent pursuit of a mischievous child, in consequence of his having stolen a boat, by "a huge Cliff" that moved "As if with voluntary power instinct" (*Prelude,* I, 406–7): all of these episodes, first recounted in the V manuscript of 1799,[8] are defined sensorily in language of the most striking particularity. These episodes possess the mind so deeply and adhere to the memory so fixedly, not because they evoke feelings of the world's immateriality that threaten the young Wordsworth with what in an 1843 note to the *Immortality Ode* he is ready to speak of as an "abyss of idealism," [9] but because they touch him with an extraordinary sensory power and vividness that set them apart from experiences less palpably felt.

The most important of these moments, for it is the only one that Wordsworth invests with explicit moral consequences, is the incident of the stolen boat and the pursuing mountain, an episode in which a moment of heightened sensory experience is the result of obvious perceptual distortion. In almost any empirical scheme, optical illusions or any other nonveridical perceptions are bound to create perplexity: they must be numbered among our ideas; but they are felt to be inaccurate and distorting representations of the unknowable objects that are their source; and hence these ideas are assumed to be, in a significant sense, unreal ideas. By asserting that ideas and objects agree as to their primary qualities, Locke had believed that these perplexities could be eliminated, at least in connection with "solidity, extension, figure, and mobility." The phenomenon of the moving mountain was plainly illusory, for in this instance the visual image fails to coincide, according to common sense, in the primary quality of mobility with the movements of the object itself. But the difficulty here, as Berkeley recognized, was that since the mobility of objects was a matter to be settled only by an appeal to facts and circumstances that lay beyond the possibilities of human knowledge, any such judgment as Locke makes rests, at best, on probability and inference, or, as is more likely, on the needs and desires of one seeking to continue in the tradition of an increasingly vulnerable philosophic realism. For Berkeley, of course, the problem of perceptual distortion could never truly arise. Since to be is to be perceived, the existential status of the nonveridical perception, the bent stick in the water or the cliff hastening after us, can in no way differ from the existential status of the veridical perception, the straight stick in the air or the cliff immobile and fixed in its customary place.

Wordsworth's explanation of his childhood experience of the mountain's pursuit of him would seem to place Wordsworth midway between Locke and Berkeley. The appearance of movement certainly has as one of its causes a disorientation of the senses, but we cannot therefore dismiss this movement merely as a baseless aberration. From the evidence of Wordsworth's commentary upon the incident, the unsettling appearance of the moving cliff is clearly regarded by him as the intended effect of nature's causal powers rather than as the accidental by-product of a distortion of the senses. The parenthetical reference to nature that begins the passage, "(surely I was led by her)" (I, 372)—a phrase that has no qualifying modifier attached to it in the V manuscript's animistically phrased variant, "They guided me, one evening led by them"—leaves little doubt that it is external nature that knowingly and purposefully draws the young Wordsworth to this corrective confrontation, so that it may use one of the forms available to it as sensory image to upset the child's normal perceptual observations, the "familiar shapes / Of hourly objects" (I, 423–24) and thereby disturb the moral complacency and indifference bred by an excessive self-regard. Similarly the hymn of praise to the powers ultimately responsible for these appearances again underlines the role Wordsworth believes that external causation has played in this episode and in its consequent moral effects.

> Wisdom and Spirit of the universe!
> Thou Soul that art the Eternity of Thought!
> That giv'st to forms and images a breath
> And everlasting motion! not in vain,
> By day or star-light thus from my first dawn
> Of Childhood didst Thou intertwine for me
> The passions that build up our human Soul,
> Not with the mean and vulgar works of Man,
> But with high objects, with enduring things,
> With life and nature, purifying thus
> The elements of feeling and of thought,
> And sanctifying by such discipline,
> Both pain and fear, until we recognize
> A grandeur in the beating of the heart.
>
> (I, 428–41)

These lines, quoted from A, differ in one important way from the early manuscripts, JJ and V, where the powers apostrophized are animistic presences rather than, as they become in A, Wordsworthian abstractions. But in this one case, at least, revision philosophically clarifies the meaning of an event in terms consistent with the point of view held by Wordsworth at the time he first described it. The abstractions addressed by Wordsworth, somewhat overly idealized versions of what in 1798 were described in terms of motion, force, and power, form the underlying substratum of reality, the substantial objects that are the productive cause of "forms and images," that give them being, constantly replenish it, and determine both the activities and appearance of the perceived phenomena of sense. The mountain moves, Wordsworth would seem to contend, because the reality it represents invests it with "a breath / And everlasting motion."

But the incident upon which these lines comment actually describes the processes involved in the formation of this remarkable illusion with considerably more subtlety than any simple emphasis on external causation alone would seem to suggest. Nature, understood here not just as a collection of objects or forms but as a total system of being including all its ends and purposes, produces these exceptional effects by the collaborative dealings this larger nature arranges between mind and the world. Again such arrangements are not to be confused with the forms of epistemological interchange contained in transcendentalism. The contribution of the mind is essentially through its psychological states, the enactment of a pattern of mental behavior that culminates in the responsiveness or receptivity necessary for the elements of external causation to produce these kinds of rare and intense perceptual experiences. Such experiences, moreover, seem restricted, for the most part, to childhood, because the behavioral pattern on which they depend has its basis in the interests and feelings dominant in our earliest years. Since childhood in Wordsworthian terms is the stage of deepest self-absorption and the most intense sensory and emotional awareness, there are occasions when the child focuses on those objects that feed his pleasure with a degree of concentration that excludes all else in the perceptual field from having noticeable significance for him. Yet such moments of the most intense self-regard are, paradoxically, the moments when the child is most susceptible to nature's influence or instruction. When concentration relaxes—as it does in *There Was a Boy* and *Nutting*—or when the perceptual field surrounding the focus of interest undergoes a marked or violent change—as it does in the incident of the stolen boat or Book I's other instances of the ministry of fear—the images subsequently implanted in the mind are, Wordsworth indicates, somehow endowed with an extraordinary vividness and power. Moreover, with the exception of the account of the boy hooting at the owls, all of these episodes present the child's quest for pleasure as a violation of the rights of others, either the property of man or the sanctity of nature, so that the psychological pattern of concentrated attention followed by the counter-thrust of a distinct and conflicting perceptual experience can be readily translated into the moral pattern of act and consequence.

This does not mean, however, that the pursuing mountain is to be taken, as it so often is, as an illustration of the incipient workings of conscience. The image is still derived essentially from the productive powers of the external world and the subsequent moral effect is still that intended by nature "when she would frame / A favor'd Being." But the notion of external causation must itself be modified to make clear the fact that nature must economically and, it would seem, almost knowingly make use of the varied behavioral patterns of man if the operations of external power are to produce their desired perceptual and ethical results. In the incident of the stolen boat, the child is led to the temptation of the unguarded boat by nature because nature can assuredly predict that the child will indulge himself, that he will take the boat and use it in an adventure that absorbs him sufficiently to allow the sudden appearance of the mountain to generate the shock and ensuing distortion needed to make the episode morally determining. Just as in the earlier episode of the plundered traps, Wordsworth describes himself as "Scudding away from snare to snare" (I, 319) and "hurrying on / Still hurrying, hurrying onward" (I, 320–21), so too in the later episode he partially secures the effect of concentration by the device of repetition: "I push'd, and struck the oars and struck again / In cadence" (I, 385–86). Another device used to convey the absorbed attention this self-gratifying enterprise requires is a simile that compares the boat's movement to that of "a Man who walks with stately step / Though bent on speed" (I, 387–88), that is, it is a movement that fosters great excitement but at the same time requires that the boy restrain and guide it by exercising over this condition of excitement the strictest and psychologically most demanding kinds of self-will and self-control.

Finally, Wordsworth directly expresses in visual terms the degree of concentrated attention that such an episode induces, when he tells how the boy

> fix'd a steady view
> Upon the top of that same craggy ridge,
> The bound of the horizon, far behind
> Was nothing but the stars and the grey sky.
> (I, 397–400)

It is the attentiveness with which the child fixes his gaze upon what he assumes to be "The bound of the horizon" that, of course, makes the sudden apparition of the cliff seem such an intrusive presence. The cliff seems to thrust itself between act and goal "As if with voluntary power instinct" (I, 407), because under these troubling circumstances the entry into what he took to be a fixed perceptual field of so unexpected and so spectacular a presence becomes explicable only by endowing it with a life and purpose of its own. There then follows a sequence of reversals, first in perception and then in conduct. The fixed object of attention gives way to the new and unexpected presence that thereupon seems quickly and ominously to fill the child's entire field of vision:

> the huge Cliff
> Rose up between me and the stars, and still,
> With measur'd motion, like a living thing,
> Strode after me,
> (I, 409–12)

and almost immediately the child tremblingly reverses his course and returns the boat to its original mooring-place. But there are more lasting consequences too, for the effect of the sudden reversal of expectations is that the image that immediately succeeds the initial object of attention and desire impregnates the mind with such power that it thereby acquires a lifelong authority over subsequent acts and feelings. As its direct aftermath, the spectacle observed by the young Wordsworth creates a violent dislocation of normal habits of thought and memory, displacing "familiar shapes" with "a dim and undetermin'd sense / Of unknown modes of being" (I, 419–20). But more distant effects of a more enduring moral significance are also produced by this complex incident. Since forms so indelibly imprinted are subject to ready recall, and since associational psychology holds that an act repeating or resembling an earlier one is likely to arouse in the mind the train of events and images that followed the earlier one, it becomes apparent that nature has led the child to the unguarded boat to instill for the future in the storehouse of memory a highly effective moral censor. In later life, similar temptations to disregard the rights and property of others will automatically call forth the unsettling image of the pursuing mountain and the sense of dislocation that succeeded it, until the repeated checks of association inculcate that permanent habit of self-restraint required before one can undertake the life of true moral benevolence.[10]

As long as the child's knowledge is almost entirely a knowledge of sensible forms, it clearly follows that incapable of, or unready for, any additional metaphysical inference, he will take the world at face value, regarding the externally impressed ideas that come before his consciousness not as representations but as objects in themselves, independent entities whose existence can be explained without recourse to any further agent of causation. Under normal circumstances, we experience this world as inanimate, as material for our will to mold in accordance with humanly desirable and desired ends. On occasion, however, especially in childhood, and most especially in Wordsworth's childhood, the world seems to behave as if it were the active agent and man the material to be molded; and on such occasions, it is easy for someone un- aware that these objects of consciousness are representations produced by metaphysically remote causes to interpret the activity of sensible objects as willed activity, emanating di- rectly from a conscious life that subsists independently and individually in the sensory image itself. In the tendency toward this interpretation of nature's activities (the tendency of the primitive, but for our purposes important only as the tendency of the child), we can find, I think, the basis for one of the most puzzling aspects of Wordsworth's thought, the unalloyed animism of certain passages in *The Prelude* and in *Nutting*. All of them are written in the period under discus- sion, and many of them are either excised completely in later revisions or are altered sufficiently to provide a less radically animistic and more abstractly philosophic presentation of nature and its effect on man. Moreover, all of the passages that can with certainty be called animistic are associated with childhood, some passages simply calling attention to the role played by nature's spirits and presences in drawing the unsuspecting child into self-indulgent acts that nature shall ultimately turn to his benefit, while others furnish a more extended commentary of praise to those same spiritual pres- ences for the general concern they exhibit for man's welfare.

Discussion of Wordsworth's animism has usually confined itself to the question of belief.[11] When Wordsworth in the earliest manuscripts of *The Prelude* addresses

> ye Beings of the hills,
> And ye that walk the woods and open heaths
> By moon or starlight,[12]

or some lines further

> Ye Powers of earth, ye genii of the Springs
> And ye that have your voices in the clouds

And ye that are familiars of the Lakes
And standing pools,[13]

did he actually hold that a local, personalized soul resided in individual natural objects, animating them, endowing them with purpose, and determining their behavior to man? On the strength of the metaphysical sophistication of the more speculative passages of *Tintern Abbey, The Ruined Cottage,* and the earliest segments of *The Prelude* itself (passages written at the same time or even earlier than the animistic statements), it seems most improbable that Wordsworth could have adopted so naïve a reading as consistent doctrine and highly unlikely that even at random moments, moments of the highest exhilaration, he would have substituted such local spirits and genii in his articles of philosophic faith for the abstractly conceived "something far more deeply interfused" that as a metaphysically depersonalized "motion and a spirit" is understood to roll "through all things." A more probable explanation of Wordsworth's animism can be derived from the fact that all of the passages in question, those undeniably animistic, occur in the first book of *The Prelude* and in those sections of it dealing with his earliest childhood. (*Nutting,* of course, was at the time of its composition intended as an episode in Book I.) What the animistic passages tend to do is to reproduce the judgments of childhood, when a limited capacity for metaphysical thinking forces the child to account for his experiences of natural agency as the workings of localized powers, presences and genii, which, though hidden from view, nonetheless still have their home in the immediate world of sense phenomena. Wordsworth repeats these judgments—in childhood prime articles of faith and fear—not because in later life he once more believes in them or even because by repeating them he hopes to renew for himself the uncomplicated intuitions and feelings of the past but because he intends the metaphysical argument of *The Prelude* to

evolve generally in a pattern of progressive revelation. From
the parts of the poem written between 1798 and 1800, we
can plainly distinguish two stages of this unfolding pattern:
first, the animistic inferences of childhood; then, the deepened metaphysical awareness that comes in youth and that
leads Wordsworth to regard nature's most intense and turbulent activities as the expression of depersonalized energies
that he terms a "sentiment" or "pulse of Being." And going
a stage beyond this, we can hypothesize that the poem was
supposed to conclude originally—as it did eventually—with
a dramatic epiphany of final discovery, a revelatory episode
similar to the ascent of Mount Snowdon, or perhaps that very
episode. But this earlier hypothetical episode, whether the
ascent of Snowdon or some other event, would presumably
have been given at this earlier date a philosophic construction
much more closely akin to the basically naturalistic speculations of *Tintern Abbey* than to the theistic and transcendental conclusions drawn from the culminating episode that
Wordsworth later actually wrote.

Earlier, the metaphysical correlative to the second stage of
human development, youth, was described as impulse. This
is probably too restrictive a label, imposing too rigid a
schematism at the cost of Wordsworth's imaginative freedom,
to describe the actual recognitions and insights of this period.
Certainly the claim of correlation between metaphysical understanding and developmental stage does not mean that the
youthful Wordsworth ever perceived directly the elementary
particles assumed to exist according to the corpuscular theory;
for whatever credibility might be given to the idea that such
particles did, in truth, exist derived from the postulate that
such particles were empirically undiscoverable, operating as
they did at a level below the threshold of normal sense perception. Instead, the common denominator that links the
two, the Wordsworthian awareness and the Lockian scheme,
might be more loosely defined as activity, an activity express-

ing itself through sense phenomena but one that we consciously recognize as originating in forces and movements that take place in an objective reality beyond our senses. Though Coleridgean vitalism and custom have dictated that we bleakly regard the world posed by the Lockian scheme as cold, inanimate, and dead in all respects that really matter, that world is, in fact, one of energy and movement, a place of constant activity that, though mechanistic rather than vital, offers to a poet of Wordsworth's temperament much in the way of imaginative possibility. The key elements in this metaphysical activity are power and impulse, power being understood as the qualities or modifications in objects themselves (in Locke only the original or primary qualities actually exist in objects) that "produce simple ideas in us," [14] and impulse as the imperceptible particles by means of which bodies convey resemblances of themselves (in the case of primary qualities) and representations of themselves (in the case of secondary qualities) to us as ideas. That during this empirically oriented period Wordsworth conceived of the activity of the external world in precisely this way is evident from the familiar sixth stanza of *Expostulation and Reply:*

> Nor less I deem that there are Powers
> Which of themselves our mind impress;
> That we can feed this mind of ours
> In a wise passiveness.
>
> (21–24)

The argument of *Expostulation and Reply* is essentially deductive, grounded in the need to provide some form of power and some kind of act that would reasonably explain how ideas that come to the mind originate. In *The Prelude,* however, the experience of those activities that in metaphysical terms underlie the phenomenal world results from a direct cognition, the revelation that comes to Wordsworth in those moments of transport when a "pulse of Being" becomes an immediate object of knowledge, engaging consciousness by a kind of penetration of the sensory world, so that

> all the several frames of things, like stars
> Through every magnitude distinguishable,
> Were half confounded in each other's blaze,
> One galaxy of life and joy.[15]
>
> (VIII, 628–31)

A more detailed and familiar account of this wakened consciousness is provided in the second book of *The Prelude:*

> I felt the sentiment of Being spread
> O'er all that moves, and all that seemeth still,
> O'er all, that, lost beyond the reach of thought
> And human knowledge, to the human eye
> Invisible, yet liveth to the heart,
> O'er all that leaps, and runs, and shouts, and sings,
> Or beats the gladsome air, o'er all that glides
> Beneath the wave, yea, in the wave itself
> And mighty depth of waters. Wonder not
> If such my transports were; for in all things
> I saw one life, and felt that it was joy.
> One song they sang, and it was audible,
> Most audible then when the fleshly ear,
> O'ercome by grosser prelude of that strain,
> Forgot its functions, and slept undisturb'd.
>
> (II, 420–34)

The "pulse" or "sentiment of Being" the young Wordsworth perceives in nature is a notion neither sufficiently clear in itself nor sufficiently illuminated by surrounding detail to be subjected to careful philosophic analysis or even to be tentatively assigned to any traditional philosophic system. Yet what the term would seem to designate is a form of activity that, like impulse, is essentially mediating. On those profound occasions when the young Wordsworth becomes conscious of a "sentiment of Being spread / O'er all that moves, and all that seemeth still" he directly intuits, according to the larger Wordsworthian scheme, a presence that is not to be taken as an end in itself but only as the means to metaphysically still more distant ends, the unified and quietistic reality developed in *Tintern Abbey*. A distinction of this sort between mediating consciousness and ultimate knowledge seems suggested by the passage in MS. RV that directly follows the account of the "sentiment of Being":

> By such communion was I early taught
> That what we see of forms and images
> Which float along our minds and what we feel
> Of active, or recognizable thought
> Prospectiveness, intelligence or will
> Not only is not worthy to be deemed
> Our being, to be prized as what we are
> But is the very littleness of life
> Such consciousnesses seemed but accidents
> Relapses from the one interior life
> Which is in all things, from that unity
> In which all beings live with God, are lost
> In god and nature, in one mighty whole
> As indistinguishable as the cloudless east
> At noon is from the cloudless west, when all
> The hemisphere is one cerulean blue.[16]

As de Selincourt prudently notes, this passage, troublesome in itself as the most unqualifiedly pantheistic Wordsworth ever wrote, "was not transcribed in MSS. U and V and was never used in the published text of *The Prelude*." [17] Whether Wordsworth finally suppressed these lines because of their speculative unorthodoxy or because his speculations lacked philosophic precision, they, nonetheless, indicate several ways in which the immediate knowledge given in these moments of transport differs from the more significant metaphysical truths later deduced from this direct cognitive activity. Both passages speak of the consciousness of nature as a consciousness of one life, but they record that consciousness in very different ways. The first bases its knowledge of the one life upon the felt presence of a common "sentiment of Being" that diffuses itself through and animates a group of sensory particulars that still, however, preserve unchanged their clearly determinate character. Each particular thus engages in its own activity, sings its own song. But Wordsworth adds, such activities, though individually distinct, are ultimately alike in character and operation, so that all created beings are to be understood as manifestations of the "one life," and their separate voices heard as a blended harmony, the "One song they sang" to the spiritual ear. The unity described in MS. RV, however, is of an unquestionably different sort. Turning from auditory imagery to an extended spatial metaphor,[18] Wordsworth characterizes reality as a boundless whole, from which all marks of perceptible separateness and individuation have disappeared. The simple consciousness of nature as impregnated by one life described in the first passage has in the second given way to a fuller and truer knowledge of how the life therein described is in itself constituted. Further, the second passage also conveys that atmosphere of quiescence, of profound tranquillity, that denotes Wordsworth's most meaningful experiences during this period; and here, as in *Tintern Abbey,* it is "the quiet of the sky" that merges all things into "one mighty whole." But the "sentiment of Being" expresses itself as joy, and life, and song, the means best suited to evoke a response from the youth, who lives by appetite and passion. This is not to say that so vital and joyous an experience is without value, but only that it possesses a lesser value and yields a lesser knowledge according to the Wordsworthian scale. Although nature's song sounds most clearly

> when the fleshly ear,
> O'ercome by grosser prelude of that strain,
> Forgot its functions, and slept undisturb'd,

and although the "sentiment of Being" awakens the adolescent poet to a consciousness of regions "lost beyond the reach of thought / And human knowledge," Wordsworth at this point still has yet to experience that tranquillity which lies at the heart of things and which the poem's progressive revelation was ultimately to disclose.

The close relationship between the activities generated by the "sentiment of Being" and the emotional pitch of youth becomes more evident when the passage in question is set in a context even earlier than MS. RV. For these lines finally published in the second book of *The Prelude* first appear in manuscript in the 1798 version of *The Ruined Cottage*, in that poem's account of the Pedlar's youth, an account quite obviously modeled on Wordsworth's own early life. In this initial context, consciousness of the "sentiment of Being" is seen, above all, as fulfilling a special need posed by the turbulent passions of youth, and hence as another instance of nature's economy in disclosing its being and forms to man in ways appropriate to the distinct and separate stages of his development. Here, as elsewhere, youth is defined as the season of life in which nature exercises control over man's interests and feelings:

> Nature was at his heart, and he perceived
> Though yet he knew not how, a wasting power
> In all things which from her sweet influence
> Might tend to wean him.

(202–5)

If the eventual effect of this attachment to nature is that it frees the youth from his earlier bondage to the self and thus

prepares him for a later sympathetic involvement with the
world of man, its immediate effect is to induce feelings in the
youth requiring a corresponding turbulence in nature that
nature as it is normally perceived cannot always satisfy. Thus
Wordsworth tells how the Pedlar

> was o'er power'd
> By Nature, and his mind became disturbed,
> And many a time he wished the winds might rage
> When they were silent;
>
> (223–26)

or again how

> at this time he scann'd the laws of light
> With a strange pleasure of disquietude
> Amid the din of torrents, when they send
> From hollow clefts, up to the clear air
> A cloud of mist which in the shining sun
> Varies its rainbow hues.
>
> (230–35)

Such demands, however, must go unanswered:

> But vainly thus
> And vainly by all other means he strove
> To mitigate the fever of his heart.
> From Nature and her overflowing soul
> He had received so much, that all his thoughts
> Were steeped in feeling.
>
> (235–40)

With this account of his youthful turbulence and nature's
failure to pacify it, Wordsworth prepares the ground for the
awakening of the metaphysical consciousness. Only in rare
moments of transport can the desire for correspondence between the self and the world be fulfilled, and then only by a
form of activity not given in ordinary perception.

He was only then
Contented, when, with bliss ineffable
He felt the sentiment of being, spread
O'er all that moves, and all that seemeth still.
(240–43)

Transplanted back to its first setting in *The Ruined Cottage,* the experience Wordsworth describes here can be fitted into his developmental pattern in much the same way as the animistic experiences of childhood. Just as nature, by leading the child to an unguarded trap or boat, had initiated a process destined to evolve into the moral life, so also by steeping youthful thought in feeling, nature had forced the mind to go beyond the forms of sense-perception, to require for its satisfactions states of awareness that must inevitably lead it to a comprehensive and direct knowledge of the real essences of things. But experience of the "sentiment of Being" is of instrumental rather than intrinsic benefit, a state of awareness fitted to the specific conditions of youth but fundamentally designed to draw the mind to its mature perception of nature's essential calm. Indeed, the famous formula, "Love of Nature Leads to Love of Man," by which Wordsworth sought to explain the transitional role that the feelings of youth play in acquisition of a moral consciousness, might have as its metaphysical corollary an analogous formula, awareness of nature as activity—that is, apprehension of the "sentiment of Being"—leads to awareness of nature as calm.

The problem of such a formula, as I indicated earlier, is that the portions of *The Prelude* written when Wordsworth might have endorsed it take his life only through the stage of youth, so that the poem's progressive revelation never fully unfolds. Any detailed exposition of the quietistic metaphysics that the mature Wordsworth arrives at in his personal development must be looked for, not in *The Prelude,* but in

Tintern Abbey. But it may be well to remind ourselves that if Wordsworth never elaborates such views in *The Prelude,* he does anticipate them in the questioning of the river Derwent with which the poem commences. There, as we saw earlier, nature is presented as deliberately purposeful, essentially changeless, and, in its changeless being, inherently calm. Man, however, left to his own devices, lives outside this tranquil order; but fortunately—a further proof of ultimate design— he is sufficiently susceptible to nature's benevolent influences to have the conduct of his life brought eventually into harmony with that order. Amplified both discursively and symbolically, this is, in essence, the argument of *Tintern Abbey,* and we can only conjecture that what is foreshadowed here in the lines on the Derwent would have been the argument of *The Prelude* as a whole had Wordsworth continued his personal history beyond youth into maturity. Nature in its activities here is clearly conceived of as a purposeful agent, because it is from motives of love, Wordsworth tells us, that the river Derwent "sent a voice / That flow'd along my dreams." Such a voice, moreover, always present at the threshold of consciousness with "ceaseless music" and "steady cadence," serves, like the landscape of *Tintern Abbey,* as an emblem of the changeless, as much of an equivalent of eternity as the philosophic naturalism of Wordsworth will ever metaphorically accommodate. And against this background of changelessness, human nature—at least human nature uninformed by the goals and purposes of a superintending nature—is seen to be essentially disordered: man's conduct wayward and his dwellings "fretful." It is to temper "Our human waywardness," to compose the poet's earliest thoughts "To more than infant softness," in effect, to initiate the process that will carry him from the disordered community of man to the ordered community of nature, that the Derwent so lovingly acts upon the poet's infant consciousness.

Yet even the tranquilizing power of the Derwent's song

and the state of composure it instills are only momentary representations of the calm that is the abiding state of nature and that can, under nature's auspices, become the most fundamental characteristic of man. In the concluding lines of this segment, nature's power and the effects that flow from it, though unquestionably conferring immediate pleasures and benefits, are in their most important sense foreshadowings when regarded from time's larger perspective. The "more than infant softness" of earliest thoughts point to an even more tranquil future for the poet by giving him "A knowledge, a dim earnest, of the calm / That Nature breathes among the hills and groves." In closing the passage in this anticipatory way, Wordsworth reveals just how closely the presuppositions with which composition of *The Prelude* was originally undertaken resemble the beliefs that *Tintern Abbey,* in its autobiographic fullness, managed so thoroughly to develop and to express. First, it is clear that retrospection here serves no regressive desires or needs; from its opening episode *The Prelude* is to be unmistakably developmental in its presentation of man. Second, in *The Prelude,* just as in *Tintern Abbey,* the growth of metaphysical awareness has as its final goal a fundamentally quietistic knowledge. We fulfill our being, according to nature's scheme, when the self, made tranquil by nature's efforts, pierces the veil of image and activity to discern a corresponding tranquillity as the essence of the irreducibly real and the ultimate source from which all succeeding impulses and ideas emanate.

In addition to calm, the attribute that best defines the final Wordsworthian reality is unity. But apart from very rare apprehensions of metaphysical unity such as the consciousness recorded in RV of

> that unity
> In which all beings live with God, are lost
> In god and nature, in one mighty whole,

the unity of being in which Wordsworth believes is ordinarily projected symbolically as a harmonious arrangement of sensible particulars like that depicted in the landscape of *Tintern Abbey*. In at least one case, *Lines written in early Spring*, Wordsworth expressly points to nature's symbolic expression of essential unity as a norm that is at once real, existent in the sensible world, and ideal, a norm conveyed by nature that reflects the ideal order's judgment upon, and condemnation of, the waywardness of man. The grove is very much a natural palace of pleasure, but the pleasure Wordsworth finds there is created out of an interaction of harmonious parts, the joint enterprise of the creatures of the grove cooperating with one another to produce such an atmosphere of pleasure.[19] Tone and theme are sounded, the harmonious ordering of the grove expressed, by the "thousand blended notes" (1) overheard by the poet in the opening line. The spirit of such enterprise is carried out by the twigs and flowers interacting with the moving breeze in what Wordsworth describes as a form of mutual aid:

> Through primrose tufts, in that green bower,
> The periwinkle trailed its wreaths;
> And 'tis my faith that every flower
> Enjoys the air it breathes;
>
> (9–12)

and again,

> The budding twigs spread out their fan,
> To catch the breezy air;
> And I must think, do all I can,
> That there was pleasure there.
>
> (17–20)

That the embrace of sentient being by the breeze could be intended as something more than metaphor, that it could serve, in fact, as foundation for Wordsworth's faith in nature's unity becomes more plausible when we recognize that space in Wordsworth is never merely relational, the air never merely a backdrop against which the acts and movements of man and nature take place. Instead, the air in Wordsworth is itself a living presence, carrying with it qualities of the metaphysical reality underlying all natural forms. And in its reciprocal interplay with these forms, the Wordsworthian atmosphere conveys to them—and hence to us—a reinforced awareness of that reality's most basic characteristics, its deep pulse of joy, and its abiding and divine calm. In the most meditative of moments, we experience the atmosphere as "the quiet of the sky," the presence that in *Tintern Abbey* binds the particulars of landscape in tranquillity. At other times, the day of natural harmony presented in *Lines written in early Spring* or "the first mild day of March" when the excursion of *To my Sister* is suggested, the Wordsworthian atmosphere acts as unifying agent through the spirit of animation it seems to implant in surrounding objects. In *To my Sister,* Dorothy is called out so that she may share in this atmosphere of animated pleasure:

> There is a blessing in the air,
> Which seems a sense of joy to yield
> To the bare trees, and mountains bare,
> And grass in the green field.[20]
>
> (5–8)

And from this blessing conferred by the air, Wordsworth says,

> Love, now a universal birth,
> From heart to heart is stealing,
> From earth to man, from man to earth:
> —It is the hour of feeling.
>
> (21–24)

This last quatrain confirms a belief already familiar to us from *Tintern Abbey:* the harmony of nature, whether expressed quietistically or joyfully is a harmony that in any full and accurate presentation, must include man as one of its necessary components. So too in *Lines written in early Spring* Wordsworth's insistence that man need never be an alien from the community of nature, that, in fact, the way in which he best fulfills his goals and achieves the happiness potentially available to him lies in participation in that community, is clearly reiterated, this time by nature's active and successful attempt to draw the poet's spirit into the "sweet mood" of his natural surroundings, the way in which "To her fair works did Nature link / The human soul that through me ran" (5–6). It is this fact of achieved harmony for himself, an experience that suggests that all men are potentially members of a community whose cooperative means produce pleasurable ends, that leads Wordsworth to judge and find wanting the larger human community set apart from nature, "What man has made of man" (24).

The symbolic representation of metaphysical unity by nature's sensory particulars is not confined solely to those poems in which such unity is seen to have direct and immediate moral or social application. For unity, the blending of nature's separate parts into a composed whole, is so prominent and persistent a feature of Wordsworth's poetry as to seem as much a habit of style as a vehicle of thought, so that instances in which descriptive techniques suggest natural unity are confined to no single phase of the years between 1797 and 1805 nor, indeed, even to those years themselves. The most frequent means by which Wordsworth secures the impression of unity is by having a single element in a given setting possess the appearance of suffusing with its own characteristics those other objects that appear within the setting, thus imparting to a group of disparate particulars a seemingly common quality. The air itself, whether seen as the calm of the heavens or as an animating breeze, is, of course, one important means of securing this effect. But utilized with equal frequency and significance as agents that suffuse and unify the typical Wordsworthian landscape are water and the twilight glow of sunrise and sunset. Like the air, the sound of waters may, as in *Tintern Abbey,* deepen the calm of an already quiet scene by infusing it with the harmonies of "a soft inland murmur"; or, as it later does in the *Immortality Ode,* the sound of waters may heighten the joy of an already animated prospect by sounding forth its "trumpets from the steep" (25). Another way in which water sometimes serves as an agent that unifies the natural setting is by composing together the separate features of landscape in their reflected forms into a single image perceived upon the surface of sea, or lake, or stream. One of the best-known instances of this is the famous account of the boy of Winander who, in the moment of intense silence that interrupts his mimicry of the owls, has imprinted upon his consciousness the grandeur of his surroundings, which unified by the mirror of reflection

> Would enter unawares into his mind
> With all its solemn imagery, its rocks,
> Its woods, and that uncertain Heaven, receiv'd
> Into the bosom of the steady Lake.
> *(Prelude,* V, 410–13)

Sunrise and sunset are comparable emblems, investing natural objects, colored and seemingly exalted by the same rich, suffusing light, with a common glory, a unity and grandeur in which all objects seem to share. It is because he had watched the sun

> lay
> His beauty on the morning hills, had seen
> The western mountain touch his setting orb,
> *(Prelude,* II, 188–90)

Wordsworth tells us, that he felt his first stirrings of love toward the sun and thereby fixed the basis, according to associational psychology, for his later and more disinterested love of the sun. In much the same manner, Wordsworth's later love for man derives, at least in part, from his childhood observation of a mountain sunset in which placed amidst the luminous natural setting he had spied a distant shepherd equally "glorified / By the deep radiance of the setting sun" (*Prelude,* VIII, 404–5).

Where the presence of water and of sunrise or sunset does most to convey the impression of unity—the unified ground that underlies all being—are those occasions in which both are observed as prominent features of setting. One such instance of unelaborated but implicitly profound importance occurs during a youthful excursion "Upon the Eastern Shore of Windermere" (*Prelude,* II, 145). Rowing gently "ere the fall / Of night" (*Prelude,* II, 170–71) to the music of a companion's flutings, Wordsworth experiences a moment of extraordinary consciousness as the elemental presences of sky and water converge to affect deeply both the receptive mind and the responsive feelings:

> Oh! then the calm
> And dead still water lay upon my mind
> Even with a weight of pleasure, and the sky
> Never before so beautiful, sank down
> Into my heart, and held me like a dream.
> (*Prelude,* II, 176–80)

Again, in two of Wordsworth's finest sonnets, compositions of 1802, we find this same combination of elements: sunrise and the quiet Thames in *Composed upon Westminster Bridge;* and sunset and the "eternal motion" of the waters of the English Channel in *It is a beauteous evening, calm and free.* In the first sonnet, Wordsworth radically extends his customary insight into the essential harmony of man and nature by granting a variant of that harmony to the forms of urban life. Products of human enterprise and places of human habitation at the greatest conceivable distance from Wordsworth's usually normative rural environment are dramatically revealed to be participants in the same general life of harmony and tranquillity as the cosmic presences of sky and sun, earth and water. Possibly, Wordsworth favored this insight with only the briefest credence, founded as it was upon the view of a moment rather than, as with his beliefs drawn from nature, upon the repeated observations of a lifetime. But that he held such a belief at all is probably owing to the presence, in this urban prospect, of his two major agents of natural harmony: the rising sun bathing all in a common tint—"Never did sun more beautifully steep / In his first splendour, valley, rock, or hill" (9–10)—and "The river" that "glideth at his own sweet will" (12) and that functions in the poem as a natural point of focus, gathering to itself the features of the city surrounding it in an image of unity fashioned by the binding flow of the Thames. In the sonnet addressed to his daughter, Caroline, these same recurrent figures create less a unity of specific particulars than a unity of mood and atmosphere that directs our attention to the metaphysical ground of all such natural unity, which in this poem of 1802 is already beginning to draw to itself transcendental overtones. That such images can refer to immanent as well as transcendental concepts of ultimate reality, that they are, in truth, simply sensory referents by which Wordsworth characteristically signifies the advent of some form of metaphysical consciousness, becomes evident when we recall the prominence Wordsworth gives to sunset and water (as well as the earlier noted atmospheric images of sky and air) in his most famous metaphysical description, the awareness he achieves in *Tintern Abbey*

> Of something far more deeply interfused,
> Whose dwelling is the light of setting suns,
> And the round ocean and the living air,
> And the blue sky, and in the mind of man.

From this range of examples, the imagery of sunset or sunrise and water as vehicles for indicating unity is clearly a habit of mind, a figurative staple that survives the discarding of old philosophies and accommodates itself to the development of new ones. Indeed, this range of examples could easily be extended backwards in time to the earliest of the juvenile work Wordsworth himself chose to publish (*Extract from the Conclusion of a Poem, composed in anticipation of leaving School*), a pledge of future sympathy, whatever later circumstances may bring, for his "Dear native regions" (1), a notion developed through the simile of the setting sun and the "lingering light he fondly throws / On the dear hills where first he rose" (13–14). And other illustrations can be found in poems written well after the completion of the golden decade, for example, in *Composed upon an Evening of extraordinary Splendour and Beauty,* an elegy for the lost gleam, occasioned by the special qualities of "the tranquil hour" of "purpureal Eve!" No more detailed account can, in fact, be given of the unifying function of this sunset image than this relatively late example of it:

> No sound is uttered,—but a deep
> And solemn harmony pervades
> The hollow vale from steep to steep,
> And penetrates the glades.
> Far-distant images draw nigh,
> Called forth by wondrous potency
> Of beamy radiance, that imbues,
> Whate'er it strikes with gem-like hues!
> (21–28)

If use of these images to create an effect of unity is not limited to the period under present discussion but has, instead, a long and continuing history in Wordsworth's poetry, we can, nonetheless, distinguish something of the special quality of Wordsworth's thought between 1797 and 1800 by comparing an experience in *The Ruined Cottage* that contains this cluster of images with an episode in *The Prelude,* remarkably alike in setting and circumstance, the morning of dedication presented in Book IV and composed in 1804.[21] The latter, autobiographically ascribed to Wordsworth's first vacation from Cambridge, follows an evening of casual and careless pleasure. Returning home, the young Wordsworth is greeted by a morning of "memorable pomp," a morning characterized by the familiar imagery that so often in Wordsworth precedes episodes of spiritual insight or awakening—"The solid Mountains were as bright as clouds, / Grain-tinctured, drench'd in empyrean light" (IV, 334–35). Unsurprisingly, the only major addition by nature to this scene of visual splendor comes from the voice of waters, the sounds of the sea "laughing at a distance" (IV, 333). And as the inward corollary to this splendid landscape, Wordsworth tells us, he felt himself at that very moment endowed with a consciousness of grace, but a grace whose origin and meaning Wordsworth leaves veiled in obscurity:

> I made no vows, but vows
> Were then made for me; bond unknown to me
> Was given, that I should be, else sinning greatly,
> A dedicated Spirit. On I walk'd
> In blessedness, which even yet remains.
>
> (IV, 341–45)

The long controversy over what we are to understand to be the object of Wordsworth's spirit of dedication may, I think, be partially resolved by turning from *The Prelude* of 1804 to

The Ruined Cottage and its description and discussion of an experience so markedly similar to that of *The Prelude* that it seems safe to assume that they have a common basis in some single event in Wordsworth's own life.[22]

In *The Ruined Cottage*, Wordsworth dates the event at an earlier period in the Pedlar's boyhood as a shepherd and presents it as a recurrent experience brought about by the required activities of his occupation rather than as a solitary moment in the life of a youthful college student:

> Ere his ninth summer he was sent abroad
> To tend his father's sheep, such was his task
> Henceforward till the later day of youth.
> Oh! then what soul was his when on the tops
> Of the high mountains he beheld the sun
> Rise up and bathe the world in light. He looked,
> The ocean and the earth beneath him lay
> In gladness and deep joy. The clouds were touched
> And in their silent faces did he read
> Unutterable love.
>
> (119–28)

Similar, too, in both works, is the immediate effects of the spectacle on its solitary observers. The sense of how "to the brim / My heart was full" (IV, 340–41) that Wordsworth reports in *The Prelude* is paralleled in *The Ruined Cottage*, though there the power of the visual scene captures the child's inner self even more intensely and more expansively:

> his spirit drank
> The spectacle. Sensation, soul and form
> All melted into him. They swallowed up
> His animal being; in them did he live
> And by them did he live. They were his life.
>
> (129–34)

Finally, both occasions close sacramentally with a consciousness of grace bestowed. The afterglow of immediate and overpowering perceived experience Wordsworth speaks of as "blessedness," a state of mind shared by his autobiographic and fictional heroes. (Of the Pedlar, Wordsworth says at the end of the episode that his mind "was blessedness and love" [141]; about his own subsequent feelings he writes in the 1804 account, "On I walk'd / In blessedness, which even yet remains" [IV, 344–45].)

Where the two passages significantly differ is in the application of the key term *love* to the scenic and psychological effects of the earlier account, and in the inclusion in *The Ruined Cottage* of prefatory material that explains the origins of the child's apprehension of love on empirical and naturalistic grounds. Until this event—"Ere his ninth summer," as Wordsworth loosely dates it—nature, though actively engaged in fostering the child's development, had with apparent foresight withheld its most crucial and essential property from him:

> **In his heart**
> Love was not yet, nor the pure joy of love,
> By sound diffused, or by the breathing air,
> Or by the silent looks of happy things,
> Or flowing from the universal face
> Of earth and sky. But he had felt the power
> Of nature, and already was prepared
> By his intense conceptions to receive
> Deeply the lesson deep of love, which he
> Whom Nature, by whatever means, has taught
> To feel intensely, cannot but receive.
> (108–18)

Omission from the later passage of the concept of love and, even more, of the naïve principle of external causation from which Wordsworth derives the feeling of love tells us much about the course of philosophic change he underwent between composition of *The Ruined Cottage* and composition of Book IV of *The Prelude* in 1804; and additionally, it may explain why the account of 1804 provides so little assistance to us in the form of significant commentary that might help to elucidate the real meaning for Wordsworth of the scene and his reaction to it. For the event first described in 1798 discloses an occasion understood by Wordsworth to be too formative in his own development; or, perhaps, what might be an explanation more closely approximating psychological truth, it brought forth from memory an episode that too deeply possessed him to be safely eliminated from his own personal history. What remained for him in 1804, with the empiricist explanation necessarily rejected by him in the light of later beliefs, was to reproduce the earlier scene in a relatively skeletal version, with its pictorial form essentially preserved but with an account that largely divested the scene of its interpretative comment and commentary. He chose to give the episode an aura of significant meaning, to adhere to his felt conviction of its abiding centrality, by setting it apart from all other events as that special moment in his life of personal dedication, the moment from which all succeeding events can be assumed to receive their direction. But dedication from what source, and dedication to what end? These are the questions that in *The Prelude* go unanswered.

More relevant to our present purposes than as an object for comparison or as a standard by which to measure changing beliefs is the way in which the sunrise occasion of *The Ruined Cottage* is used to project what for Wordsworth is the aspect of his metaphysics that is most significant in itself and most significant for man, that power of love which resides in and emanates from nature. And though love is a quality not often associated with the scientifically measurable, real existents of Locke's world of objects, Wordsworth clearly treats love as if it were such a real existent, accounting for its mental counterpart by the same sense-oriented theory by which a more conventional empiricism explains our ideas of extension, or figure, or mobility. Love is a perpetual presence in the real world and a ceaseless emanation from it

> By sound diffused, or by the breathing air,
> Or by the silent looks of happy things,
> Or flowing from the universal face
> Of earth and sky.

Diffusion and "flowing," if not the precise terminology of Lockian empiricism, nonetheless convey that philosophy's basic notions: external agency emitting its own properties to a mind dependent upon those properties for formation of its ideas. One further way in which the empirical assumptions of the passage are qualified is in its teleological regard for the developing characteristics of man; until the expanding powers of the child reach the point where he can grasp the idea or at least sustain the consciousness of love, the love that flows from the "universal face / Of earth and sky" never truly enters into his psychological or emotional life. Such love is purposefully withheld from the child until nature's preparations for its reception are completed, in much the same way that disinterested attachment to nature or benevolent regard for man are withheld from man by nature until man, through nature, has gained the appropriate condition of psychological readiness to carry on these relationships. Once readied for the experience of love, however—and the child, Wordsworth here adds, is readied for it by nature—the relation between mind and the external world in which love dwells is defined from an unmistakably empirical point of view. Just as Locke observes that "whether or no" the understanding will have the "materials of knowledge" given it through the senses "is not in its own power," since "the objects of our senses do many of them obtrude their particular ideas upon our minds, whether we will or no," [23] so Wordsworth also regards love as a similarly irresistible idea impressed upon us by external objects, one

                                                which he
            Whom Nature, by whatever means, has taught
            To feel intensely, cannot but receive.

Our feelings of love are thus shown to be derivative, and, if
we are exposed in childhood to an environment like that of
the Pedlar, necessary. Once more Wordsworth resolves the
split between knowledge and value by again maintaining that
value inheres objectively in the external world and communi-
cates itself to man through a process no different from that
through which he gains his knowledge of all else in the objective world.

   Appropriately enough, the means by which the child receives his first overwhelming impression of love is a sunrise
scene in which sky, mountains, and sea all basically are tinged
by the same coloration and thereby express "gladness," "deep
joy," and "unutterable love." What makes this scene a fitting
emblem of love is not merely its impregnating power as spectacle but also the use to which Wordsworth generally puts the
image of the diffused light of sunrise or sunset as a way of expressing nature's harmonious relational structure. For at this
point in his career, the idea of love and the idea of harmony
are concepts inextricably linked to one another, harmony
being the metaphysically descriptive term that characterizes
this relational structure, and love the value term that defines
it. Or we may instead wish to regard harmony as the com-
posite effect given us by the particulars of nature when they
are perceived within the context of relationship, and thereby
understood truly and fully, and love may be taken as the expression of that ultimate power which compels such relationship and as the binding agent that preserves it. The intercon-
nectedness of these concepts, and perhaps their interchange-
ability, is nowhere more evident than in *To my Sister*. The
animating breeze that wakens into life "the bare trees, and

mountains bare / And grass in the green field" (7–8), rousing
them into a single vital harmony, is presumably the mode by
which, several stanzas later, the power of love is conveyed to
all beings to link them together in sympathetic union:

> Love, now a universal birth,
> From heart to heart is stealing,
> From earth to man, from man to earth:
> —It is the hour of feeling.
>
> (21–24)

Eventually Wordsworth turns from effect to cause, from the
perception that nature and ourselves constitute a single relational order, to recognition of the productive source of that
order, which here, as in *Tintern Abbey,* he treats as a common component of all being, a single generative force that
"rolls through all things." And again, the term of value that
Wordsworth employs as the correlative to metaphysical power
is *love.*

> And from the blessed power that rolls
> About, below, above,
> We'll frame the measure of our souls:
> They shall be tuned to love.
>
> (33–36)

In dealing with the role of love in Wordsworth's metaphysics, we pass from fact to motive. Nature is as it is, harmonious and tranquil, because love—simply a term that
describes the teleological aims of nature's impelling force—
desires nature to be so. It is nature's scheme of harmonious relationship—whether such relationship occurs among the objects of nature, between man and nature, or among men
themselves—that most clearly serves the principle of love.
How love exists both as a real attribute of what is for Wordsworth ultimate substance and as a part of the phenomenal

appearances of the perceived world; how it blends that world's seemingly disparate particulars in a unified whole, dramatically rendered by the lights and colors of an almost visionary dawn and by the joyful motions stirred by nature's animating breeze; and how, finally, it transmits itself to man so that he too may be bound within this harmonious chain of relationship: these are the matters taken up and the metaphysical argument summarized in the key statements on love that occur in *The Ruined Cottage* and *To my Sister*. But there is also another place in which Wordsworth assigns to the motive of love a major function in the detailed elaboration of his philosophy: where love appears as the initiating agent that brings man to his first perception of, and hence knowledge of, the world.

In the second book of *The Prelude,* Wordsworth offers an unusually full account of the beginnings in infancy of the most fundamental of all relationships between man and the external world, that relationship established in our simple and immediate acts of perception. A relatively rare instance in *The Prelude* where theory does not grow out of personal experience, since the occasion described predates rememberable time, Wordsworth's account of the origins of perception obviously has its basis in attitudes shaped by his general philosophic orientation at the time he wrote the passage. For those who find that orientation to be, at its most meaningful, essentially transcendental, the lines on the blessed babe and his expanding perceptual life become, despite the unsystematized argument and the frequent obscurity of detail, a central statement of Wordsworth's transcendental theory of mind and his transcendental theory of imagination. The transcendental, and hence traditional, reading of these lines is probably best exemplified by Havens, who sees in them "the idea of the active or creative power of the mind," which constitutes for him "the most marked of Wordsworth's departures from the associationalism of Hartley and other eighteenth-century philosophers." [24] Indeed, such readers often see these lines not only as anti-Lockian and anti-Hartlian, an imaginative recoiling from the mechanistic thought of the eighteenth century, but also as a case of direct influence by a transcendental Coleridge whose yet unwritten theory of imagination they poetically predict. D. G. James, for example, says of this passage that "the activity of the imagination in the life of the child clearly derives its substance from Coleridge. The 'first poetic spirit of our human life' is Coleridge's 'primary imagination', the condition of perception." [25] And Havens, too, writes of the passage as Coleridgean in essence, the power of mind described here being the same as that which "is termed by Coleridge 'the primary imagination' " and which "is as universal and as commonly used as any faculty, since it enters into all perception, and is therefore employed by every person almost every moment, even in the most ordinary and utilitarian acts." [26] But identification of the workings of the child's mind presented in Book II of *The Prelude* with the primary imagination as Coleridge conceives of it, a faculty so universal and so necessary that it constitutes the "prime agent of all human perception," becomes most doubtful in the light of Wordsworth's tracing of the later history of the babe's first mental operations. For universality and necessity are concepts clearly incompatible with a process that Wordsworth tells us is "By uniform controul of after years / In most abated or suppress'd" (II, 277–78).

What Wordsworth gives us in Book II is his own speculative attempt, original and personal, to come to terms with epistemological problems that engaged Locke deeply but that he left, certainly as future generations have seen them, basically unresolved. Building on Lockian foundations, Wordsworth, nonetheless, discovered himself here, as elsewhere, considerably altering Locke's conclusions, recasting them into forms more closely allied with the imaginative premises of the poems of 1798 and 1799. But altering Locke does not mean, of necessity, transcendentalizing him or even transcending him. Rather, it involves the adoption of an alternative perspective by Wordsworth, well within empiricist limits, from which to regard these fundamental epistemological problems, a perspective created out of the assumption that the primary attributes of the universe are value and purpose, not force and motion.

The epistemological problems treated by Wordsworth here are, of course, perennial ones: how the mind puts together complex ideas from the simple materials of sensation and how it can be determined that our complex ideas are actually counterparts, mental representations, of substantial objects in the external world. These matters, philosophically always very troubling, were especially so for an age that had so widely accepted Locke's general analysis of the origins and character of human knowledge. For that analysis posed a special impediment of its own to their solution. This was the basic axiom of the corpuscular hypothesis that the world, as it is given to us in experience, is given us atomistically, in single, elemental units. As Locke himself states it, the ideas produced in the mind by the primary qualities of objects acting upon the senses initially enter the mind "by the senses simple and unmixed." [27] Although all of our ideas of objects are of figured, colored objects, that figure and that color enter the mind separately as unmixed, simple ideas of sensation. The mind then out of these primary materials of sensation fashions new complex wholes through its power of compounding. Obviously, this account of the formation of ideas runs counter to common human experience; for we know no unalloyed simples, no colors that do not inhere in figure, no figure that does not contain within it some idea of color. Our knowledge is a knowledge not of simple ideas but of objects, a collection of simple ideas no one of which can be perceived in itself, apart from objects. Furthermore, the fact of compounding leaves unanswered the question of how we are to know that the figured, colored objects put together by the mind truly represent a single unitary substance located in the external world.

Eventually, the Lockian impasse was breached or, perhaps, circumvented in the idealistic solution of Kant. For Kant, knowledge began with our awareness of a manifold, which the mind then ordered by the powers of the productive imagination operating at a level of activity below consciousness. Imposing on the manifold the forms and categories that are the mind-originated, a priori conditions under which knowledge is possible, we create for ourselves a world of intelligible objects, existing substantially in space and time and acting upon and acted upon by other intelligible objects in causally necessary connections. The reality of such objects, Kant insists, lies in their existence as empirical fact and not in some shadowy congruence with a corresponding set of objects in the external and hence objective world. But in the second book of *The Prelude,* Wordsworth nowhere indicates that the problem of perception necessitates a Copernican reversal, the revolutionary Kantian shift from the activity of the world to the activity of the mind, to explain how objects as we perceive and know them come to be formed.

Like his metaphysics, Wordsworth's treatment of perception grows out of the historical situation created for the eighteenth century by Locke; and certainly when measured by the standard of Kant's revisions of Locke, Wordsworth's departures from, and modifications of, the Lockian scheme seem moderate enough. To that scheme, retained by Wordsworth in its general details, are added two concepts that have already been seen to function significantly in Wordsworth's general approach to the problems of philosophy: belief that the particulars of the external world are entwined in a relational structure that, independent of the mind's acts—its projective power or unifying needs—actually subsists within the world as it really is; and belief that all relationships and all relational knowledge are made possible by the motivating force of love, presented in Book II of *The Prelude* not as a diffusive energy that spreads itself through the entire cosmos, as in *The Ruined Cottage,* but, in more practical terms, as a force that, localized and concentrated in the maternal presence, stimulates the babe to his first relationship with, and knowledge of, the world. For the problem of the perception of objects is a problem in relations: compounding the simple ideas that come to us through sensation into relational structures that match the relational structures that exist in and constitute the individual objects of the external world. And in love, specifically maternal love that awakens us to the habit of perception, Wordsworth finds an initial guarantee that, freeing us from solipsistic dangers, assures us that our ideas can conform to their external counterparts.

In turning to this first stage in "The progress of our being" (II, 239), Wordsworth again emphasized the value-oriented character of his thought by requiring an awareness of love as the preliminary and necessary condition before any complex acts of knowledge can take place. Despite this, the generally Lockian disposition of the passage is evident almost from the outset. The mind is clearly devoid of significant content at birth, a *tabula rasa* in the familiar empiricist sense, and its capacities, defined as little more than receptivity and retentiveness, are scarcely developed. It is a feeling of love, Wordsworth tells us, that first alerts the mind to the world around it and to the necessity for developing its capacities for knowing it. Such feeling, however, is itself not an inborn constituent of the infant life but plainly derivative, dependent upon sensation in the same way as those later ideas of the world it makes possible. Wisely, nature (that is, nature as a comprehensive system of universal design) has made certain, with the purposeful economy it shows everywhere in guiding human development, that life for the babe begins under conditions of love:

> blest the Babe,
> Nurs'd in his Mother's arms, the Babe who sleeps
> Upon his Mother's breast, who, when his soul
> Claims manifest kindred with an earthly soul,
> Doth gather passion from his Mother's eyes.
>
> (II, 239–43)

"Such feelings" are not just the condition under which the child's mind develops; they are, in fact, the stimulus that actuates the child's otherwise inert being, and, indeed, they may well be one with the sustaining breath of life itself. For "Such feelings," as Wordsworth describes their first effect upon the infant, "pass into his torpid life / Like an awakening breeze" (II, 244–45). The caution implied by introducing this claim through the qualifying medium of a simile is absent from a still earlier manuscript version of these lines, RV, where Wordsworth asserts the power of this externally derived consciousness of love even more assuredly: "This passion is the awakening breeze of life." The epistemological consequence of having life's first stirrings engendered by love is that the child desires to know the world as a collection of distinct and individuated particulars, to locate in space, for example, as a single, unified presence, the source of this maternal love:

> hence his mind
> Even [in the first trial of its powers]
> Is prompt and watchful, eager to combine
> In one appearance, all the elements
> And parts of the same object, else detach'd
> And loth to coalesce.
>
> (II, 245–50)

It is here that Wordsworth speaks of knowing—at least the knowing of objects—as an essentially relational act, a drawing together of parts "else detach'd / And loth to coalesce" into unity and wholeness. Despite Wordsworth's own indications of its doctrinal importance, the passage obviously suffers as philosophic argument from its looseness of terminology, particularly in its failure to fix upon any clearly stipulated meaning for the term *object,* which seemingly may refer here to either a mental existent or an external substance. In this case, however, such looseness is critically rewarding for it helps us to discover by its very inexactness (an inexactness that almost always accompanies the rendering of difficult epistemological concepts in ordinary language) those presuppositions which, though logically indefensible, nevertheless, govern Wordsworth's understanding of the transaction by which mind comes to know the world. By *object,* Wordsworth here, in one sense, means an appearance in the mind, since only in this way can we speak of the parts of an object as separable, having entered the mind as simple ideas "detach'd / And loth to coalesce." At the same time, the term *object* seems to refer to something outside the mind that exists prior to the mind's knowledge of it (the point at which the difficulties of Locke's empiricism become apparent); and in the object intended in this sense, those elements that the mind directly perceives only as simple ideas truly inhere, and inhere collectively and inseparably. Knowledge of objects, then, is for Wordsworth simply an exact correspondence between the idea formed when these elements coalesce within the mind and the pre-existing object located in the external world. And in a more general way, this proposition can be extended to Wordsworth's larger theory of knowledge during these years, when knowledge for him was essentially conformity of the mind's ideas to the actual structure of the external world.

In addition to stimulating the child to attend to external objects, love also plays an indispensable part in training him in the sorting out of individual objects from the confusion of undifferentiated sense-experience in this earliest stage of knowledge. Since love is a quality that attaches itself to ideas of sensation, the mind can choose among the multitude of ideas given it those that share the common attribute of love and that can thereby be identified as belonging to the same object. Once identified, these ideas can be gathered together and unified into mental representations of objects as they truly exist, differentiated and individual, in the external world. The most obvious example of this is what Wordsworth considers to be our first object of perception, the mother, whom we seek because of the love that she has given us and that has become an active force in our own lives, and whom we set apart from all else and all others by the love expressed in her every act, the love involved in every sensation connected with her, the love that, in essence, defines her for us. And the love imparted to us that moves us to attend to the maternal presence also moves us to attend sympathetically to the other objects of the world that we have come to associate with that presence:

> In one beloved Presence, nay and more,
> In that most apprehensive habitude
> And those sensations which have been deriv'd
> From this beloved Presence, there exists
> A virtue which irradiates and exalts
> All objects through all intercourse of sense.
>   (II, 255–60)

Perception, as Wordsworth explains it, grows out of this affective base: feelings that, once transmitted to us, move in a kind of reciprocal circulation between ourselves and the world. From the mother, and later from nature, we derive sympathies that then, in turn, spread outwards from ourselves to engage us with the world. It is in this sense of reciprocal flow and sympathetic involvement, rather than in any Coleridgean sense of imaginative transformation, that Wordsworth can say of the child "From nature largely he receives;

nor so / Is satisfied, but largely gives again" (II, 267–68). Through this reciprocal flow, first expressed by the interaction between mother and child, the child is assured that he too belongs to a world that, as a relational structure, is sustained by the energy of love:

> No outcast he, bewilder'd and depress'd;
> Along his infant veins are interfus'd
> The gravitation and the filial bond
> Of nature, that connect him with the world.
>   (II, 261–64)

By this Wordsworth would seem to indicate that *love* and *life* are virtually convertible terms. Life itself begins, according to Book II, not with some inward consciousness informing us of our autonomous self-identity but with a sense of being in and belonging to the world. When maternal love stirs the child as "the awakening breeze of life," Wordsworth treats such love as the actuating principle, as the substance of life itself, because possessing love, the child finds himself at home in, and sympathetically attracted to, a world that also possesses love sympathetically "flowing from the universal face / Of earth and sky." Love is the common essence that, present in all things, constitutes the "filial bond" among them, linking the objects of nature with themselves and linking man with nature. It is the gravitational force whose hidden powers hold together all of the disparate particulars of the world in a single, unified relationship. Our entry into the world is marked not by "a sleep and a forgetting" but by an acquisition of love that fixes life's proper beginnings.

Much the same point is made by a manuscript entry in JJ (a portion of which later appears in Book I of *The Prelude*) that has a close bearing on Wordsworth's speculations about the development of the "infant Babe." Speaking of what must surely be these same initial sympathies, felt inwardly as "hallowed & pure motions of the sense," Wordsworth traces their derivation, not to the maternal presence, but to a more distant and abstract source:

> th' eternal spirit, he that has
> His life in unimaginable things
> And he who painting what he is in all
> The visible imagery of the world
> Is yet apparent chiefly as the soul
> Of our first sympathies—Oh bounteous power
> In childhood, in rememberable days
> How often did thy love renew for me
> Those naked feelings which when thou wouldst form
> A living thing thou sendest like a breeze
> Into its infant being.[28]

Omission of the mother from this account of life's beginning does not really contradict anything said in Book II. Eliminating all concrete and circumstantial detail, above all, the mediating role of the mother in nurturing the child to involvement in the world, Wordsworth, intending here not a precise description of epistemological process but an elevated hymn of praise, treats the problem of life's beginnings from the broadest possible perspective as a transaction between the infant and the "eternal spirit." But it is the same problem that is treated in Book II, and it is treated in essentially the same way. Life and love are still interdependent: when the "eternal spirit" "wouldst form / A living thing" his instrument is those "feelings"—earlier alluded to "as our first sympathies" —that he "sendest like a breeze / Into its infant being." Though we may assume that in any concrete and detailed elaboration of this we would find a mother's "beloved Presence," an "apprehensive habitude," and an outpouring of love from the child, in this more generalized instance "our first sympathies," when stripped of any mediating agency, are seen by Wordsworth as the most apparent manifestation to us of the life of the "eternal spirit." Indeed, according to the passage, that spirit constitutes the soul of such sympathies. Not that we are to draw any idealistic or theistic conclusions from the fact that the eternal spirit's composition is identical with mind, for he lives elsewhere as well: in "unimaginable things," that is, in things that offer no images to the mind, real objects in the external world that, while acting as the productive cause of our sensible ideas, are themselves unknowable as ideas, the Wordsworthian version of Locke's substance to be spoken of only as "an uncertain supposition of we know not what." But because such objects are the productive cause of our sensible ideas, Wordsworth, preserving here the distinction between the object and its mental representation, finds the life of the "eternal spirit" expressed also in ideas impressed upon the mind, in what we receive as well as what we give, "painting what he is in all / The visible imagery of the world."

What Wordsworth discusses here, the workings of the "eternal spirit" dualistically in mind and object, sheds a helpful light upon some of the otherwise less accessible matter in the speculations on infancy in Book II. The flow of sympathy from mother to child acts as "The gravitation and the filial bond / Of nature" not only because it joins the child to the world's general circulation of love but also because, having as its soul the "eternal spirit," such sympathy sanctifies the child by its acquisition and raises him to equality with external nature, which as another vessel of the "eternal spirit" is also divine. The lines from JJ are even more helpful for their elucidation of Wordsworth's rather perplexing discussion of the creativity of the infant's mind, the way in which it

> Even as an agent of the one great mind,
> Creates, creator and receiver both,
> Working but in alliance with the works
> Which it beholds.
>
> (II, 272–75)

Again we find a tendency to read these lines as a premature or perhaps prophetic intimation of views that did not receive full public expression until publication of the famous thirteenth chapter of *Biographia Literaria:* Wordsworth's infant would act in his earliest perceptions as "an agent of the one great mind" by exercising upon the chaos and flux of pure sensation creative and ordering powers that are "a repetition in the finite mind of the eternal act of creation in the infinite I AM." But knowledge that our first sympathies involve the being of the "eternal spirit" explains why the infant mind enacts its role as "agent of the one great mind" in terms that raise no discrepancy between this statement and Wordsworth's general epistemological beliefs at this time. The mind of the infant creates, "gives again" after it has received, as the preceding lines state it, because "feeling has to him imparted strength" (II, 269). Under the impetus of feeling, that is, that power of sympathy whose acts Wordsworth identifies with those of the "eternal spirit," the infant mind, "powerful in all sentiments of grief, / Of exultation, fear, and joy" (II, 270–71), attends to the world in a continually widening circle of interest, apprehends the elements of the world as they come to the mind through sensation, and combines these elements into compound ideas that hopefully reproduce accurately the objects that these elements represent. (It is in this sense, it should be added, that the mind can be characterized as "Working but in alliance with the works / Which it beholds.") The creativity that Wordsworth here celebrates is by post-Kantian standards a very limited form of creativity, acts of mind that by the yardstick of mind-projected forms and categories scarcely deserve to be called creative in any sense. But since these empirically restricted powers of apprehending and compounding derive from feelings of love toward the babe and act out of feelings of love by him, a love that in all its manifestations is the primary expression of the purposes of the "eternal spirit," the "infant mind" may therefore be spoken of, and truly spoken of, as "an agent of the one great mind."

Though perception is analyzed here in fundamentally Lockian terms, with the Lockian emphasis upon the machinery of sensation and the physiological processes involved in perception, Wordsworth, free of any idealistic bias, clearly finds nothing in such machinery or such processes to object to or to disparage. Not only does he confer upon these earliest perceptual activities a sanctity befitting "an agent of the one great mind," but he also invests the mind with an aesthetic dignity, identifying in this first display of the mind's powers "the first / Poetic spirit of our human life" (II, 275–76). Once more we may explain this by concepts habitually used by Wordsworth rather than by appealing to later Coleridgean categories, such as the similarity in kind of the primary and secondary imagination. Why Wordsworth should consider the act of perception a poetic act becomes evident in the "Preface" to *Lyrical Ballads,* where the poet himself is described in language already familiar to us from Wordsworth's epistemological statements as "upholder and preserver, carrying everywhere with him relationship and love." [29] Like poetry, the beginnings of perception, the mind's earliest formation of objects, is the relational act of a mind urged forward by feelings of love. Most men, however, Wordsworth complains, exhaust their poetic spirit at life's beginning: the formation of objects, once learned, becomes a habitual act and affection ceases to accompany it; their knowledge of the relationships that bind the external world in unity is narrowly limited to those which enable the mind to know objects individually so that the necessary affairs of human life may be conducted. But some few, those in whom the poetic spirit remains "Pre-eminent till death" (II, 280), do not view the objects of the external world "In disconnection dead and spiritless" (*Excursion,* IV, 962); but moved by the force of love, they continue to build larger and larger relational structures from their experience. His own adolescence, Wordsworth tells us in a passage to which the digressive account of the "infant babe" is the explanatory preface, illustrates the continuance of this "infant sensibility, / Great birthright of our Being" (II, 285–86). Then, first loving nature for its own sake, he perceived what habit had obscured for so many others, "a register / Of permanent relations" (II, 311–12) among

> A store of transitory qualities
> Which, but for this most watchful power of love
> Had been neglected.
>
> (II, 309–11)

Like so much else from these years, the entwined clues to Wordsworth's conception of relationship and love are generally lost sight of in the later written books of *The Prelude*, submerged in the final portion of the poem by a heavy tide of transcendental speculation. But even there the concepts of relationship and love surface occasionally, a kind of vestigial presence that still sustains him during episodes when his faith in the unity of all is most severely threatened. So it is that in London, amidst a "press / Of self-destroying, transitory things" (VII, 738–39), by retaining that which is "of all acquisitions first" (VII, 713), Wordsworth is yet able to find "diffused" through the city's "blank confusion" (VII, 695) a spirit of "Composure and ennobling Harmony" (VII, 740). Later the still more potent pressures of the first phase of the French Revolution also fail to subdue the "genial feelings" (X, 740) originally implanted in him; and Wordsworth, even from a later and more conservative vantage point, looks indulgently upon those years of revolutionary zeal as a time in which he remained

> a child of nature, as at first,
> Diffusing only those affections wider

That from the cradle had grown up with me,
And losing, in no other way than light
Is lost in light, the weak in the more strong.

(X, 753–57)

Not until England had declared war on France did Wordsworth leave "the pale of love" (XI, 761), and then for the
first time he allowed the mind to engage the world without
the prompting and guidance of the heart. Indeed, though
Wordsworth's beliefs altered in almost every particular in
the years following the passage on the growth of the infant
mind, there is evidence to suggest that he continued to
possess a deep-rooted and perhaps unshakable adherence to
the doctrine of relationship and love. It may well be that in
The Prelude he never altogether discarded the poem's first
aim, to record the progress of those two interdependent concepts in his own development; for even as late as 1804, it
was with the recollection of the earliest of his intentions for
The Prelude still in mind that he spoke to Coleridge of
"This History" as one "Of intellectual power, from stage to
stage / Advancing, hand in hand with love and joy" (XI, 42–
44).

1. Earl Wasserman, *Shelley's Prometheus Unbound: A Critical Reading*
(Baltimore, 1965), pp. 5–6.

2. Ibid., p. 7. The reason that Wordsworth's philosophical thinking was
cast so firmly in this mold may well have been, as John Jones suggests, Wordsworth's failure—at least in comparison to Coleridge—to grasp the way in
which the currents of eighteenth-century philosophy were to run: "His feeling
for the history of ideas led Coleridge to look upon eighteenth-century
philosophy as moving inevitably toward Humeian scepticism; but Wordsworth, lacking both Coleridge's sense of history and his intellectual finesse,
could not see things this clearly: he was unselfconsciously living the pattern
of ideas within which he had grown up" (*The Egotistical Sublime* [London,
1954], p. 42).

3. Recent speculation about Wordsworth's metaphysics (most notably
H. W. Piper in *The Active Universe* [London, 1962] and Jonathan Wordsworth in his influential study of *The Ruined Cottage, The Music of Hu-*

manity [New York and Evanston, Ill., 1969]) has tended to concentrate almost exclusively on the panvitalistic theory of the "One Life." But reduction of the metaphysics to this single doctrine results in a too narrow focus, distorting Wordsworth's relationship with the tradition of Locke by substituting a part for the whole in treating Wordsworth's characterization of the physical universe. As we shall see, Wordsworth in attributing value and purpose to the underlying reality of substance departs significantly from Locke; but nonetheless, the mechanisms by which the attributes of substance become the content of consciousness clearly derive from the corpuscular theory. Moreover, there is an obvious philosophic compatibility between the corpuscular theory developed by Locke and an empirical theory of mind emphasizing receptivity and development that renders unnecessary the importation into the poetry of a concept of the active imagination (the indispensable corollary for Piper of the metaphysics of the active universe), for which little evidence can be found between 1797 and 1800.

4. Locke, p. 67.

5. Ibid., p. 156.

6. Ibid., p. 39.

7. Ellen Douglas Leyburn has taken Wordsworth's references to nature as constituting a "visible language" as evidence for a significant influence of Berkeley upon Wordsworth. However, Wordsworth's repeated use of such terms as *impulse* and *impression* in his discussions of perception are clearly inconsistent with any firmly held belief in Berkelian immaterialism. See "Berkelian Elements in Wordsworth's Thought," *JEGP* 47 (1948):14–28.

8. Though the incident of the drowned man and the two events used in Book XI as "spots of time" first appear in the V manuscript, the passages of commentary in books V and XI explaining the significance of these recollections (as an illustration of the salutary influence of books in the first instance and of the mind's mastery over "outward sense" in the latter) are not added until 1804 when the incidents are incorporated into the A manuscript. This matter will be treated more fully in chapter 7.

9. *PW*, IV, 463.

10. I have labored so long over what might well seem obvious because in this case the obvious has so often been disregarded or dismissed. Ferry, for example, argues that the boy feels himself a trouble to his natural surroundings because, at their deepest level of meaning, the passages that describe the ministry of fear record the inherent and inescapable alienation of man from nature; "for a human being, as a creature of time, is by definition a stranger to the 'unknown modes of being' which at the same time he is uniquely equipped to apprehend, and of which moon and stars are the outward expression" (p. 116). Bloom discounts the ethical implications of these incidents for very different reasons. Such incidents describe the boy's "participation in other modes of being," and in them "he belongs more to the universe of elemental forces, of motions and spirit, than he does to ours" (p. 157).

11. The fullest discussion of Wordsworth's animism appears in chapter 5 of Raymond Dexter Havens's *The Mind of a Poet* (Baltimore, 1941). As to the question of whether Wordsworth believed in the animistic beings he de-

scribed, Havens affirmatively concludes (though not without some hesitancy and tentativeness) that Wordsworth "tended to think that woods, lonely places, and individual natural objects are not only permeated by the One Spirit, but that each has feelings, purposes, and powers through which it cooperates with the One" (p. 83).

12. *Prelude*, I, 428–33 (MS. V.).

13. Ibid., pp. 490–92 (MS. V).

14. Locke, p. 67.

15. Because it is a retrospective summary, Book VIII, although written in 1804, remains reasonably faithful to the philosophic attitudes of 1799 and 1800 when it recapitulates earlier episodes.

16. *Prelude*, p. I, 525 (II, 434–35, MS. RV).

17. Ibid., p. 525.

18. This is probably another aspect of the running conflict between the auditory and visual that is one of the relatively few features that remains constant throughout Wordsworth's poetic career. Sometimes these faculties are arranged hierarchically and sometimes contrastingly, but they almost always reflect a clash in values, with the visual, in most cases, representing the more important and the more desirable of these values. We have already observed this conflict in *Tintern Abbey* both in terms of a contrast in values —the idealized landscape of nature opposed to "the din of towns and cities" —and in terms of a hierarchy of values—the idealized landscape of maturity and "the sounding cataract" of youth. And we shall see this feature present again in the great opposition of visual and auditory imagery in the *Immortality Ode*. Hartman also discusses this conflict in connection with *Descriptive Sketches* (pp. 106–15) and the ascent of Snowdon in *The Prelude* (pp. 184–86).

19. Joseph Warren Beach believes the poem exemplifies Wordsworth's principle of pleasure. "The means by which 'fostering' nature leads birds to function as birds he finds to be pleasure, the gratification of their instincts. Man too he knows to be a creature so organized as to realize his nature through the gratification of his instincts (and his higher powers), and such gratification is pleasure. He realizes how far man has fallen short of his capacity for such gratification" (*The Concept of Nature in Nineteenth-Century English Poetry* [New York, 1936], p. 87). But surely when Wordsworth laments "What man has made of man," he laments a failure of sympathy and benevolence, a refusal to act concertedly in a spirit of mutual aid to create a human community as harmonious as that of the grove. Nowhere, however, does he lament the refusal of individual men to seek instinctual gratification. Jack Stillinger seems to me much nearer the truth when he writes, "The point of the poem (esp. in lines 1–8, 21–24) is that everything in nature is blended in harmony and pleasure, and only man is a cause of discord" (William Wordsworth, *Selected Poems and Prefaces*, ed. by Jack Stillinger [Boston, 1965], p. 505).

20. Wordsworth continued to regard the air as an animating force after 1800 as well. For example, in *The Green Linnet*, seeking a figure to express the way in which the bird's song spreads itself throughout the scene, he

speaks of the linnet as "A life, a Presence like the Air / Scattering thy glad-ness without care."

21. The similarity between these two episodes is discussed by Havens (pp. 156–57). Piper believes the two take their origin from a single personal experience (p. 111).

22. The majority of critics have traditionally interpreted Wordsworth's emergence from that morning as "A dedicated Spirit" to be a statement of his dedication to poetry. The persistence of this view is illustrated by Hart-man, who writes "Though he does not realize the full meaning or inner force of the experience ('bond unknown to me / Was given') it makes him a dedicated poet" (p. 223). This view, prevalent since de Selincourt's edition of *The Prelude,* has been carefully and convincingly refuted by Havens, who, among the several objections he makes to it, points out "that the writing of poetry is neither mentioned nor implied in the entire passage or in the lines that precede and follow it" (p. 365); and that "if this experience was a momentous one for his poetry it is strange that he never refers to it in any of the passages in which he speaks of his art, of his decision to be a poet, or of the kind of verse he wishes to compose" (p. 366).

23. Locke, p. 52.

24. Havens, p. 322.

25. D. G. James, *Scepticism and Poetry* (London, 1937), p. 141.

26. Havens, p. 207. Even so recent a commentator as Stillinger in his notes to the passage refers readers of his recent edition of Wordsworth to "Coleridge's statement that the primary imagination is 'a repetition in the finite mind of the eternal act of creation in the infinite I AM' " (p. 546). The only noteworthy exception to this view is the important essay by Francis Christensen, "Creative Sensibility in Wordsworth," *JEGP* 45 (1946): 361–68.

27. Locke, p. 53.

28. *Prelude,* p. 636 (a passage from MS. JJ).

29. *PW,* II, 396.

4

The Empirical Phase:
Theory of Morals

The third major feature of Wordsworth's philosophic scheme in the early years of the golden decade, the empiricist phase, is an empirically based ethical theory that is the logical outgrowth of the theory of mind and the metaphysics of nature just traced. Though most writers on ethics in the eighteenth century would have termed themselves empiricists and did, in fact, continually submit their moral propositions to the validating test of human experience, Wordsworth's ethics are empirical (that is, grounded in the philosophy of Locke) in a far more restrictive sense of that term than the ethics of David Hume or Adam Smith. For in the empiricism of Wordsworth, what determines individual behavior is primarily environmental conditioning. A system of external objects endowed with value and moved by its own teleological will acts with cumulative effect to impress itself upon the essentially receptive tablet of mind and to produce a moral existence that, grounded in sensations, follows a clearly distinguishable developmental pattern and fulfills itself in a life of benevolence, conduct proceeding from purely disinterested motives.

Once again the model given Wordsworth by his age is fundamentally sensationalistic. It derives in some degree directly from Locke but more substantially from Locke's more radically sensationalistic successors. Such a model, it must be understood, is not an inhibiting form to be imitated in every detail so that Wordsworth may bring to his poetry a fully assembled system of moral doctrine; it is rather a broadly conceived foundation and framework—perhaps that ordered and shaping condition which alone makes freedom possible—that gives direction and context to the ethical structure, personal and idiosyncratic, that he builds from the materials of his own experience and desires. Moreover, in describing this model, a description based, of course, on the writings of Wordsworth's sensationalist predecessors, we need not concern ourselves with questions of direct influence. What is to be sought in turning to the ethical statements of those writers in whose metaphysics and epistemology we have already found loose analogies and rough parallels with Wordsworth is a general pattern of explanations of and assumptions about moral behavior that can guide our expectations when we come to Wordsworth's empiricist ethics.

By implication, at least, two major features of a sensationalist ethic, environmental conditioning and diversity of behavior, are already present in Locke. In the famous polemic against innate ideas that takes up the first chapter of the *Essay,* Locke had pointed to the great variety of customs and moral opinions among men as proof that moral principles do not arise innately but are "something that we, being ignorant of, may attain to the knowledge of, by the use and due application of our natural faculties." [1] But the diversity Locke observes is primarily that which exists among disparate cultures rather than that which exists between the separate stages of the developing individual, and his argument anticipates the ethical relativism of the anthropologist far more than it does the Wordsworthian theory of moral growth. Moreover, Locke in his view of human nature—unlike some of his eighteenth-century followers more congenial to Wordsworth—still held to an egoistic interpretation of moral behavior, limiting the application of the terms *"Morally good and evil"* to "the conformity or disagreement of our voluntary actions to some law, whereby good or evil is drawn on us from the will and power of the law-maker." [2]

Much closer in time and temper to Wordsworth is the familiar name of David Hartley, who combines a sensationalistic theory of knowledge with a benevolistic ethics. To Hartley, man is a creature capable of purely altruistic actions; but such altruism, Hartley maintains, is based wholly on the effects of prior sensations, for it is from "the Doctrine of Association" alone that he derives his evidence "that there is, and must be, such a Thing as pure distinterested Benevolence." [3] Yet in reaching such conclusions about man's moral nature, conclusions usually thought to be at variance with strict empirical principles, Hartley in no way relinquishes or even modifies his empiricism. Indeed, if anything, the philosopher of benevolence is in this case a far more than thoroughgoing sensationalist than his guide and predecessor. For Locke, though presenting the mind as a *tabula rasa* initially devoid of all ideas, did endow the mind with reflective powers capable of raising their own ideas, and these ideas of reflection together with those contributed by sensation were understood by Locke as comprising the materials of all human knowledge. Hartley, however, rejected this internal and secondary source of ideas, claiming "that all the most complex Ideas arise from Sensation; and that Reflection is not a distinct Source, as Mr. Locke makes it." [4] By attributing to the mind inborn powers of reflection, Locke to some extent offsets the determinism implicit in the new way of ideas, since variation in the mind's reflective powers could offer some explanation of the differences among men. Hartley, by eliminating these powers as original principles of the mind and by reducing the mind's role in thinking essentially to perception alone, made man completely the creature of his environment, his destiny totally dependent upon the character of his sensations. But Hartley saw in this inescapable determinism no cause for alarm; for associational psychology was the psychology of Utopia, having within it "a Tendency to reduce the State of those who have eaten of the Tree of the Knowlege of Good and Evil, back again to a paradisal one." [5]

Another point at which the Hartleian scheme resembles Wordsworth's in broad outline, if not in every specific detail, is in the developmental pattern, with its well-demarcated stages, which Hartley establishes as the natural and proper order of human life. Although all knowledge is rooted in simple sensation, Hartley sees the individual's mental and behavioral history as a progress through a hierarchy of increasingly complex states of mind molded by the laws of association, passing from the pleasures and pains of simple sensation to those of imagination, ambition and self-interest, and, finally, to the most spiritual and praiseworthy, those of sympathy, theopathy, and the moral sense. Hartley, unlike Wordsworth, leaves the chronological sequence of this ascent unspecified; but since the pleasures of the final stages are an aggregate of all earlier stages, it is apparent that man must receive a relatively large quantity of sensations before the intellectual pleasures become predominant. Childhood, with its comparatively meager accumulation of experience and its imperfect "connecting Consciousness," is, therefore, a time of grosser pleasures and of "Affections and Actions disproportionate to the Value of the Things desired and pursued." [6] One of the strongest arguments put forward for associationism by Joseph Priestley, Hartley's editor and disciple, is, in fact, the obvious amorality of children: "I will venture to say that any person who has attended to the ideas of children, may perceive that the ideas of moral right and moral obligation are formed very gradually and slowly, from a long train of circumstances; and it is a considerable time before they become at all distinct and perfect." [7] All men, in their earliest years, according to Hartley, must submit to the tyranny of the sensible pleasures and pains; but this in no way impairs man's inevitable progress, for nature, wisely economical, transfers these pleasures and pains "more and more every Day, upon things that afford neither sensible Pleasure nor sensible Pain in themselves, and so beget the intellectual Pleasures and Pains." [8] Thus, Hartley, happily unmindful of the materialism implicit in his system, triumphantly concludes, "Some Degree of Spirituality is the necessary Consequence of passing through Life." [9]

For a rare and exemplary few, this spirituality culminates in the formation of the moral sense, and nowhere does Hartley seem closer to the Wordsworth of *Tintern Abbey* than in his account of this faculty. Both Shaftesbury and Hutcheson, the originators of the moral sense theory and its best-known exponents, had considered the moral sense an originally implanted faculty, although they spoke of it as "connatural" rather than innate to escape the strictures of Locke's celebrated polemic against innate ideas. Hartley, however, whose scheme left no place for such original sources of ethical judgment, had converted the moral sense into man's final mental acquisition, the aggregate of all preceding pleasures and pains. Once acquired, however, the moral sense exercises a virtually total control over the behavior of its possessor, and since it is actually the net result of man's accumulated sensations—the only source Hartley acknowledges for the formation of character—in a very real sense, the acquired moral nature becomes the man himself. "This Moral Sense therefore carries its own Authority with it, inasmuch as it is the Sum total of all the rest, and the ultimate Result from them; and employs the Force and Authority of the whole Nature of Man against any particular Part of it, that rebels against the Determinations and Commands of the Conscience or moral Judgment." [10]

As passing references to Wordsworth's ethics in preceding

chapters indicate, almost all of the general tenets of the sensationalist theory set forth by Hartley could, with very little modification, be subscribed to by Wordsworth. In fact, viewed from a purely ethical perspective, *Tintern Abbey* conforms to the sensationalist model in virtually every significant feature and serves, as in so many other respects, as a kind of exemplary instance. There is moral determination by the sensory environment, "the mighty world / Of eye, and ear" (105–6) constituting the "soul," Wordsworth says, of his "moral being"; there is a developmental pattern dividing the individual life into clear and progressive stages, which in *Tintern Abbey* appear as childhood, youth, and maturity, stages that, rendered in ethical terms, can be distinguished by an evolution from love of self to love of nature to love of man; and finally there is, as the aggregate and crown of all our sensory experience, the moral sense that enables man to conduct himself with a selfless and spontaneous benevolence, a faculty that in *Tintern Abbey* expresses itself in our "little, nameless, unremembered, acts / Of kindness and of love" (34–35). Even apart from *Tintern Abbey,* which does, however, possess a kind of paradigmatic status for these years, almost every poem or passage that has been already noted can be drawn upon (and in some measure has been drawn upon) to illustrate the shaping role that one or another of the key concepts of this form of sensationalism—environment, development, and benevolence—has in Wordsworth's thought between 1797 and 1800. What remains to be done in this treatment of Wordsworth's ethics is less a confirming of his adherence to broad theoretical principles than a filling in of the details needed to transform the sensationalist framework into a uniquely Wordsworthian structure whose every characteristic expresses the poet's personal vision. The course and pattern of individual development must be observed and analyzed with far greater discrimination than *Tintern Abbey* alone provides; the goals implied for both the indi-

vidual and society by Wordsworth's developmental hypothesis
need to be stated explicitly; and the practical consequences,
apart from all metaphysical ramifications, of Wordsworth's
sensationalist ethics must be isolated and examined. And a
convenient point of entry into these more complex ethical
issues in Wordsworth—convenient both as a point at which
to begin the study of the chronology of individual development and as a representative statement of Wordsworth's
moral views—is *Nutting,* a poem that recent scholarship has
made into something of a test case for judging Wordsworth's
ethical attitudes.[11]

In *Nutting,* Wordsworth tells how, as a child seeking hazel-
nuts, he had come upon "a virgin scene" (21), a rich bower
of hazels previously unnoticed by men. After a moment's
"wise restraint / Voluptuous" (23–24), he had gathered his
plunder by dragging "to earth both branch and bough, with
crash / And merciless ravage" (44–45). Both David Perkins
and David Ferry reject any developmental possibilities for
Nutting and bring to their readings of the poem the assumption that for Wordsworth the behavior of children and adults
is fundamentally alike, so that what seems a simple account
of the way in which children will wantonly deface the beauty
of nature is, at bottom, an example of the inherent conflict
between man and nature. Thus, Perkins describes such children as "little prototypes of human nature, passionately
greedy and desirous," [12] and Ferry a priori insists: *"All* men
are like this in their relation to nonhuman nature, since *even*
this innocent young child is a libertine and a destroyer." [13]
Certainly nothing we have seen earlier lends support to such
assumptions, nor does *Nutting* itself, upon closer examination, seem to stand apart as an exception to Wordsworth's
general developmental hypothesis. Here too we see Wordsworth, committed to an empirical interpretation of human
behavior, denying any such self-identity among life's unfolding stages. This is not to say that one's childhood experiences

are without influence upon one's later conduct. In fact, the paradox at the heart of the poem is that the calm devotion to nature Wordsworth felt at that time of its composition had evolved from just such turbulent and destructive moments of childhood as the poem describes. Neither can we accept the second major assumption of Perkins and Ferry that nature and man, even if only during childhood, can ever stand in a relation of fundamental hostility to each other. For in the denial of this, *Nutting* provides a second and still stranger paradox. As we have seen, nature actively solicits man's devotion; and Wordsworth here implies that nature, far from being a passive victim in this tale of mutilation, knowingly and lovingly leads the child to her quiet bower to receive his merciless ravage. So determined is nature to make a moral agent of this passionate child who roams her woods that even the loss of her quiet beauty seems not too great a sacrifice to achieve her purpose.

Nutting is, of course, most intimately connected with the opening books of *The Prelude,* since Wordsworth tells us that it was originally "intended as part of a poem on my own life," [14] and since it bears so obvious a resemblance to such scenes as the stolen boat and the plundered nest. In the opening book, Wordsworth makes clear at least two of the distinctions that separate the child from the man. First, as a child he came to nature through "extrinsic passion" (I, 572), the games and interests that bring the child into constant contact with nature even before he has developed the aesthetic response to her beauty that led the mature Wordsworth to love nature for her own sake. Second, Wordsworth regards the child as fundamentally amoral, so caught up in his own passions and pleasures that he commits acts hostile to nature and man, undisturbed by guilt until rebuked by nature. Only in maturity does guilt truly become an attribute of conscience, and only then does man discover that benevolent action leads to pleasures that are deeper and more lasting than the pleasures derived from the gratification of selfish passion.

In *Nutting,* Wordsworth again points to the aesthetic and moral difference between the adult and the child. What draws the child to the woods is an extrinsic passion, the sport of nutting—an activity that by definition cannot but be fundamentally destructive of nature. The source of the boy's joy upon discovering the bower is not its tranquil beauty but the profusion of untouched hazels, which closes his mind to any other values the scene might offer. Even in his moment of restraint, indulged in only to increase the pleasure of his triumph, his "heart luxuriates" among what he judges to be only

> indifferent things,
> Wasting its kindliness on stocks and stones,
> And on the vacant air.
>
> (41–43)

What intrigued so many commentators on the poem is the way in which Wordsworth has intensified our response to the act of desecration by using a metaphor of sexual violation. But if he had presented the episode in its bare outlines, as a despoiling of nature by a child whose passions blind him to the scene's loveliness, the wrongdoing would be at most an aesthetic lapse resulting from the child's still underdeveloped sense of beauty. To Wordsworth, however, such early contacts with nature mean more than that, nourishing man's moral as well as his aesthetic sense, so that by employing a metaphor of sexual violation he is able to draw ethical implications and elevate the judgments of the poem from an aesthetic to a moral level. By his offense against the property of nature, the boy expresses his fundamental disregard for any claims upon him other than those of his own desires, a disregard that might easily take the form of an offense against human property, just as in *The Prelude* the plundered nest and the stolen boat serve equally as an index to the child's moral deficiencies. It is because nature has finally remedied these deficiencies, so that the mature Wordsworth is no longer dominated by selfish passions, that the poet is able to give his thanks (in a manuscript passage intended as a beginning to *Nutting*) to

> powers
> That teach philosophy and good desires
> In this their still Lyceum.[15]

In Book I of *The Prelude,* the child's ethical instruction comes largely through fear, as nature puts on her sternest aspect to rebuke him and deter him from further wrong-doing. But in *Nutting,* nature appeals to gentler feelings in the child and employs gentler methods. By simply leading him to a scene that supplies the mind with an image of harmony and beauty that he can later set against the destruction worked by his own hands, nature hopes to awaken the child's sensitivity to the consequence of acts motivated solely by a passionate self-interest. And nature apparently does achieve its ends, for Wordsworth tells us "I felt a sense of pain when I beheld / The silent trees, and saw the intruding sky" (52–53). Such discomfort is, however, only momentary and dissolves quickly as the youth turns away from the scene, "Exulting, rich beyond the wealth of kings" (51). Moreover, so great is the distance between the child's moral responses and those of the adult that Wordsworth qualifies even this limited possibility of moral responsiveness by questioning whether such a lesson—far subtler than any in *The Prelude* —did actually arouse feelings of remorse or pain or whether "I now / Confound my present feelings with the past" (48–49).

Although the emotions of the poet reflecting upon the incident and those of the child who participated in it are dissimilar, the experience is, nevertheless, a formative one of a kind frequently employed by nature "when she would frame / A favor'd Being" (*Prelude*, I, 363–64). From such experiences the older Wordsworth has learned, as he tells us in the closing lines of *Nutting*, that nature's quiet bowers house not dumb, insensate things but active moral and spiritual powers anxious to communicate their indwelling calm to man. In no sense do these lines say that man should not intrude upon these previously unvisited corners of nature, since the poem's admonition to the "dearest Maiden" who accompanies him on a later excursion among similar scenes is that she should "move along these shades / In gentleness of heart" (54–55)—a prohibition against violation not intrusion. But the assumption by Perkins and Ferry of a fundamental enmity between man and nature makes man an intruder incapable of such gentleness, an intruder against whom nature must defend herself by putting "pathless rocks and matted ferns and tangled thickets in his way" in order to make it "difficult for him to find the glade." [16] Surely the earlier and more extended account of *Nutting* contained in a letter to Coleridge makes it clear that it is nature herself, as I have indicated, that leads the child to the site of his act of desecration. Here Wordsworth begins,

> Among the autumnal woods, a figure quaint,
> Equipped with wallet and with crooked stick
> They led me, and I followed in their steps,

and he continues some lines farther on,

> They led me far
> Those guardian spirits, into some dark nook
> Unvisited.[17]

The omission of these lines should certainly be attributed to Wordsworth's habit, seen in evidence in other works, of removing some of the more boldly animistic statements that appear in manuscript from the published versions of his poems, a practice that seldom, however, impairs the meaning expressed by the original. So too in *Nutting*, meanings made explicit in the letter to Coleridge still remain implicit in the poem given the public through the retention in the closing line of that familiar Wordsworthian nature spirit, who, as the original manuscript puts it, has expressed her love for the youthful poet-to-be by leading him to her most secret haunts.

The problem still remains, however, of how nature used the episode to direct the poet's growth and how it achieved sufficient significance to become a subject for later meditation. Perkins contends that "we do not discover here an approach to nature with the receptivity Wordsworth would have conceived formative." [18] Yet we have already seen a more intense form of receptivity in Wordsworth than even that mood of reverential contemplation he calls wise passiveness. This heightened receptivity occurs during momentary relaxations from activities that so absorb the mind that it is no longer conscious of the settings in which these activities take place. It is in such moments that nature most fully impregnates the mind, leaving behind images that will haunt it for years to come. De Quincey's famous description of Wordsworth suddenly turning from listening absorbedly for the sound of the wheels of a coach and catching sight of a star, the skating scene in *The Prelude,* and *There was a Boy* are all examples of this form of receptivity. In connection with the last poem, Wordsworth in his *Preface* of 1815 gives a brief account of this mode of perception: "The Boy, there introduced, is listening, with something of a feverish and restless anxiety, for the recurrence of those riotous sounds which he had previously excited; and, at the moment when the intenseness of his mind is beginning to remit, he is surprised into a perception of the solemn and tranquillizing images which the Poem describes." [19] As the incident of the stolen boat discussed in an earlier context illustrates, every aspect of the mind's operation, including its most unreflective acts, is, within the general economy of things, fitted to nature's final purposes, and even this relatively rare yet seemingly minor form of perception has a significant function in determining man's final behavior. It is the child who is most frequently intent upon activities solely designed to meet the needs of his self-gratifying passions and who is, therefore, most indifferent to the beauty of his environment. But because nature's forms imprint themselves even more strongly upon the mind when it is inattentive to them and deeply absorbed in other things than when it is observant, these extrinsic passions are not to be construed as wasteful of the opportunities for development of the child by nature. Thus, although *Nutting*'s protagonist seems wholly preoccupied with the joy of his plunder, a brief suspension of the mind's activity prior to the act itself stamps the scene unconsciously but indelibly upon the poet's memory. The question of whether or not he actually felt pain at the time of the incident is then of secondary importance. The primary value of the day's excursion is that it has given the poet an image of pristine beauty whose loss as the result of his own misconduct is a source of guilt and pain to the fully developed moral and aesthetic sense. Years later, another woodland excursion has recalled, through the workings of the laws of association, memories of this earlier incident now accompanied by feelings of remorse that nourish good desires. These have not only freed him from bondage to his own passions but have led to so active a concern for preservation of nature's loveliness that he calls upon his companion, who, as a manuscript version tells us, possesses many of the turbulent emotions of the child, to stay her hand from nature and walk among these scenes in "gentleness of heart" (55).

This, then, is the implication of those closing lines that Ferry dismisses and Perkins ignores. Ferry, who is deeply aware of the disparity between his reading of the poem and Wordsworth's own stated conclusion concerning it, protests somewhat stridently, "Surely the moral of this is not 'Keep off the grass!' or 'Don't pick the flowers!' " [20] But the moral is, I think, something like this, and it should not be altogether surprising coming from a man who assures us he "would not strike a flower / As many a man will strike his horse." [21] Wordsworth would defend his moral in *Nutting* for its relevance to man's dealings with other men, in much the same way that he justifies the lines just quoted:

> For can he
> Who thus respects a mute insensate form,
> Whose feelings do not need the gross appeal
> Of tears and of articulate sounds, can he
> Be wanting in his duties to mankind
> Or slight the pleadings of a human heart? [22]

What emerges most strikingly from *Nutting* is a sense of moral distance between the unthinking self-interest of childhood and maturity's reflective concern for others, a concern that, though directed to nature here, can, as we have seen, be quite readily extended to man. Underlying this contrast in ethical motivation and ethical response is a still more fundamental contrast in the root principles of moral behavior. For self-interest and benevolence are not two aspects of a single mode of acting, evolving stages, widely separated in time but organically connected, that share, at the deepest levels, a common essence or that can be explained by a single moral concept. Ethical change and development in the Wordsworth of these years is dramatic and essential, a transformation, not in degree but in kind, of the interior grounds of conduct. The basis of childhood behavior is hedonistic, pleasure and pain, generally a predominantly physiological presence, being the regulative criteria by which the child governs his actions. The vocabulary by which Wordsworth characterizes the determination of childhood acts is, for the most part, a vocabulary of pleasures and pains, implicitly quantitative and, often, explicitly corporeal: childhood is the season of "vulgar joy," "giddy bliss," and "coarser pleasures"; then nature acts to impress "upon all forms the characters / Of danger and desire" (*Prelude,* I, 497–98) so that these characters may induce responses in the child of "triumph, and delight, and hope, and fear" (*Prelude,* I, 500); and in the most tellingly hedonistic phrase of all, Wordsworth speaks of his childhood experience in the V manuscript as a "medley of aversions and desires." [23] But adulthood—at least, adulthood in the moral sense Wordsworth intends—does not mean that the pleasures of childhood are refined, that hedonism is shifted from a quantitative to a qualitative base. Instead, with the attainment of a true maturity, a new faculty of ethical judgment is called into play, and perhaps into being, that makes possible conduct, both in creed and in practice, that is motivated by an enlightened and disinterested regard for the welfare of other men.

The obvious aim of moral development, then, is to shift the grounds upon which the individual acts from pleasures and pains, felt literally upon the pulses, to a faculty of judgment that moves one to acts that it deems intrinsically good. Ordinarily, from pursuit of such an aim, there inevitably follows a theory of moral education that attempts to show how a proper manipulation of the pleasures of childhood can effect such an end, carrying one from behavior determined by self-interest to behavior determined by benevolence. Hartley, Priestley, and, later, Godwin are all educational theorists in this sense, believing that man is to be morally improved by a calculated ordering of his sensations in ways conducive to virtue. It is at this point that Wordsworth who, though following such a developmental hypothesis in its broadest outlines, most markedly departs from those contemporaries of his with whom I have sought, in general terms, to identify him. Although he believes that man must be placed in an atmosphere of sensation conducive to virtue, Wordsworth repudiates any excessive human ordering of that atmosphere, any tampering with what he takes to be natural process. Nature is to be left alone to do its own work, to operate according to its own scheme of good; and any attempt by man to intervene and to accelerate nature's timetable of development can only be morally damaging.

The most detailed exposition of these views appears in Book V of *The Prelude*, with its satiric thrust at the prodigy "Engender'd by these too industrious times" (V, 293) and those educational experimenters who, rigidly controlling the child's environment, have formed his mind and character on what they take to be the principles of empiricism.[24] Curiously enough, the child whose upbringing Wordsworth so severely criticizes seems exemplary not only in knowledge but in conduct:

> selfishness
> May not come near him, gluttony or pride;
> The wandering Beggars propagate his name,
> Dumb creatures find him tender as a Nun.
>   (V, 301–4)

Yet even if this modern paragon's "moral part / Is perfect" (V, 318–19), Wordsworth rejects him as a model for childhood behavior, choosing, instead, children like himself or children like those he had lived among and played thoughtlessly with during his own childhood, "A race of real children, not too wise, / Too learned, or too good" (V, 436–37). This reference is to be explained, however, not by simple nostalgia for his own past or by a conservative unwillingness to alter things as they are. Right conduct for Wordsworth is to be judged finally by disinterestedness of motive rather than by the utility of the act itself. The determining motive, however, for the virtuous acts of the wondrous child, the "dwarf

Man," as Wordsworth so scornfully characterizes him, is vanity:

Vanity

That is his soul, there lives he, and there moves;
It is the soul of everything he seeks;
That gone, nothing is left which he can love.

(V, 354–57)

In acting solely from principles of self-regard, the prodigy in no way differs from those other children of his own age who are neither "too wise" nor "too good," for Wordsworth regards childhood itself as a time of essentially selfish pleasures, when each considers "his own person, senses, faculties, / Centre and soul of all." But where the real child finds his self-gratifying pleasures among the objects and activities encountered during the course of a normal childhood, objects and activities that are in most cases of negligible moral consequence, the child who is compelled to undertake prematurely adult responsibilities and to display adult virtues before his time must come to identify these self-gratifying pleasures with matters of such vital moral significance as charity. Those virtues formed too early and instilled by external compulsion, Wordsworth thus claims, are little more than sham virtues, devoid of all disinterested motive, dependent solely upon habitual association with feelings of vanity, and fitted to survive only for as long as they continue to supply materials for self-applause.

Moreover, those who would impose an adult regimen upon the child necessarily deprive him of those rare but invaluable opportunities provided in the ordinary pursuits of childhood when the child may feel pleasure without reference to self-interest, moments that help to prepare the child for that later stage of life in which moral action will be disinterested and virtue prized for its own sake. These habits of self-forgetfulness have their beginnings in the commonest past-times of childhood: the games played by the young poet and his friends against a background of natural beauty whose effect was to soften the competitive spirit so that "selfishness / Was mellowed down"; [25] the reading of fairy tales from which "The Child, whose love is here, at least, doth reap / One precious gain, that he forgets himself" (*Prelude*, V, 368–69). The apparent moral superiority of the child trained according to the precepts of the "mighty workmen of our later age" (V, 370) must in the end prove illusory, for his moral actions will never possess that acquired disposition to pursue only the intrinsically good, a disposition found only in those whose growth has gradually proceeded by natural process from love of self to love of others in accordance with the will of the "wiser Spirit" who "is at work for us" through "the unreasoning progress of the world" (V, 384–85) and "studious of our good, / Even in what seem our most unfruitful hours" (V, 387–88).

Two shorter poems, *We Are Seven* and *Anecdote for Fathers,* familiar works that made their first appearance in *Lyrical Ballads,* also deal with attempts to tamper with a natural process of development and with the consequences of intrusion into the child's world by an adult who compels him to deal with issues that the child is not yet ready to comprehend. In *We Are Seven,* the child holds fast, her convictions unshaken. These convictions, so stubbornly maintained, rest finally upon animal faith rather than any precocious understanding of some form of transcendent human imperishability. Despite the persistent efforts of her interrogator to force her to accept the fact of the deaths of her brother and sister, the girl—too intensely aware of the feelings of life that flow through her to conceive of its cessation—refuses to accept a notion so alien to the far more compelling facts of her immediate sensory experience.[26] But in *Anecdote for Fathers,* adult persistence finally wins out. By his father's repeated questioning,[27] the child is coerced into attempting a rational

explanation of why he prefers Kelve to Liswyn farm. In the
simplicity of his answer, the child's incapacity to form such
judgments is readily apparent, but equally apparent is his
inability to form ethical judgments, his failure to recognize
that falsehood should be an object of moral disapproval.
What the poem dramatically illustrates is a problem raised
by an educational theory based upon the premises of associational psychology. When he failed to satisfy his father the
boy had "blushed with shame" (46), but once he came upon
an answer that he thought would relieve these pressures—
and the absence of a weather-cock at Kilve seemed as good an
answer as any—the child "eased his mind" (54). In an act
that has important bearings for the future, he has learned to
associate uneasiness with the inability to answer difficult
questions and pleasure with any form of answer, however
little relevance it may have to truth. Thus, as Wordsworth
tells us in a subtitle that further clarifies the poem's purport,
"the art of lying may be taught." The poem certainly offers
no grounds upon which to regard the child as endowed with
"a kind of knowledge or insight usually denied to the adult
with his confined and fading imagination" or to take the
child's answer "as a rebuke to the mental processes of age,
tethered and straitened as they are by the restless desire of
rational explanation." [28] What the father learns from the
child is that we must treat all things according to their
natures, and, more important, we must treat all persons as
persons, demanding no more from them than their natural
endowments allow. In establishing a relationship with his
child, a father (the poem is, after all, an anecdote *for* fathers)
must consider the child's interests and competence; for if
he interferes with the natural development of the child's
intellect, he runs the risk of gravely impairing the child's
moral development as well. Wordsworth makes this most
clear in a letter in which he explains that his intention in the
poem "was to point out the injurious effects of putting in-

considerate questions to Children, and urging them to give answers on matters either uninteresting to them or upon which they had no decided opinion." [29] *Anecdote for Fathers* states, though with considerable subtlety, the point we saw made earlier in Wordsworth's broad satire upon the youthful prodigy. The too insistent prodding of a child aggravates his moral imperfections, permits him to employ motives or engage in actions that an insufficiently developed moral judgment fails to condemn or check, and finally, as an implied corollary, thwarts nature's efforts to transform him from the passionate, self-centered creature we see in childhood into a truly responsible moral agent.

Danger to the child's moral future is not the sole consideration in Wordsworth's warnings against this sort of adult tampering. Though childhood treated primarily from the moral goals of the developmental point of view has a primarily instrumental value, Wordsworth also attaches an intrinsic importance to natural process and quite obviously displays a deep affection for the condition of childhood (to be distinguished, however, from worship of childhood), which he regards as being, in its proper season, undeniably a good in itself. The eye he casts upon the "race of real children" who, like himself as a child, are "not too wise, / Too learned, or too good," does not simply view their behavior in terms of future moral possibilities but also looks appreciatively upon activities that have their own substantial values. Wordsworth sees in these children "doing wrong, and suffering" (V, 441) a moral carelessness that must not be persisted in beyond childhood; but he also perceives in their behavior an unreflecting innocence that enables them to be "yet still in happiness / Not yielding to the happiest upon earth" (V, 443–44). There is a complexity of attitude here (a term in this case greatly preferable to ambivalence) that is not to be ignored. In taking issue with the conventional assumption that Wordsworth in his approach to childhood was uniformly reverential, we need to exercise considerable caution against falling into the opposing error of taking Wordsworth's description of the child's underdeveloped moral consciousness as an unduly severe reproach to childhood. In lines from the JJ manuscript of *The Prelude* that offer the most reliable commentary upon these complex attitudes toward childhood that he held between 1797 and 1800, Wordsworth, reflecting upon the episodes from his early years that he has just described, expresses an obvious retrospective satisfaction toward the enjoyments of these years; but he does so within a clearly defined developmental context that assures us that the pleasures of childhood, though real and intrinsically worthwhile, are not the final good at which life aims:

> The beauteous colours of my [our] early years [time]
> Which make the starting-place of being fair
> And worthy of the goal to which they tend.[30]

The developmental course that carries Wordsworth from "the starting-place of being" to life's distant moral goal is not, at least in theory, a passage free of obstacles. For to reach that goal requires that ethical acts and judgments that in our earliest years could have no basis other than self-interest must eventually be determined on some disinterested basis, a change not in degree but in kind that involves a leap over what would seem to be a psychologically impassable barrier. To surmount this barrier, Wordsworth turns to the agency of nature, which, in providing man with a basis for disinterested conduct, performs its most morally significant function. Though nature's efforts to check and inhibit the child's passions during his most aggressively self-interested and most irresponsible acts are unquestionably vital to the child's moral progress, nature, in this, its monitory guise, performs a predominantly negative function. Only in youth, when it becomes "all in all," does nature's positive bearing upon the ethical life fully manifest itself by shifting the focus of interest for man, which in childhood had been the self, "Centre and soul of all," to "Another soul, spring, centre of his being, / And that is Nature." [31] Through the power of its attractions, nature effects a transfer of man's attention and concern to an object whose value is determined without reference to any considerations of self-regard. Though possessing no intrinsic moral status in itself, this concern for nature establishes the foundations of the moral life by calling forth feelings untainted by self-interest and thus proving that there does exist in man a capability for genuinely disinterested action. Moreover, Wordsworth indicates that the disinterested concern man demonstrates toward nature is ultimately convertible—the proper level of personal development having been reached—into behavior motivated by an equally disinterested concern for man:

> Not useless do I deem
> These quiet sympathies with things that hold
> An inarticulate language; for the man
> Once taught to love such objects as excite
> No morbid passions no disquietude
> No vengeance, and no hatred needs must feel
> The joy of that pure principle of love
> So deeply that unsatisfied with aught
> Less pure and exquisite he cannot choose
> But seek for objects of a kindred love
> In fellow-natures and a kindred joy.[32]

Though nature is the instrument that first fosters disinterestedness in man, and thus is the mediating agent for his engagement in the moral life, there is in this, as in all other relations between nature and man, a collaborative arrangement required. Nature's effects are dependent upon man's growth, the development in him of sympathetic faculties, powers through which he can project himself into the lives and feelings of others, first, according to Wordsworth's developmental scheme, into sympathetic involvement with the affairs of men. The "quiet sympathies" man feels "with things that hold / An inarticulate language" lead him eventually to desire to extend those sympathies and to "seek for objects of a kindred love / In fellow-natures." In the attempts to isolate a benevolistic principle as the basis of moral action, theories of sympathy occupied a conspicuous position in eighteenth-century ethics. By its very nature, the sympathetic principle, according to those who advanced the theory, was incompatible with any form of self-love. "Sympathy," Adam Smith argues in *The Theory of Moral Sentiments,* the fullest exposition of an ethic based on this doctrine, "cannot in any sense be regarded as a selfish principle." For what occurs in sympathetic projection is that we find ourselves experiencing "an imaginary change of situations with the person principally concerned"; but this, Smith adds, "is not supposed to happen to me in my own person and character, but in that of the person with whom I sympathize." [33] For proponents of the theory of sympathy like Smith, the sympathetic impulse is universal among men and, when forcefully stimulated, acts upon the individual with what seems virtually an irresistible compulsion. As illustration of the universality of the power of self-projection and the strength of its effects, Smith, in a famous passage, cites the behavior of the mob looking up at the rope dancer: That this [sympathy] is the source of our fellow-feeling for the misery of others, that it is by changing places in fancy with the sufferer, that we come either to conceive or be affected by what he feels, may be demonstrated by many obvious observations. . . . The mob, when they are gazing at a dancer on the slack rope, naturally writhe and twist and balance their own bodies, as they see him do, and as they feel they themselves must do if in his situation." [34]

Whether the concept of sympathy reached Wordsworth

from such ethical theorists as Smith and Hume, or, as seems more likely, from eighteenth-century literary materials in which the moral effects of sympathetic projection serve as a staple of sentimentalism, sympathy is a concept that very clearly plays its part in Wordsworth's moral scheme. Indeed, on occasion he describes the individual moved by the power of sympathy to a necessary response in ways that seem not very different from the act of imaginative transferral by the mob watching the ropedancer. In *The Old Cumberland Beggar,* probably the poem of this period that deals most explicitly with man's relations with man from the perspective of a highly developed and relatively abstract theory of ethics, many of the acts of charity or kindness to the beggar clearly proceed from sympathetic responsiveness to his situation. The beggar, like the vagrant soldier of *The Prelude,* and, somewhat later, the leech-gatherer of *Resolution and Independence,* provides a critical focus for observing the nature and extent of man's moral concern, his capacity for true disinterestedness. All of these figures are absolutely dependent, yet absolutely alone, requiring the charity of others for their very sustenance but lacking any claim of kinship or friendship to foster that charity. Man, Wordsworth contends, does respond: even those who seldom look beyond their own personal interests and needs find themselves impelled by powerful and unfamiliar sympathies to a sense of genuine fellow-feeling for those lonely outcasts who express in their plight the depth of human dependence upon the potential for benevolence in others. Moreover, the act of charity that occurs in such a poem as *The Old Cumberland Beggar* goes beyond mere alms-giving in ways that reveal an authentic solicitude on the part of the donor. "The sauntering Horseman" interrupts his journey and

> throws not with a slack
> And careless hand his alms upon the ground,

But stops,—that he may safely lodge the coin
Within the old Man's hat; nor quits him so,
But still, when he has given his horse the rein,
Watches the aged Beggar with a look
Sidelong, and half-reverted.

(26–32)

The general habits of such a man can scarcely be termed
virtuous, for his usual charities, those ordinarily bestowed
"with a slack and careless hand," would seem to be the product of custom rather than of any spontaneous outflowing of
generous feeling. In this, his behavior differs little from the
normal conduct of the average man; yet the desolation of the
aged and lonely wanderer does touch the heart, so that the
horseman, acting under the virtually compulsive pressures
of his powers of sympathy, departs from custom and neglects
his own purposes from an unselfish concern for the welfare
of another. Even the coarse postboy who usually reacts to
any interruption of his progress by "a curse / Upon his lips
or anger at his heart" (42–43) has his feelings softened by
the image of helplessness that the beggar puts before him, so
that if the old man fails to hear the shouted warning when
the cart's "rattling wheels o'ertake / The aged Beggar in the
woody lane" (37–38), the postboy "Turns with less noisy
wheels to the roadside, / And passes gently by" (41–42).

Sympathy, then, stands as the most basic and most common
of man's moral resources, the seminal beginnings for Wordsworth of the ethical life. Even among those ordinarily indifferent to the needs of others, the power of sympathy, when
acted upon by a sufficiently compelling object, can in most
cases prove stronger than the barriers of habit and thus dis-
pose man to acts of true disinterestedness. And if sympathy
is the most basic and the most common motive of benevolent
conduct, it is also—unsurprisingly—in the scheme of man's
development to be numbered among the earliest of man's

motives to benevolence. Even those who in their lives eventually realize the highest and most far-reaching of man's moral aspirations and prove

> authors of delight
> And happiness, which to the end of time
> Will live, and spread, and kindle,
> (107–9)

have had the course of their future development shaped by the childhood sympathies that such a figure as the Cumberland beggar so compellingly calls forth:

> even such minds
> In childhood, from this solitary Being,
> Or from like wanderer, haply have received
> (A thing more precious far than all that books
> Or the solicitudes of love can do!)
> That first mild touch of sympathy and thought,
> In which they found their kindred with a world
> Where want and sorrow were.
> (109–16)

Sympathy for Wordsworth is thus the basis for all subsequent moral endeavor, the basis of the moral possibilities not only of the individual but of humanity at large. For underlying Wordsworth's hope of general social reform is an ethical uniformitarianism founded upon trust in the strength of the sympathetic emotions and their prevalence or potential prevalence among all mankind, faith "That we have all of us one human heart" (153).

Though sympathy may be seen to carry us into the ethical life, it, nonetheless, occupies a relatively subordinate position within the larger framework of Wordsworth's general view of human development. Within this context, man's moral reliance upon his powers of sympathy constitutes a necessary but elementary and, in some respects, primitive phase in the growth of his capacity for benevolence. If the operation of the sympathetic emotions seem irresistibly potent in their immediate effect, they are by that very fact limited in the range and extensiveness of the moral relations to which sympathy can lead us. The sympathetic response requires for its evocation a directness of experience like that provided when the horseman or postboy bear personal witness to the desperate deprivation of the beggar, a requirement that thereby precludes sympathy from being expended upon a more generalized object, such as the abstract idea of man himself. This is not to question the disinterestedness of the sympathetic response, but it is a disinterestedness so narrowly circumscribed by what goes on within the bounds of directly perceived or at least familiar experience that, taken in itself, the emotion of sympathy can scarcely be expected to raise in us that more elevated motive to conduct in the benevolence, at once abstract and universal, that Wordsworth speaks of as love of man.[35]

There is also another sense in which a moral theory based purely on a concept of sympathetic disinterestedness fails to conform to the goals for man established within Wordsworth's developmental scheme. For Wordsworth's view of nature and of man, as we have already seen, is essentially quietistic, and the end of human development is the attainment by man of a tranquillity comparable to nature's own. Such tranquillity is marked in part by a negative characteristic, the waning power exercised by the emotions in the determination of conduct. Sympathy, however, rests upon a fundamentally affective base: the ability of an observer to project himself into the situation of another is in direct proportion to the intensity of emotion that the situation arouses in him. If man is to complete his moral development, sympathy, grounded as it is in the emotions, must give way as the initiating agent in man's altruistic acts to qualities of mind that are more tranquil and reflective, qualities of the kind that Wordsworth refers to when he praises "The calm existence that is mine when I / Am worthy of myself" (*Prelude,* I, 360–61). Indeed, so distinct is powerful emotion from the mature Wordsworth's ideal of right conduct that fulfillment of man's moral nature would seem necessarily to require the sacrifice of an earlier ardor: thus it is, says Wordsworth, that "the wisest and the best / Of all mankind" cannot bring to his dedication "to duty and to truth / The eagerness of infantine desire" (*Prelude,* II, 22–26). The insistence here that attainment of this highest form of virtue is contingent upon the loss of man's earliest and most intense emotions further indicates that for Wordsworth the truly ethical life is a product, not of the feelings, but of some more dispassionate faculty of man.

In this connection, too, *The Old Cumberland Beggar* provides a major statement of Wordsworth's moral ideas. The first awakening of sympathetic feeling that the beggar, or others like him, calls forth, culminates for a rare and exemplary few in a mature ethical life governed by reason, a faculty whose far-reaching light falls not only upon the directly perceived needs of the specific individual but also upon the general condition of man. It is of these few Wordsworth speaks when, in a manuscript version of *The Old Cumberland Beggar,* he describes those who are

> By their good works exalted, lofty minds,
> And meditative, in which reason falls
> Like a strong radiance of the setting sun
> On each minutest feeling of the heart,
> Illuminates, and to their view brings forth
> In one harmonious prospect.[36]

What the earlier cited passages from *The Prelude* imply and these lines make plain is that love of man, at least in the form such love takes among "the wisest and the best / Of all mankind," requires not simply feelings of good will but a benevolence that is tranquil, reflective, and generalized: in short, a rational benevolence. But this last term introduces us to a new scheme of moral theorizing (indicating in the process how eclectic Wordsworth was in the ethical ideas he attempted to accommodate within his empiricist framework), a scheme whose principal exponent for Wordsworth's age was William Godwin.

The larger question of Wordsworth's total relations with Godwin need not concern us here.[37] The matter to be immediately considered is that in those few instances between 1797 and 1800 where Wordsworth delineates his ideal moral agent, the figure that emerges is the man of rational benevolence, a figure inescapably associated by Wordsworth's contemporaries with the teachings of Godwin. Indeed, even the formation of such "lofty minds"—that is, those whose "good works" are performed in accordance with the illuminations of reason—from such embryonic moral acts as those described in *The Old Cumberland Beggar* entails a process that has its obvious counterpart in Godwin. Speaking of the contribution of conduct inspired by morally inferior motives to what is eventually to be a truly rational virtue, Wordsworth writes,

> Where'er the aged Beggar takes his rounds,
> The mild necessity of use compels
> To acts of love; and habit does the work
> Of reason; yet prepares that after-joy
> Which reason cherishes. And thus the soul,
> By that sweet taste of pleasure unpursued,
> Doth find herself insensibly disposed
> To virtue and true goodness.
>
> (98–105)

The pattern traced here of man moved by some non-moral interest to perform habitually a virtuous action that he finally comes to regard as intrinsically worthy of rational approval is markedly similar to the account given of man's moral evolution in the third edition of *Political Justice:*

> A disposition to promote the benefit of another, my child, my friend, my relation, or my fellow being, is one of the passions; understanding by the term passion, a permanent and habitual tendency toward a certain course of action. It is of the same general nature, as avarice, or the love of fame. . . . But it is the nature of the passions, speedily to convert what at first were means, into ends. The avaricious man forgets the utility of money which at first incited him to pursue it, fixes his passion upon the money itself, and counts his gold, without having in his mind any idea but that of seeing and handling it. Something of this sort happens very early in the history of every passion. The moment we become attached to a particular source of pleasure, beyond any idea we have of the rank it holds in the catalogue of sources, it must be admitted that it is loved for its own sake. . . . If this be the case in the passion of avarice or the love of fame, it must also be true in the instance of beneficence, that, after having habituated ourselves to promote the happiness of our child, our family, our country or our species, we are at length brought to approve and desire their happiness without retrospect to ourselves. It happens in this instance, as in the former, that we are occasionally actuated by the most perfect disinterestedness, and willingly submit to tortures and death, rather than see injury committed upon the object of our affections.[38]

In *The Old Cumberland Beggar,* Wordsworth seems to agree with Godwin in two important particulars: both regard rational benevolence as the highest form of moral activity, and both assign to habit the function of converting "What at first were means, into ends" and thus disposing the mind "To virtue and true goodness."

One serious objection may seem immediately to present itself to this interpretation of the part played by Godwinian rational benevolence in Wordsworth's mature thought. Although scholarship has long recognized that reason holds a valued place in Wordsworth's system, it has also noted that he tends to use the term *reason* in a twofold sense. Reason as a tool of analysis (the form of rationalism habitually attributed to Godwin by critics of Wordsworth) Wordsworth invariably held suspect, regarding it as meddlesome or destructive and associating it with a type of abstract theorizing wholly divorced from the experiences of actual life. But Wordsworth also wrote of reason as a means of intuition that enabled the mind to apprehend spiritual and moral truths so profound that the senses alone were incapable of perceiving them. In *The Prelude,* Wordsworth clearly distinguished between these two operations of reason, describing the intuitive faculty as "the grand / And simple Reason" (XI, 123–24) and the analytical reason as a "humbler power" (XI, 124) to be employed cautiously since it is

> A Function rather proud to be
> The enemy of falsehood, than the friend
> Of truth.
>
> (XI, 135–37)

The majority of critics have held with Havens that this division can be explained most plausibly as a reflection of the Kantian distinction between the *Verstand* and the *Vernunft,* a distinction that Wordsworth presumably derived from Coleridge.[39]

But a distinction between reason as intuitive and reason as analytic is also central to the tradition of English rationalism, and the interpretation of reason offered by Richard Price and Godwin may help to explain why Wordsworth saw fit to treat reason under both of these headings—to distinguish between reason as a means of spiritual illumination and reason as a tool of the meddling intellect—as early as 1798, and why he gave reason in its more important and more valued sense a specifically ethical application in *The Old Cumberland Beggar*. Price, one of the central figures in late eighteenth-century radicalism and a major influence upon Godwin, had presented a full and careful exposition of the doctrine of rational benevolence in his *A Review of the Principal Questions in Morals*. One of the points that he had there insisted upon is that reason "is different from the power of *reasoning,* and ought, by no means, to be confounded with it." [40] *"Reasoning"* for Price involves only comparison and analysis and "consists in investigating certain relations between objects, ideas of which must have been previously in the mind: that is, it supposes us already to have the ideas we want to trace; and therefore cannot give rise to new ideas." [41] "Reason," on the other hand, provides the mind with insight into moral truths that are "eternal and immutable." [42]

Price's separation of the activities of the rational mind into "reason" and "reasoning" has as its precedent a somewhat similar distinction by Descartes between intuition and deduction.[43] But by the middle of the eighteenth century, the reestablishment of this important distinction and the reaffirmation of the superiority of "reason" to "reasoning" as a means of acquiring certitude had become a clear necessity, since English rationalists, particularly the influential Samuel Clarke and, to some extent, Locke himself, had apparently ignored the distinction in their writings on ethics and treated moral judgments as matters solely involving deduction.[44] To offset these tendencies, Price turned for his interpretation of reason to the Cambridge Platonists and eventually to Plato's *Theaetetus,* thus adding a new and vital current of thought to eighteenth-century rationalism.[45] Students of Wordsworth have overlooked this important development, assuming generally that reason as used by eighteenth-century writers referred always to that "humbler power" that analyzes and compares, ignoring the fact that a strongly Platonic tradition existed among the rationalists, and nowhere more noticeably than in Godwin's *Political Justice,* a work deeply indebted to Price's interpretation of reason and his rationalistic ethics. For Godwin too, the use of reason is not limited to the unraveling of the syllogism or to mere comparison and analysis; its powers instead extend far beyond that by providing man with a means of "communication with the common instructor, truth" [46] and a knowledge of those principles of morality that to Godwin are "if anything can be, fixed and immutable." [47] That Platonism presumably underlies this conception of reason has already been suggested by F. E. L. Priestley, who in his authoritative introduction to *Political Justice* has stated, "Mr. Middleton Murry is probably right in believing that Godwin always meant more by 'Reason' than the discursive reason; certainly the 'sudden and irresistible conviction' seems to be thought of as the final stage in a Platonic process in which the flash of illumination follows patient examination." [48] The moral judgments of the rationally benevolent man according to Price and Godwin derive their certitude not from the faculty devoted to logical analysis but from the workings of "the grand / And simple Reason," which lends conviction to the truth it asserts.

Plainly, Wordsworth's portrait of the man of rational benevolence is an incomplete one. References are too few and too scattered to draw from them either a comprehensive system of ethical theory or a detailed code of practical conduct that would instruct us in how the man of rational benevolence actually lives. The relative infrequency of such references suggests that Wordsworth adopted the notion of rational benevolence less because he was an ardently committed Godwinian than because the notion itself, with its basic assumption that moral achievement is somehow conditional upon the slackening of one's youthful intensity, served his purposes so well. For it enabled him to preserve an ethics of benevolence in the face of such a lessening of emotion by locating in judgment rather than in feeling the impelling source of conduct of those he regarded as "the wisest and the best / Of all mankind." And Godwin's prominence, his indisputable humanitarianism, and his strong appeal to those among whom radical sentiments still lingered made Godwinism a logical and obvious choice for Wordsworth in his quest for a form of the ethical life in which meditative habits issued in benevolent actions.

As a moralist, however, Wordsworth is clearly more concerned with process than with product, with retrospection than with prophecy. His primary aim is the presentation of an exemplary pattern derived mainly from his own life that has made eventual attainment of the moral life possible for him and that, if imitated, can make the same moral life possible for others. At the end of this process that is the ground of so much of Wordsworth's hope for man and society stands the man of rational benevolence. But though such a figure certainly exists as the logic of Wordsworth's scheme demands and the evidence of the poetry confirms, he exists for the most part as an unbodied concept rather than as a concrete presence, a far less substantial figure in Wordsworth's poetic world than the passion-driven child and the genie of the woods, figures with whom the moral abstractions of Godwin have little connection.

1. Locke, p. 32.
2. Ibid., p. 201.
3. Hartley, I:474.
4. Ibid., p. 360.
5. Ibid., p. 83.
6. Ibid., p. 391.
7. Joseph Priestley, *Introductory Essays to Hartley's Theory of the Human Mind*, in *Works*, III:195.
8. Hartley, I:82.
9. Ibid.

10. Ibid., p. 497.

11. For recent interpretations of *Nutting,* see Ferry, pp. 22–28; David Perkins, *The Quest for Permanence* (Cambridge, Mass., 1959), pp. 14–16; Bloom, pp. 136–39; Hartman, pp. 73–75; and Roger Murray, *Wordsworth's Style: Figures and Themes in the Lyrical Ballads of 1800* (Lincoln, Neb., 1967), pp. 63–68. My argument here is directed primarily against Perkins and Ferry, for it is in their readings of *Nutting,* readings that are most representative of the general cast of their books, that we find the view of the mutual incompatibility of man and nature in Wordsworth argued most forcefully.

12. Perkins, p. 79.

13. Ferry, p. 25.

14. *PW,* II, 504.

15. Ibid., p. 505.

16. Ferry, p. 26.

17. William and Dorothy Wordsworth, *Early Letters,* ed. Ernest de Selincourt (Oxford, 1935), pp. 206–7.

18. Perkins, p. 15.

19. *PW,* II, 440.

20. Ferry, p. 25.

21. *Prelude,* p. 612 (a passage from MS.18a).

22. Ibid., p. 613 (a passage from MS.18a).

23. *Prelude,* I, 356–57 (MS. V). The omission of this phrase, the only phrase so omitted from I, 351–72 when Wordsworth incorporated V into the A text, seems to me another example of Wordsworth's efforts to cover his tracks where statements in V exhibiting a radically empirical bias— or here a radically hedonistic bias—would clash most jarringly with the far different epistemological or ethical positions that Wordsworth had reached by 1804 and that consequently dominate the later-written books of the A text. Once again I am indebted to Mr. Michael Jaye for his assistance.

24. Most of this section of Book V was written in 1804. But the root idea, the criticism of educational theorists, is already present in 18a, so that clearly the general point of view stated in Book V was conclusively developed by 1798 or 1799. The catalyst may very well have been Thomas Wedgwood's attempt to secure the services of Wordsworth and Coleridge as guardians for the education of a genius through proper training and environmental conditioning. Wedgwood's choice of Wordsworth as tutor for a child to be educated in the best modern way, free of the influences of nature and fairy tales, may not have been as ridiculous as it at first would seem. For in the broadest sense, Wordsworth's educational views paralleled Wedgwood's in being radical, empirical, and developmental, directed to the production, if not of a genius, at least of a favored being. What Wedgwood probably did not know when he approached his fellow radical was how conservative Wordsworth was in regard to method, placing his faith not in human wisdom but in nature's larger teleological scheme.

25. *Prelude,* II, 69 (MS. V).

26. Obviously my reading of *We Are Seven* does not agree with the view

that the child rejects the speaker's imperatives because of some intimation of immortality. I discuss this matter further in chapter 7, where *We Are Seven* is treated in connection with the *Immortality Ode.*

27. Until 1845, the question is repeated five times in every printed version of the poem. In the 1845 edition, the number of times the father repeats it is for unexplained reasons reduced to three.

28. Perkins, p. 72. Perkins takes both the subtitle and the letter discussing Wordsworth's intentions in the poem to be instances of "Wordsworth's anxiety to discover a rational and edifying motive for the emotions expressed in his poetry" (p. 72). Although it seems to me at least arguable, particularly in light of the *Immortality Ode,* that the girl in *We Are Seven* possesses some kind of intuitive knowledge, I find no intelligible grounds for taking her counterpart's preference for Kilve as the expression of a "visionary capacity" that he owes to his proximity to "God, who is our home." To strengthen his argument, Mr. Perkins refers to the child's answer as "unhesitating," but the text scarcely supports this:

> At this my boy so fair and slim
> Hung down his head, nor made reply,
> And five times did I say to him,
> "Why, Edward, tell me why?"
>
> (1798)

Although Wordsworth said nothing about the "visionary capacity" of Basil Montagu, upon whom the child in *Anecdote for Fathers* is modeled, in a letter to Francis Wrangham, Wordsworth did discuss the child's moral short-comings, particularly his addiction to falsehood: "Basil is quite well, *quant au physique mais pour le moral il-y-a bien à craindre.* Among other things he lies like a little devil" (*Early Letters,* p. 154). Neither internal nor external evidence seems to me to justify Mr. Perkins's interpretation.

29. *The Letters of William and Dorothy Wordsworth, The Later Years,* ed. Ernest de Selincourt (Oxford, 1939), I:253.

30. *Prelude,* p. 641 (a passage from MS. JJ).

31. Ibid., p. 575, ll. 138–39 (MS. Y, VIII, 159–72).

32. *PW,* V, 400–401 (Addendum to MS. B of *The Ruined Cottage,* ll. 1–11).

33. Adam Smith, *The Theory of Moral Sentiments,* in Smith's *Moral and Political Philosophy,* ed. Herbert W. Schneider (New York, 1948), p. 53.

34. Ibid., p. 74.

35. According to Hume, sympathy exerts its "influence immediately by a direct tendency or instinct, which chiefly keeps in view the simple object, moving the affections, and comprehends not any scheme or system, nor the consequences resulting from the concurrence, imitation, or example of others" (David Hume, *An Enquiry Concerning the Principles of Morals,* ed. L. A. Selby-Bigge [Oxford, 1902], p. 303).

36. *PW,* IV, 237 (a passage from the Alfoxden MS.). The introduction of reason into a strongly sensationalist view of human development may cause some philosophic discomfort. But in treating reason as a derivative of earlier experience, Wordsworth has ample precedent in Hartley who sought to prove "all Reasoning, as well as Affection, is the real Result of Association"

(I, 499). This, I suspect, is less a matter of influence or borrowing than of their common need to make allowance for rational process within their schemes, a need felt so strongly that it swept aside all of the epistemological objections that the construction of the faculty or process of reasoning from the materials of sensation would so obviously raise.

37. For a more comprehensive examination of Wordsworth's relations with Godwin see my "Wordsworth and Godwin: A Reassessment," *Studies in Romanticism* 6 (1967): 98–119.

38. William Godwin, *Enquiry Concerning Political Justice*, ed. F. E. L. Priestley (Toronto, 1946), I: 424–27.

39. Havens, pp. 138–39.

40. Richard Price, *A Review of the Principal Questions in Morals*, ed. David Daiches Raphael (Oxford, 1948), p. 40.

41. Ibid.

42. Ibid., p. 5.

43. René Descartes, *Rules for the Direction of the Mind, Philosophic Works*, trans. Elizabeth S. Haldane and G. R. T. Ross (New York, 1955), 1:7–8.

44. Price, p. xiv.

45. Ibid.

46. *Political Justice*, I:215.

47. Ibid., II:250.

48. Ibid., III:93.

5

The Empirical Phase:
Anthropocentrism

Between 1797 and 1800 the autobiographic example is Wordsworth's primary, though certainly not his only, means of expressing his hopes for human improvement. There is also an important body of poetry that rests more broadly upon a wider range of social observation that also tends toward the same conclusions and offers the same hopes and promises. Of the major works written during this period, *Home at Grasmere* most successfully bridges these two modes of expression, moving from the predominantly personal to the predominantly social so that it may examine the effects of nature not just upon a single, gifted individual but also upon a larger community of men whose interests and occupations more nearly resemble those of men everywhere.

Home at Grasmere does begin with the purely personal. But the tone of its early sections is, for Wordsworth, uncharacteristically defensive. Where *Tintern Abbey* had assumed as virtually self-evident the superiority of the contemplative life amidst nature to the "fretful stir / Unprofitable" of the city, Wordsworth here acknowledges that in withdrawing to the seclusion of nature he has made himself liable to charges of having shirked his responsibilities to mankind, of having betrayed poetic gifts granted him for use in the service of the common good for the sake of a pastoral illusion with no real relevance to the great issues and events now confronting man and transforming his destiny. The poem begins with the admission that the desire to live at Grasmere had been initially called forth by a child's fancy, the yearnings of a "roving School-boy," who, arrested by the valley's beauty, had

> sighing said,
> "What happy fortune were it here to live!
> And if a thought of dying, if a thought
> Of mortal separation, could intrude
> With paradise before him, here to die!"
> (10–14)

Wordsworth, however, carefully separates childhood impulse from his mature decision to return permanently to Grasmere, a decision requiring more mature and significant motivation than a simple sense of nostalgia. On that first visit, he tells us, nature had aroused in him feelings of "unfettered liberty" and "power and joy"; but such feelings had little future consequence, since he had employed his newly found consciousness of freedom

> only for this end,
> To flit from field to rock, from rock to field,
> From shore to island, and from isle to shore,
> From open ground to covert, from a bed
> Of meadow-flowers into a tuft of wood.
> (38–42)

Only after a sufficient passage of time does the beneficent influence of nature upon man's spiritual development become evident. Then, as its first salutary effect, the vision of Grasmere, preserved by memory, works to dispel the "damp and gloom" of the poet's "splenetic Youth." Only then, too, as childhood passions subside and as reflective powers mature can the deepest values of the remembered scene unfold and the valley of Grasmere become "As beautiful to thought, as it had been, / When present, to the bodily sense" (48–49). Even this implanted image of beauty provides insufficient grounds for the final step Wordsworth contemplates of permanent withdrawal to Grasmere. Not only does such an act run counter to the conventional wisdom of the majority of men but even the poet himself feels that such a decision may be only "A condescention or a weak indulgence / To a sick fancy." [1] To merit Wordsworth's unqualified approval, his choice must rest not upon the sanctions of the heart but upon a more reflective determination: it must be "an act / Of reason that exultingly aspires." [2] Only after the authority of the mature judgment has confirmed his choice does Wordsworth justify his return to Grasmere and his renewed commitment to nature, asserting in a passage that pointedly recapitulates the developmental assumptions of *Tintern Abbey*

> That in my day of Childhood I was less
> The mind of Nature, less, take all in all,
> Whatever may be lost, than I am now.[3]

His decision made, Wordsworth proceeds to a more expansive consideration of the benefits that rural life confers. The most assured proof of such benefits still comes to Wordsworth through introspection, and the personal history of his stay at Grasmere is largely a record of an increasing happiness fed by a sense of "glad emotion and deep quietness" (231). Such introspective assurances are by themselves not enough to support the poem's larger claims and anticipations: that a return to nature would be universally beneficial and that the "blessedness" that he and his sister have secured at Grasmere will at some future date belong "To all the vales of Earth and all mankind." [4] Confirmation of so sweeping an assumption requires more than an avowal of personal happiness and

of personal achievement. Wordsworth must also demonstrate
that the general habits of those who have lived at Grasmere
are superior to the habits of men elsewhere, and he must
demonstrate, moreover, that this superiority is in some way
dependent upon nature. Thus, in the middle section of
Home at Grasmere, Wordsworth turns from personal to
social analysis, confident that observation will substantiate
the conclusions of introspection. But just as at the outset of
the autobiographic section Wordsworth had been careful to
separate childish fancy from reasoned judgment, so here too
Wordsworth inserts qualifications that would forestall criticism of his claims by carefully distinguishing the rural character as it emerges in the poet's dream from the actual conduct of the real inhabitants of Grasmere. Neither "tenderness of mind" nor "romantic hope," he insists, distorts his
observations of his neighbors, for what he looks for among
the shepherds of Grasmere is not some rare being moved by
"perfect love" but

> Man,
> The common Creature of the brotherhood,
> Differing but little from the Man elsewhere,
> For selfishness, and envy, and revenge,
> Ill neighborhood—pity that this should be—
> Flattery and double-dealing, strife and wrong.
>
> (352–57)

By introducing such qualifications into his account of life
at Grasmere, Wordsworth, of course, is simply employing
tactics that will enable him to claim for himself a fidelity to
fact that he can later draw upon when he argues in behalf of
the virtues of his rural neighbors, virtues that, we are to assume, are founded upon realistic observation rather than
upon the naïve conventions of an idealized pastoralism. But
the virtues Wordsworth claims derive, in no small part, from
economic conditions that, if not idealized fictions, are,

Wordsworth acknowledges, rapidly disappearing elsewhere in England. At Grasmere, the land belongs, almost entirely, to those who till it; and though great wealth is largely unknown there, so also is the unrelieved poverty increasingly common in so many other parts of the nation. Because the inhabitants of Grasmere have maintained "kindred independence of estate" (380), so "That they who want, are not too great a weight / For those who can relieve" (366–67), charity still occupies an important place in the lives of the members of the community; and the sympathies so vital to man's moral growth are provided with a sphere in which to develop. The significance of this aspect of rural life does not become fully apparent, however, until Wordsworth contrasts the relatively manageable demands of Grasmere with those made by the "Vast Metropolis"

> Where pity shrinks from unremitting calls,
> Where numbers overwhelm humanity,
> And neighbourhood serves rather to divide
> Than to unite.
>
> (598–601)

For Wordsworth, then, urban life impairs our moral development not because it contains social evils and social needs from which an idyllic rural society is free but because "the increasing accumulation of men in cities" produces social evils and social needs on a scale of such magnitude that our power of sympathetic responsiveness, unable to cope with these "unremitting calls" upon it, becomes frozen in indifference.

Beyond the advantages that the simpler structure of rural society affords its members, there is another feature of life at Grasmere that encourages the growth of the affections in a still more positive way. In its permanence, or at least its relative permanence when viewed from the perspective of the changing life of man, nature acts as an important chronicler of human events. Episodes of joy or sorrow that would otherwise be lost to memory are spared from oblivion and remain a source of comfort and instruction by having been associated with natural objects that survive such episodes and, in many cases, even survive those who participated in them. For example, a grove of firs planted years earlier by her husband, now dead, helps an aged woman to keep alive memories of the happy years they had spent together. The life lived among the objects of nature, Wordsworth claims, strengthens rather than weakens our ties to others, because the deeds of those we have known and loved are perpetuated by the natural surroundings in which they took place. Much of the remainder of *Home at Grasmere* is given over to extending the lesson of the grove of firs to the larger community of Grasmere, until Wordsworth, looking out at the fields, finds such histories present virtually everywhere:

> Joy spreads, and sorrow spreads; and this whole Vale,
> Home of untutored Shepherds as it is,
> Swarms with sensation, as with gleams of sunshine,
> Shadows or breezes, scents or sounds.
>
> (445–48)

This morally indispensable relationship between human event and natural form derives, of course, from the basic assumption of associational psychology that conceives of a perceived object not as a mere isolated entity but rather as the gravitational center for a cluster of objects or events that had previously been connected with it by similarity, causality, or contiguity in time or space. To the experienced observer, therefore, the world of men and the world of nature are not radically dichotomized realms, since even when in apparent solitude such an observer finds that a familiar natural object calls to mind images of those he lives among and of their activities. Where solitude truly exists, says Wordsworth, is among the multitude confined to the city

> whose eyes are doomed
> To hold a vacant commerce day by day
> With objects wanting life, repelling love.
>
> (594–96)

There even the living

> Are ofttimes to their fellow-men no more
> Than to the Forest Hermit are the leaves
> That hang aloft in myriads.
>
> (606–8)

But the world of nature continually calls our attention to the joys and sufferings of our fellows, so that those who live close to nature may find their affections strengthened and their sympathies enlarged even by such unlikely presences as a twisted thorn or an abandoned sheepfold.

It is in this coalescence of object and event that Wordsworth's pragmatic argument for the moral utility of nature finds its strongest justification. Without minimizing the contributions made by nature to Wordsworth's own personal development through admonishing the wayward impulses of childhood or turning youth's interests outward from a pure self-concern, we may still see that nature's most direct and most widespread benefit to the rural community is in its preserving, and hence recounting, the significant experience of that community. In this regard, Wordsworth's interpretation of nature or of objects assimilated to nature, like the sheepfold or the ruined cottage, is deeply anthropocentric. To observe the objects of nature properly is to experience these objects in conjunction with the human incidents associated with them. How persistent this tendency is on the part of those who live in rural surroundings is indicated in its

most basic form by the common rustic habit of naming places
for the persons or events or occupations most intimately connected with them. And, correspondingly, the strength of this
tendency in Wordsworth himself is illustrated by the inclusion in his collected poems of a special category called simply
"Poems on the Naming of Places." In the poems given this
classification, the mountains and dells of Grasmere evoke
for Wordsworth, even in solitude, the remembered presence
of the brother, the sister or the friends for whom he has
named them. Or a given place may, in more didactic fashion,
derive its name from some morally instructive event that has
occurred there. One such place appears in "Poems on the
Naming of Places" as Point Rash-judgment, called that by
Wordsworth and his friends to rebuke themselves for having
thoughtlessly misjudged a peasant seen fishing in harvest
time as " 'Improvident and reckless' " ("Poems on the
Naming of Places," IV, 50). Upon learning that the peasant
was actually too ill to labor in the fields, Wordsworth tells
how

> unwilling to forget that day,
> My Friend, Myself, and She who then received
> The same admonishment, have called the place
> By a memorial name
> ("Poems on the Naming of Places,"
> IV, 74–77)

to remind themselves reproachfully each time they pass the
place to be called Point Rash-judgment, "What need there is
to be reserved in speech, / And temper all our thoughts with
charity" ("Poems on the Naming of Places," IV, 72–73).

Wordsworth's anthropocentrism also serves more complex
purposes. One such purpose is the employment of the object
with its attendant associations less as focal symbol than as
impulse to narrative, but to narrative of a characteristically
Wordsworthian kind: simple, humanized, pathetic, and mor-

ally instructive. Implicitly, or even at times overtly, such narrative stands contrasted with the violent imaginings that the Gothic and kindred forms of sensationalism could be expected to attach to objects like those described by Wordsworth. There is something of this even in *The Thorn* and *Michael,* since neither the desolate natural setting of the first nor the crumbling human ruin of the second ever quite give rise to the tales of "extraordinary incident" that might have been expected of them. In *The Thorn,* the sensationalism of the child murder is diverted and muted by the uncertainties and indirection of the narrator's account of it, and in *Michael,* the sensationalism likely to arise from any full recounting of Luke's dissolute course is plainly subordinated to the poem's major theme of love and endurance. But it is in *Hart-Leap Well* that Wordsworth's unwillingness to exploit the Gothic possibilities of place becomes explicit. Despite the ominousness of the "doleful place" with its emblems of waste and decay, the gray trees and "square mound of tawny green," Wordsworth is careful to reject any excessively lurid explanation of nature's desolation, such as the tale of murder against which " 'blood cries out for blood' " (138). Indeed, such an explanation is expressly precluded by the stance that Wordsworth takes at the beginning of Part Second as anti-Gothic, anti-sensationalist poet:

> The moving accident is not my trade;
> To freeze the blood I have no ready arts:
> 'Tis my delight, alone in summer shade,
> To pipe a simple song for thinking hearts.
> (97–100)

Instead of the curse of bloodguiltiness, Wordsworth's explanation for the dreariness of Hart-Leap Well is found in nature's sympathy divine for the beast who fell there; and the lesson to be drawn from the setting and the tale that attaches to it is the simplest of moral admonitions: " 'Never to blend our pleasure or our pride / With sorrow of the meanest thing that feels' " (179–80).

Probably the most conspicuous example of the way in which the humanized object of the Wordsworthian landscape leads to a sense of meditative pathos rather than to the Gothic shudder occurs in *The Ruined Cottage*. Initially Wordsworth arouses only expectations of the sensational, describing the cottage as a place to be shunned:

> 'Twas a spot
> The wandering gypsey in a stormy night
> Would pass it with his moveables to house
> On the open plain beneath the imperfect arch
> Of a cold lime-kiln.[5]
>
> (32–36)

But as the Pedlar's narrative develops, the young poet comes to learn the proper construction that is to be placed upon the signs of abandonment and decay around him. They stand as evidences not of the strange or the marvelous but of a suffering commonly experienced—but no less tragic for its commonness—by ordinary human nature. To the young poet's perfected moral understanding, the landscape has become so thoroughly humanized that even the silvered weeds and the spear grass that cluster around the ruined cottage help to memorialize the love that Margaret bore her husband and the unhappy outcome of that love. At the end, setting and event have so fully merged that the cottage viewed first as an object of fear has been transformed into an object of reverence. The part that Wordsworth's anthropocentrism plays in assessing the experience described in the poem becomes clear in the poet's closing response to the Pedlar's completed narrative:

> my friend
> Your words have consecrated many things.

And for the tale which you have told I think
I am a better and a wiser man.[6]

What the young poet has gained in addition to an increased appreciation of the pathos of ordinary life and a deepened sympathy for the misfortunes of others is a new understanding of how objects neglected or avoided by the majority of men can actively further the individual's moral growth. By his friend's tale the poet has finally come to see the ruined cottage as consecrated by the suffering undergone there, a place whose very desolation can provide morally fruitful associations for the feeling heart.

His belief that the natural world functions most significantly as a repository of human values and moral interest also helps to clarify Wordsworth's rather perplexing attitude toward science. Critics, following the lead of Whitehead, have generally viewed Wordsworth's opposition to the methods of science as the normal reaction of a vitalist to the scientific "fallacy of misplaced abstraction." [7] But examined within the context of Wordsworth's anthropocentric and ethical interpretation of external nature, science is simply another force in modern life that, like the city, threatens to retard man's moral progress by divesting the objects of experience of their human associations. The scientific observer to be faithful to his discipline must, of course, necessarily commit himself to ignoring the moral and spiritual meanings of the external world and to viewing the objects that come under his scrutiny only in terms of the properties that directly inhere in them. Wordsworth's best known criticism of this separation between feeling and value occurs in *A Poet's Epitaph,* where he speaks of the man of science as

a fingering slave,
One that would peep and botanize
Upon his mother's grave.

(18–20)

The offense Wordsworth charges the botanist with is not failure to perceive the world in its concrete wholeness but an unwillingness to set aside the task of analysis and consider the important human values symbolically expressed by the silent life around him. And despite their satiric exaggeration, these lines are not, as Whitehead suggested, merely a tasteless departure from Wordsworth's usual approach to the problem of science, but rather a concentrated statement of the very substance of that approach.

A similar but more developed indictment of the procedures of science appears in lines eventually published as part of *The Excursion* but written in 1798 as an intended conclusion to *The Ruined Cottage*. Here Wordsworth's attitude toward science can be most clearly seen as an outgrowth of his anthropocentric interpretation of the nonhuman world. In lines immediately preceding his criticism of science, Wordsworth gives a full and careful account of his anthropocentric approach to nature and of the moral benefits eventually to be realized from the enlightened use of nature humanized:

> And further, by contemplating these forms
> In the relations which they bear to man
> We shall discover what a power is theirs
> To stimulate our minds, and multiply
> The spiritual presences of absent things.
> Then weariness shall cease. We shall acquire
> The [   ] habit by which sense is made
> Subservient still to moral purposes
> A vital essence, and a saving power.
> Nor shall we meet an object but may read
> Some sweet and tender lesson to our minds
> Of human suffering or of human joy.
> All things shall speak of Man, and we shall read
> Our duties in all forms, and general laws
> And local accidents shall tend alike

To quicken and to rouze, and give the will
And power which by a [   ] chain of good
Shall link us to our kind. No naked hearts,
No naked minds shall then be left to mourn
The burthen of existence.[8]

Here Wordsworth presents what is perhaps the most complete statement of the ethical aims of his poetry, the inculcation in man of a mode of associatively endowed perception by which every element of sense experience comes to possess human significance and moral interest. Men so endowed and continually aware of "The spiritual presence of absent things" have little occasion or desire to lapse into selfishness, little need of those "gross stimulants" required to satisfy that "craving for extraordinary incident" characteristic of an age in which the mind has been reduced "to a state of almost savage torpor" [9] by the pressures of urban life, since such men find that in every object they may read a "sweet and tender lesson to our minds / Of human suffering or of human joy." Only by such means can the "weariness" of modern life cease and the ethical regeneration of man begin. When man sees all things "In the relations which they bear to man," life shall be a continual exercise of sympathy, a continual reminder of the duties we owe to others; and thus, habits of benevolence shall be established that will be the paramount impulse in the conduct of men.

But opposing this habit of mind that encourages the observer to look upon "general laws / And local accidents" as a form of moral experience and as a means of linking us more closely "to our kind" are the tendencies of science with its rival claim that human improvement is possible only if man chooses to disregard the human associations intertwined with the things of the physical world and to pore, instead, "On solitary objects, still beheld / In disconnection dead and spiritless" (63–64). Science, Wordsworth charges, promotes detachment from, and indifference to, our necessary moral concerns by requiring those who pursue it to lay aside all considerations of value when dealing with the physical universe. Moreover, by keeping the eye "Chained to its object in brute slavery" (48), it places severe restraints upon the mind's "excursive power," a term that, despite the expectations it raises of powers akin to those of Coleridge's projective imagination, seems, when examined in its proper context, to refer simply to the ordinary and somewhat mechanical operations of the associative process.[10] It must be remembered though that for Wordsworth this process is the cornerstone of any foreseeable moral progress, and if allowed to work unhampered, it shall compel man, Wordsworth writes, to

>   move
> From strict necessity along the path
> Of order and of good.
>   (92–94)

Wordsworth's antagonism to science at this time arose then not because he feared the encroachment of science upon the poet's imaginative freedom but because of an intense preoccupation with ethical issues that had led him to distrust as inimical to man's welfare any occupation that tempted man to deal with the world around him in a manner wholly divorced from moral consequence. Yet Wordsworth also feels that the hostility that presently exists between science and morals need not be of permanent duration. In that future time when all objects of perception shall speak to man's moral nature, science too will serve man's best interests by relating its inquiries to moral experience and become "a precious visitant" (44) whose "heart shall kindle" (46). But science cannot itself be the instrument of this progress. Not until a general change of heart takes place among men so that their thoughts are trained to a habitual concern for the welfare of others will the utility of scientific inquiry outweigh its potential dangers: "then, / And only then" (45–46), Wordsworth insists, will science "be worthy of her name" (46).

The opinions Wordsworth expresses in *The Ruined Cottage* form the basis, I think, for the more familiar but perhaps even more puzzling remarks on science contained in his "Preface" to *Lyrical Ballads:*

> If the labours of Men of science should ever create any material revolution, direct or indirect, in our condition, and in the impressions we habitually receive, the Poet will sleep then no more than at present; he will be ready to follow the steps of the Man of science, not only in those general indirect effects, but he will be at his side, carrying sensation into the midst of the objects of science itself. The remotest discoveries of the Chemist, the Botanist, or Mineralogist, will be as proper objects of the Poet's art as any upon which it can be employed, if the time shall ever come when these things shall be familiar to us, and the relations under which they are contemplated by the followers of these respective sciences shall be manifestly and palpably material to us as enjoying and suffering beings. If the time should ever come when what is now called science, thus familiarised to men, shall be ready to put on, as it were, a form of flesh and blood, the Poet will lend his divine spirit to aid the transfiguration, and will welcome the Being thus produced, as a dear and genuine inmate of the household of man.[11]

What Wordsworth implies here is very close to what *The Ruined Cottage* had stated explicitly: that science thus far has considered the phenomena with which it deals in isolation, paying no attention to the possible connection of object and value that alone could make such phenomena matters of general human interest. Only when science begins to explore these connections and learns to make its appeal to men as "enjoying and suffering beings" can it hope to gain the assistance of the poet whose principal duty is to bind "together by passion and knowledge the vast empire of human society, as it is spread over the whole earth, and over all time." [12] It is clear that what Wordsworth would require of science before admitting it as a proper subject for poetry is that it put on a "form of flesh and blood," that contemplation of its objects somehow serve man in much the same way as the grove of firs at Grasmere or Margaret's ruined cottage have been shown to serve him. But in believing that science can eventually put on such a form and offer mankind such service, Wordsworth differed considerably from his contemporaries. Perhaps, as Marjorie Nicolson suggests, Wordsworth responded to Keats's toast to the confusion of mathematics at Haydon's immortal dinner with somewhat less warmth and enthusiasm than the other guests assembled there.[13] If so, it may well have been because he did not regard the breach between science and value as irrevocable and could entertain, at least as a theoretical possibility, the thought of science cooperating with nature in strengthening the ties between men. Of course, such hope, resting as it does on the belief that science too can orient itself to Wordsworth's scheme of natural observation, in the end serves only to illustrate how mistaken Wordsworth was in his understanding of the methods of science. For the man of science certainly cannot measure his achievement by moral criteria but must, as Bertrand Russell rightly says, recognize "the irrelevance of human passions and the whole subjective apparatus where scientific truth is concerned." [14] If Wordsworth emerges from this survey as a less formidable critic of science than writers since Whitehead have maintained, it is because his quarrel with science essentially is neither methodological nor metaphysical; instead, it is ethical and offers further confirmation of the pervasiveness of those moral considerations to which Wordsworth subordinated all else.

The anthropocentrism that *Home at Grasmere* describes is clearly neither a fortuitous nor a minor element in Wordsworth's thought, shaping as it does not only his conception of the moral utility of nature but that of literature and science as well. The way in which the vale of Grasmere serves its residents is by providing them through nature with an environment of continual moral experience, the kind of environment that Wordsworth, in the scattered comments I have cited on literature and science, says shall at some time hereafter exist for all mankind. There is a sense, too, in which *Home at Grasmere* makes this same point, in which here, as in *Tintern Abbey,* description of the process of moral development (in this case communal rather than individual development being the process described) is to be understood predictively. This is most evident in *Home at Grasmere*'s most famous passage, those lines "On man, on Nature and on human life" that, though first published in 1814 as a *Prospectus* to *The Excursion,* were conceived in 1800 as a conclusion to *Home at Grasmere.* But these lines are less a conclusion than a beginning, plainly intended as the invocation to Wordsworth's projected but abandoned epic *The Recluse,* for which *Home at Grasmere* was written as an introductory book. And in stating his argument by this transitional rather than introductory invocation, Wordsworth is drawing upon themes and concerns already stated that he intends to elaborate more fully in the epic matter that is to follow.

The most evident example of this continuity is the way in which the ethical elements that so deeply inform *Home at Grasmere* carry over into the subsequent ethical argument as defining terms. Although "the mind of man," Wordsworth states, is to be "the main region" of his song, his explorations are undertaken for reasons that are moral and social rather than psychological in the modern sense. His object is not the delineation of states of thought and feeling but the celebration of the mind's moral potentialities, for these place a seemingly Utopian social order within man's reach, one that is to be, Wordsworth confidently predicts, at some "blessed hour," attained. It is with this not altogether remote goal in mind that Wordsworth states his purpose and defends his methods, justifying his very radical departures from epic tradition on the grounds that *The Recluse* is not fiction but prophecy. For the Utopia depicted by earlier poets,

> Paradise and groves
> Elysian, fortunate (islands) fields like those
> In the deep ocean

need not be

> A History or but a dream, when minds
> Once wedded to this outward frame of things
> In love find these the growth of common day.[15]

The unconventional choice of the poet—that is, himself—as epic hero, about which Wordsworth expresses so much uncertainty, is finally defended here on much the same principle: though acknowledging that the history of such a "transitory Being" as the poem describes would seem scarcely to be of epic proportions, it may, nonetheless, perform an exemplary and predictive function and "Express the image of a better time / More wise desires and simple manners." [16] The epic matter too—the humble actions of rural life— derives much of its fitness for "great argument" from the prophetic hints these actions contain of that "great consumation" forecast by Wordsworth which will so radically alter the form of human society and thereby bring about a new and harmonious relationship among men.

Wordsworth, of course, never actually fulfilled his epic intentions and, thus, never clearly established the full relevance of the behavior of his rural neighbors to the universal social changes he foresaw. But in *Home at Grasmere,* he does give some indications of the probable direction that the finished argument was to have taken. In the lines that were later to form the *Prospectus,* Wordsworth insists that a change in man's relationship to his environment must necessarily precede any permanent change in the social order; a marriage of the mind "to this outward frame of things / In love" must take place if the Utopian ideal that had heretofore lived only in the poet's dream is ever to take place. We may assume that what *The Recluse* was to have shown is how rural life generates this necessary union, and evidence of this aim appears even in the fragmentary portion of that work Wordsworth finally did complete. At Grasmere, Wordsworth found love of nature—the motive that had first urged the poet and his sister to take up residence there—a permanent element in the lives of his neighbors, the tender marriage of the human mind and nature everywhere affirmed by the objects around them:

> Look where we will, some human heart has been
> Before us with its offering; not a tree
> Sprinkles these little pastures but the same
> Hath furnished matter for a thought; perchance,
> For some one serves as a familiar friend.
>
> (440–44)

In the establishment of such a bond between man and nature, Wordsworth sees the first stage in a larger design that will some day transform all of society. As love of nature grows, the hold of self-interest over the affections begins to decline, and newly awakened sympathies and impulses to benevolence begin to exert a rectifying influence upon conduct. Even when the inhabitants of Grasmere come to nature with imperfect motives—"From self-respecting interests" (452) and subservience "To every day's demand for daily bread" (450)—nature yet confers its grace upon them, promoting feelings that

> lift the animal being, do themselves
> By Nature's kind and ever-present aid
> Refine the selfishness from which they spring,
> Redeem by love the individual sense
> Of anxiousness with which they are combined.
>
>   (454–58)

The paradisal goals heralded by the *Prospectus* as those toward which man and society are necessarily tending are thus discernible, at least in outline, within the vale of Grasmere; for upon the benevolent feelings fostered by their daily contacts with nature, the residents of Grasmere have constructed for themselves "A true Community, a genuine frame / Of many into one incorporate" (615–16), a precursor of that social order which Wordsworth envisions as being some day the general state of all mankind.

1. *PW*, V, 315.

2. Ibid.

3. Ibid., p. 316.

4. Ibid., p. 320.

5. The text cited for *The Ruined Cottage* is that of *PW*, V, 379–404. See Jonathan Wordsworth's discussion of *The Ruined Cottage* as an expression of "Wordsworth's growing contempt for the poetry of 'moving accidents' " (p. 68).

6. *PW*, V, 400.

7. Though the sense is clearly that of Whitehead, the term I use here is actually taken from Abrams, p. 309.

8. *PW*, V, 401. (*The Ruined Cottage*/Addendum to MS.B/, 11. 24–43).

9. *PW*, II, 389.

10. In an earlier passage in *The Ruined Cottage* describing the Pedlar's education, Wordsworth speaks of the development of "Imagination" and the mind's apprehensive power in terms very much like those he applies to the mind's "excursive power." Such power—whether imaginative, apprehensive, or excursive—is given man so that he may discover the hidden moral world that is conveyed to us associatively during our perceptions of the objects of nature:

> for many a tale
> Traditionary round the mountains hung,
> And many a legend peopling the dark woods
> Nourished Imagination in her growth,
> And gave the mind that apprehensive power
> By which she is made quick to recognize
> The moral properties and scope of things.
> (167–73)

11. *PW*, II, 396–97.

12. Ibid., p. 396.

13. Nicolson, p. 2.

14. Bertrand Russell, "Science and Culture," *Mysticism and Logic* (New York, n.d.), p. 38.

15. *PW*, V, 338.

16. Ibid., p. 339.

6

The Goslar Lyrics and the
Middle Phase

Though the years between 1797 and 1800 form a very narrow span in a poetic career of more than sixty years, the relative brevity of Wordsworth's adherence to the views just sketched should not obscure their significance. The poetry of these years, more than any other segment of his work, provides us with what in originality, coherence, and scope may justly be called *the* Wordsworthian philosophy. Its underlying premises—the empirical foundations of knowledge, the teleological workings of nature, and the progressive development of man—taken together comprise a philosophic scheme of remarkable thoughtfulness and inventiveness, an epistemology, metaphysics, and ethics clearly interrelated and mutually dependent. Even those poems of the golden decade written after 1800, though recording a new set of changing and changed poetic beliefs, still testify to the potency that this earlier scheme held for Wordsworth by the very form that its negation takes. For in the majority of these poems, the older, more optimistic view with its emphasis on the benevolence of nature and the development of man survives as latent context, an unstated hypothesis to be considered, challenged, and finally cast out in favor of an alternative vision. As a result, these later works often differ from the earlier in method as well as conclusion, in being not amplified statements of belief but expressions of conflict where hard-won truths are extracted from an often harsh dialectic. From this perspective, we may speak of the poems of 1802 and after as poems of challenge that call into question the most fundamental of Wordsworth's convictions about nature, the self, and the ethical life. For it is Wordsworth's belief, of course, between 1797 and 1800, whether expressed in poems as assured as *Tintern Abbey* or as somber as *The Ruined Cottage,* that the effects of nature, acting upon man through the associative memory, must necessarily be productive of human happiness. Moreover, the self thus produced by nature emerges as relatively uncomplicated, the process of human development seemingly wholly fulfilled at that point in time which Wordsworth designates as maturity, so that the mature self narrating *Tintern Abbey* is to be looked upon as fully developed, morally and spiritually complete, and, like nature itself, apparently immune to any further change. Having passed beyond the preliminary stages of childhood and youth, the mature poet has come to the end of the difficult ascent; life's journey henceforth can be expected to continue over the far more regular terrain of that plateau of achieved maturity that stretches unbroken from the retrospective vantage point of *Tintern Abbey's* twenty-eight-year-old narrator to the serene old age of the Pedlar in *The Ruined Cottage.* That present joy may have to give way to future sorrow is a possibility explicitly rejected in *Tintern Abbey,* whose author professes certainty that nature's privilege is "Through all the years of this our life to lead / From joy to joy" (124–25). Finally, with maturity, and as its principal benefit, there is formed a faculty of moral enlargement that carries us beyond the self to a genuinely altruistic regard for mankind in general. The man of the future is to be the man of general benevolence; and if much of the meditative verse of these years examines the inward life, it is not because of the particularity or complexity of that existence but because, the accidental set aside, the essentials of Wordsworth's personal history are so suitable to re-enactment. The aim of his autobiographical endeavors, *Home at Grasmere* tells us, is to provide general instruction for others rather than to deepen his own self-understanding; and he turns to the events that befell a "transitory Being" because from them he can draw what shall "Express the image of a better time / More wise desires and simple manners." All of these beliefs rest finally upon Wordsworth's own sense of personal achievement; for loss there has been "abundant recompense," so

> That in my day of Childhood I was less
> The mind of Nature, less, take all in all,
> Whatever may be lost, than I am now.

The self as thus conceived is essentially stable. What the major autobiographic works of these years give us is the poet recollecting emotion in tranquillity, the finished product of nature whose life may serve as model for man in the society of the future.

No general and consistent pattern of reassessment of fundamental beliefs occurs until 1802, when Wordsworth's confidence in his own spiritual growth and spiritual achievement clearly begins to waver, making the need for personal stability a more pressing poetic concern for him than even his desire for amelioration of the social conditions of England. Only then does a portrait of the artist comparable in depth and subtlety to those drawn by his fellow Romantics emerge from Wordsworth's autobiographic art. But even as early as 1799, two remarkable groups of lyrics, the "Matthew" and the "Lucy" poems—atypical of the period of their composition in their attitudes toward man and nature—give some forewarning of the changes to come.

Of the two groups, the "Matthew" poems provide a fuller and more interesting delineation of Wordsworth's own self-questionings. Like *The Ruined Cottage,* the "Matthew" poems are, in one sense, dialogues between youth and age, innocence and experience. Here, however, faith in nature's benevolence and man's stability belongs to innocence, the youthful poet as yet untested by life's inescapable harshness. As the poems inform us, nature is, in itself, essentially neutral, returning to us through memory only what is our own, as ready in its neutrality to remind us of past sorrows as past happiness. Neither is life itself, as *Tintern Abbey* would have it, a process that must lead "From joy to joy" to "one who need bemoan / His kindred laid in earth" (*The Fountain,* 49–50). Nor, finally, can we assume in man that general disinterestedness suggested elsewhere, a sense of sympathy for all that is equivalent in its effects to those nearer and more compelling affections called into being by our domestic relationships. Experience, instead, offers a reckoning of accounts that implicitly refutes the optimistic predictions of *Tintern Abbey.* From the vantage point of Matthew as he nears life's close, those inescapable sorrows, which though common are, nonetheless, profound, are of far greater significance to man than any of time's incidental gains.[1]

In *The Two April Mornings* Wordsworth dramatizes this reckoning by a juxtaposition of past and present scenes, illustrating how a momentary sorrow of thirty years earlier may intrude into and impair present happiness. Paradoxically, the poem's setting, occasion, and actors would seem, at the outset, wholly in keeping with Wordsworth's prevailing vision. The beautiful natural surroundings, illuminated by the splendor of the rising sun, seem hardly the stimulus to precipitate tragic remembrance, nor are the participants in the day's excursion men whom we would normally expect to mar so cheerful an occasion with distant and seemingly forgotten sorrows. The youthful narrator's happy mood appears to correspond perfectly to the natural scene and the morning's expectations, while his companion, though "A village school-

master" who reveals "hair of glittering grey," is yet "As
blithe a man as you could see / On a spring holiday" (5–8).
Indeed, this agreement in mood between youth and age
would appear initially to affirm that joy does persist throughout the whole of life for those who have remained close to
nature. But the poem's opening mood of shared pleasure is
quickly dispelled as Matthew exclaims, "The will of God be
done" (4). To the youth, such solemnity seems obviously out
of keeping with both the mood of the morning and the character of his companion, and his surprise is evident in the
phrasing of the question he directs to Matthew:

> what thought,
> Beneath so beautiful a sun,
> So sad a sigh has brought?
> (14–16)

Matthew explains that a particular cloud with a long purple
cleft is exactly the same shape and color as a cloud he observed thirty years earlier on a morning that had begun as
this one but had concluded in sorrow. Once again, nature in
its anthropocentric aspect furnishes a reminder, through
associative memory, of significant human incident. But the
effects of nature's stimulation of memory depend not upon
nature's indwelling benevolence but upon what has been
most centrally and most profoundly formative in the experience of the beholder. Thus, the shape of a cloud and the
color of a slope of corn recall to Matthew not the joys of his
youth but the ineradicable pain of a father's loss, just as three
years later Wordsworth himself will find the objects of nature, however beautiful in themselves, a persistent source
of sorrow, a disturbing reminder of the vanished gleam that
had once apparelled them.

The recollected incident that occasions Matthew's sorrow
is another fishing expedition, thirty years earlier, that had

brought him to the churchyard containing the grave of his young daughter. Having come quite suddenly upon the burial ground while intent upon another matter, he found his normal sense of grief sharpened even further by this element of unexpectedness, so that it seemed to him that he loved his daughter more that day than he ever had before. Turning from the grave and his thoughts of the dead, Matthew comes with equal unexpectedness upon an image of animate and radiant life, "A blooming Girl, whose hair was wet / With points of morning dew" (43–44). Despite his immediate sorrows, Matthew finds himself attracted to the child's beauty and vitality and responds to her loveliness with feelings of "pure delight." But this pleasure in the living cannot supplant his memories of the dead, and with "a sigh of pain" Matthew rejects all desire for the child before him: "I looked at her, and looked again: / And did not wish her mine" (55–56). Critics have advanced a variety of explanations for Matthew's preference in *The Two April Mornings*.[2] The most likely explanation, however—and one that receives support from the similar choice made by Matthew in *The Fountain*—bases Matthew's behavior upon the special and binding character of man's domestic relationships. His rejection of the living child is less a free and reasoned judgment than an emotionally compelled and necessary acquiescence in the unalterable laws of human nature. Matthew's feelings for the girl who stands "Beside the churchyard yew" (42) are impersonal, a natural response to any such spontaneous appearance of vivacity and beauty; but the girl who lies beneath the earth is his daughter, to whom he is bound by private affections and emotions that no relationship independent of kinship can ever duplicate.

Most centrally, then, *The Two April Mornings* affirms the primacy of the domestic affections over other less binding forms of human sympathy. Through its dialectical interplay between the young narrator and Matthew, the poem also

conveys something in the nature of an initiatory movement
of innocence into experience. At the outset, the day's journey, like life itself, is for the youthful narrator a prospect
of expectation, of hopes to be realized and promises to be
fulfilled. By his nostalgia for his loss, Matthew, of course,
confounds such expectations and, moreover, in his reminis-
cences makes clear how little hope there is of realizing life's
seeming promise for anyone touched—as all inevitably must
be—by the knowledge of mortality. That Matthew's sorrow
is not an isolated phenomenon becomes apparent in the finely
understated closing stanza, where it is at last revealed that
the conversation of Matthew and the poet is itself a recollected incident, and that since that time the poet, too, has
known the pain of personal loss, so that now for him images
of a remembered April morning must convey with them, as
they had for Matthew, the consciousness of mortality:

> Matthew is in his grave, yet now,
> Methinks, I see him stand,
> As at that moment, with a bough
> Of wilding in his hand.
>
> (57–60)

The Fountain, companion piece to *The Two April Mornings,* restates much the same argument somewhat less
obliquely. Again the poem opens with youth and age in
harmony—or so the narrator assumes—through similarity of
temperament and occupation. On this pleasant summer day,
the young poet, confident that his responses are shared, indicates his own feelings of communion with a pleasantly animate nature by inviting Matthew to "match / This water's
pleasant tune" (9–10) with some song "That suits a summer's
noon" (12). But in Matthew the sounds of the fountain call
forth other thoughts, comparisons of the inner life and nature
that lead to radically different conclusions:

No check, no stay, this Streamlet fears;
How merrily it goes!
'Twill murmur on a thousand years,
And flow as now it flows.

And here, on this delightful day,
I cannot choose but think
How oft, a vigorous man, I lay
Beside this fountain's brink.
(21–28)

By its very constancy, the fountain, awakening in the aging Matthew memories of his vigorous youth, reveals the fundamental dissimilarity between the condition of man, subject to alteration and inevitable decay, and the condition of nature, so free of change as to seem virtually timeless. With these memories comes another disclosure of unlikeness where harmony was initially assumed: age and youth—hence Matthew and his companion—are so divided by their disparate experience that any genuine understanding between them is rendered impossible.

There is in this contrast between age and youth a pointed commentary upon the implied promise of *Tintern Abbey* that man can at some maximum point of development obtain permanent stability of character and thereby realize his completed self. To the guileless narrator, Matthew, a "grey-haired man of glee" (20), who despite the visible signs of age has seemed otherwise to preserve unblemished the inner attributes of youth, clearly seems a perfect type of the completed self and an exemplary model to stand for youth's own projected hopes of joy in age. Yet beneath this surface of appearance lies the realities of spent vigor and bitter sadness. And if Matthew shows himself as "a man of mirth," he does so in performance of a public role that conceals sorrows that must adhere to the private consciousness. Again the mechanism of associationism, the psychological foundation of Wordsworth's optimism, is treated as essentially neutral, as potent in its necessary workings to dispel the immediate pleasures of nature if significant memory dictates as it had been to dispel the gloom of towns and cities with the recollections of nature in *Tintern Abbey*. Just as in *The Two April Mornings* the appearance of a beautiful child compelled "a sigh of pain" Matthew could "ill confine" because the associative principle forced upon him an immediate contrast between the child before him and his remembered daughter, so here too Matthew finds he "cannot choose but think" (26) of an equally melancholy contrast between earlier years filled with vigor and happiness and a present in which these have been taken from him.

In addition to the consciousness of diminished vigor, age breeds still more complex and deeper sorrows. For "the wiser mind," Matthew claims, "Mourns less for what age takes away / Than what it leaves behind" (34–36). Once again nature in its comparative simplicity forces upon us a knowledge of the uniquely human tribulations old age bestows upon man alone:

> The blackbird amid leafy trees,
> The lark above the hill,
> Let loose their carols when they please,
> Are quiet when they will.
>
> With Nature never do *they* wage
> A foolish strife; they see
> A happy youth, and their old age
> Is beautiful and free:
>
> But we are pressed by heavy laws;
> And often, glad no more,
> We wear a face of joy, because
> We have been glad of yore.
>
> (37–48)

Nature in *The Fountain* thus points to two forms of human limitation. Inanimate and changeless nature offers man simply a point of reference by which to measure his physical decay. Sentient nature, though subject, like man, to change and decay, possesses a natural liberty denied to man. The blackbird and lark, Matthew observes, are free to follow the spontaneous urgings of their own instincts, free to rejoice only when feeling pleasure and free to be still when such feelings cease; they are not required in age to enact the emotions of youth when its gratifications have passed but are permitted, instead, a form of behavior suited to their situation. But man, a social being, is the victim of "heavy laws" that compel him to violate the innermost dictates of his private will and to act as social conventions demand. *The Fountain*, then, does not illustrate the stoical principles sometimes attributed to it. Matthew does not "wear a face of joy" because the property of fortitude has enabled him to triumph over personal anguish but because, as the man who had "been glad of yore," he is forced to act a socially determined role no longer applicable to his real feelings. In this feigned superiority to the circumstances of personal grief, Matthew does not follow nature, as stoicism commands, but wages a "foolish strife" with nature as it exists both in his own heart and in the life around him, where Matthew everywhere finds evidence that nature's way is to accept change and to allow its creatures to suit their beliefs and actions to the varying patterns of their lives.

The last and deepest of the griefs concealed beneath his mask of gaiety is here, as in *The Two April Mornings*, the fact of domestic tragedy and the melancholy remembrances by Matthew of "His kindred laid in earth / The household hearts that were his own" (50–51). Nor, as Matthew adds, can any other relationships duplicate or replace those he had held with members of his own houshold; though many now feel affection for Matthew, those affections differ not in degree

but in kind from those that flow through the bonds of kinship:

> "My days, my Friend, are almost gone,
> My life has been approved,
> And many love me; but by none
> Am I enough beloved."
>
>   (53–56)

The youth's reply, however, only serves to intensify Matthew's
isolation; for though his young companion's offer of himself as a substitute for Matthew's dead children moves
Matthew deeply, it is a gesture that, in its final effect, actually deepens our sense of the divisions that separate youth
and age, rendering any genuine communication between the
two companions impossible. The youthful narrator, as yet
untested by sorrow and now living only to sing his "idle
songs / Upon these happy plains" (59–60), has failed to
comprehend the real burden of his companion's meditation
—that what is past is irrecoverable. However deeply attached
Matthew may be to the youth, no sympathy of spirit between
them can ever hope to equal in intensity of love those sympathies fostered by kinship in relationships that for Matthew
can nevermore exist.

In the last stanza, the poem resumes its narrative form:

> And, ere we came to Leonard's rock,
> He sang those witty rhymes
> About the crazy old church-clock
> And the bewildered chimes.
>
>   (69–72)

Since Matthew does finally accede to his friend's request and
sing his "witty rhymes," it might well seem that his despondency has been only a temporary aberration and that he is,
at last, again restored to his normal frame of mind, willing

to face life, if not with tranquillity, then at least with fortitude. But the intervening meditation upon time's ravages between the youth's request and its fulfillment has colored our perceptions, and the "crazy old church-clock" has become charged with meaning. In contrast to the fountain, which is symbolic of natural time in its movements and a pitiless gauge of man's decay, the clock stands as a symbol of man's mutability. Bewildered and deranged by that which it was designed to measure, the old clock has, like the men who made it, become time's victim. Nowhere in the "Matthew" poems, then, does Wordsworth permit his spiritual preceptor to soften the harshness of personal suffering by consolations of the kind offered in *The Ruined Cottage*. The necessitarian and utopian perspective that allows the Pedlar to view time, despite the tragic history he has just related, as teleological and redemptive, man's best ally in his movement towards social perfection, is rejected by Matthew, who, as sufferer rather than observer, has found time to be an implacable and ultimately irresistible adversary whose ends bear no resemblance to our common human purposes.

Although the "Lucy" poems offer a less dialectical structure and less elaboration of argument than the "Matthew" poems, there is sufficient similarity of outlook between the groups and, in their shared outlook, sufficient contrast in point of view to the bulk of the work of this period to consider the two groups under a single heading as the Goslar lyrics of 1799. The most obvious of common qualities is their elegiac character, their concern with death, with loss, and with regret. At a deeper level, the two groups touch as well, for loss and regret are treated again as initiatory agents, offering an introduction to experience for an innocence whose illusory "slumber," the speaker in the most famous of "Lucy" poems laments, "did my spirit seal." [3] At this level, too, grief must remain private, essentially unshareable, its presence articulated, but its attributes undefined:

> She lived unknown, and few could know
> When Lucy ceased to be;
> But she is in her grave, and, oh,
> The difference to me!
>
> (9–12)

The final line, set off by an interjection and exclamation point, suggests unsounded depths of grief, incommunicable in its intensity, creating for the mourner a condition of permanent isolation from all others. The ideal of community through sympathy, the goal most frequently expressed in the poetry of this period, must acknowledge limitations, areas of the personal life that no sympathies can reach, wounds there that no substitute love can heal.

Three years she grew in sun and shower typifies the "Lucy" poems in attitude but considerably extends their range of argument in criticism of what heretofore has been described as the most basic of Wordsworthian doctrines. Apart from its statements of loss and regret, the poem discusses the fate of its object of mourning, one who in the language of *The Prelude* might, in her shaping by nature, be described as a favored being, in terms that raise serious doubts as to whether the goals of nature in its interaction with man coincide with our commonly accepted human ends. In accordance with the developmental hypothesis, Lucy moves toward fulfillment of her being under the guidance of a ministering nature that serves as "law and impulse" to her growth. Nature's aim is not, however, as in *The Prelude* or *Home at Grasmere,* to create from the favored being it has chosen an exemplary model whose pattern of development acts as the prophetic forerunner of our general human future. Lucy is chosen by nature, its attributes transferred to her, to serve nature's ends rather than man's. In *Three years she grew in sun and shower,* nature and man exist not in harmony but in conflict, a relationship figuratively asserted in the opposition between the poem's two speakers, both of whom vie for possession of Lucy and in the opposition of poetic forms of their separate statements. For structurally the poem is both epithalamium and elegy: a marriage hymn by the personified Nature, which finally claims Lucy as its own, framed by the lament of nature's human rival. But the outcome of the contest between rivals has, from the beginning, been preordained by the arrangements of time. Human time once again, as in *The Fountain,* is subject to change and loss, its harvest, by necessity, one of sorrow, whereas the natural time into which Lucy has entered by her death emerges as changeless and eternal, beset by neither decay nor loss.

The poem in its richness provides, however, a second element, a deep paradox that partially mutes the disharmony disclosed between man and nature. Lucy, as she emerges from nature's description of her, is "not so much a human being as a sort of compendium of nature," [4] and, we are led to believe, the attractions that draw her human admirer to her are, in large measure, those graces bestowed upon Lucy by nature in its desire to make of her "a Lady of my own" (6). But the poem's dominant voice is its final voice, that of the bereaved lover, who finds the knowledge of the origins of beauty no comfort for its loss, the knowledge that with her death she has sealed nature's contract with her no comfort for the permanent separation from humanity and from himself that her marriage with nature requires. For the narrator, all that remains is the comfortless presence of the landscape in which Lucy had once dwelt, the persistence of memory, the consciousness of mortality, and the unalterable processes of the associative principle that unite the first three in a permanently blighting sorrow:

> Thus Nature spake—The work was done—
> How soon my Lucy's race was run!
> She died, and left to me
> This heath, this calm, and quiet scene;
> The memory of what has been,
> And never more will be.
>
> (37–42)

The Goslar lyrics offer not a substitute vision for the one previously sketched but rather evidence that counter currents did exist within the general stream of tendency that for the most part governed Wordsworth's poetry between 1797 and 1800. As statements of personal tragedy, of losses unrecompensed and sorrows uncomforted, the "Matthew" and "Lucy" poems express serious misgivings as to whether any purely natural theodicy—the most vulnerable of Wordsworthian claims—can give meaning and purpose to such tales as that of Margaret and her ruined cottage. But the Goslar lyrics seem, at most, a momentary lapse from the dominant scheme and spirit of the poems written during approximately the same period, including even those others composed at Goslar itself. Perhaps the principal importance of the "Matthew" and "Lucy" poems, apart from their intrinsic achievement, substantial as that is, is in suggesting the presence of seeds of discontent even in a period of seemingly assured faith that makes the sequence of developments in the history of Wordsworth's thought a more orderly, evolving pattern than the chronological leaps between stages would seem to imply.

Unlike the Goslar lyrics, the poems of 1802 comprise a thorough and virtually permanent departure from Wordsworth's prior beliefs.[5] Though in itself a transitional stage in a larger movement from a naturalistic to a transcendental philosophy, the poetry of 1802 offers a conception of man and nature sufficiently different from what came before and what is to come afterwards to justify treating it as a self-contained unit in the history of Wordsworth's thought, a middle stage. One sign of these changes is the appearance in 1802 of an important new Wordsworthian genre, the lyric apostrophe to nature's more familiar and common objects. This might seem to indicate little more than that Wordsworth had chosen at that time to vary the form by which he expressed what, since *Tintern Abbey* and the earliest written books of *The Prelude,* had been one of the most central and abiding interests of his poetry, his observations of the natural world. In this case, however, form follows function as a vehicle of thought, so that the changes of 1802 involve not merely a variation in form but also a significant contraction in Wordsworth's span of vision, a narrowing of focus from the "enormous permanences of nature" [6] to a set of carefully chosen particulars, diminutive and transitory—the butterfly, the celandine, the daisy. And accompanying this transferral of interest in the object observed is an equally significant change in the conception and characterization of the observer himself. No longer does Wordsworth address nature with the authority of the morally and spiritually perfected speaker of *Tintern Abbey,* as one who, conducted by nature's guidance into union with its harmonious and tranquil order, has in maturity achieved a stability that leaves him as little subject to essential change as the landscape to which he has just returned. In the poems of 1802, maturity—the full and final completion of the self—clearly fails to immunize man against future change, so that even his moments of deepest pleasure are tinged with the threat of imminent reversal. There emerges in 1802 a new correspondence between man and nature, or at least that segment of nature which Wordsworth chooses to observe. What links man and nature now is their common involvement in temporal flux, their common subjugation to the alternating pattern of storm and sunshine and to the seasonal rhythms of loss and renewal. Under these conditions, if Wordsworth is to find in nature evidence for his own spiritual well-being, he must look not to its vast and changeless forms but to its least imposing and least enduring elements, particularly those quickened into life by the energies of the spring.

Of the brief lyrics of 1802, those addressed to the butterfly, the poem on the rainbow, and *To the Cuckoo* best illustrate Wordsworth's new concerns. The subjects of all of these are not only products of cyclical renewal but also agents of memory, whose appearance evokes for Wordsworth the experiences and emotions of his earliest years. Juxtaposing past against present, he is provided with a means of gauging the changes he has undergone in the course of life. But retrospection here is used not to measure the extent of his moral and spiritual advancement but to determine whether, amidst the flux and multiplicity of experience, some element exists within the experiencing self to which the individual can ascribe a personal and continuing self-identity. For only in that way, by possessing some such form of self-continuity, can the individual hope to revive within himself those moments of the past that would enable him to engage in an act of personal renewal corresponding to those forms of natural renewal that the poems describe.

Such emphasis on personal renewal is, of course, implicitly regressive, for what we seek to create anew is the self or the modes of experiencing of that self that dates back to our earliest history. This revised conception of the relationship of childhood to one's subsequent life forms the most significant point of departure by Wordsworth from his earlier philosophic scheme. Unlike the Goslar lyrics, which had only expressed doubts that the developmental process could result in an inner stability that could permanently secure the individual spirit from the liabilities of future change, the poems of 1802 deny the most basic premise of Wordsworth's earlier beliefs, the principle of development itself. Personal happiness for Wordsworth is now dependent upon his power to restore to himself the inner conditions of childhood rather than upon those new capabilities that emerge from having outgrown it.

In constructing this drastically revised version of his mental history, Wordsworth does not actually tamper with earlier accounts of the elemental psychic facts upon which he had based that history, at least not to the degree that so complete a reversal would seem to necessitate. The retrospective lyrics of 1802 originate, like *Tintern Abbey,* in Wordsworth's introspective observations of a dramatic falling-off since childhood in the intensity of his sensory pleasures and perceptions. Where the works of the two periods differ most is in their estimate of the significance of these feelings and of the extent to which they have been lost. *Tintern Abbey,* conveying the optimistic attitudes of the earlier period, takes intensity to be, at most, of only instrumental worth, its disappearance a permanent fact, but one amply justified by the far greater benefits derived from the sense of tranquillity that replaces it. In the poems of 1802, intensity has become a unit of intrinsic value, a spiritual resource of the utmost significance. The mood of these poems thus becomes one of passionate nostalgia for the heightened sensibility of childhood: the loss of that sensibility the occasion for the sorrow of the lyrics on the butterfly, its recurrence grounds for exultation in *To the Cuckoo* and *My heart leaps up.*

Since childhood had become so prominent a repository of human values, the problem of identity—particularly the persistence of those intense feelings and perceptions through all of life's stages—assumes a new and important status in Wordsworth's thought in 1802. In *Tintern Abbey,* where Wordsworth had judged his past and present selves to be radically dissimilar, the problem was only of minor interest, sensory experience alone being sufficient to account for man's well-being. But when Wordsworth reaches much the same conclusion about life's discontinuity in the lyrics on the butterfly, this judgment now occasions nostalgia and regret. The earlier and simpler of the two lyrics, although primarily an affectionate tribute to his sister's gentleness, conveys Wordsworth's sense of loss and a response to loss much altered from that of 1798 in his description of the childhood days that are the poem's focal center as "Dead times," irretrievable now except as recollected image. And restoration, even in this limited form, seems relatively tenuous; for memory here seems curiously independent of will, its operations, instead, apparently determined by the direct physical presence of the butterfly, a creature intimately associated with the childhood events Wordsworth describes. In the second of the lyrics on the butterfly, Wordsworth distinguishes even more sharply between past and present modes of feeling, wistfully recalling a fullness of experience that the adult can never again hope to enter into, known by the poet during "Sweet childish days, that were as long / As twenty days are now" (18–19).

The conclusion of *Tintern Abbey* that man's development is radically discontinuous, reauthenticated by the comparisons of past and present in the apostrophes to the butterfly, might seem to provide us with Wordsworth's firm and final judgment on the question of personal identity. But whether changed spiritual needs induced new beliefs or further experience actually contradicted previous assumptions, Wordsworth's opinions on identity do undergo substantial modification in the spring of 1802. Statements of loss and regret, like the two lyrics on the butterfly, are more than counterbalanced by *To the Cuckoo* and *My heart leaps up*, strenuous affirmations of life's continuity and the essential unity of the self. In these latter works, some form of cyclical renewal in the processes of nature evokes a corresponding self-renewal in the poet himself, the vividness of his earliest perceptual experiences and the intensity of his initial responses to the natural world reproduced here for the mature poet not in memory but in fact.

The lyric on the rainbow provides not only a major formulation of Wordsworth's newly acquired belief in the self-continuity of the inner life but also—by implication if not by exposition—some sense of the altered philosophic characterization of man required by this view of identity. The proclaimed constancy of response to the rainbow that runs from childhood to maturity and, expectantly, through old age identifies an aspect of the self unconditioned by the cumulative effects of sense experience. Nature plays its part in the responsiveness of the poet, but its role is no longer an epistemologically causative one in which impulse is converted into idea, producing mental phenomena from the translated materials of the physical world. The poet's repeated perceptions of the rainbow do not work incrementally to produce the changes in character, the moral or spiritual progress that Wordsworth's empiricism had prescribed. The function of nature in *My heart leaps up* is to provide, through the appearance of the rainbow, the occasion for rather than the substance of Wordsworth's consciousness of self-renewal.

The suggestion of *My heart leaps up* and other important poems of 1802 is that nature and man are related not in terms of the interactionism of Wordsworth's empirically oriented epistemology but according to a kind of psychophysical parallelism in which mental and physical events form two corresponding systems that are harmoniously united in their separate activities but with no causal interchange going on between them. Despite the admitted clumsiness of the terminology, particularly when applied to a work apparently as far removed from systematic philosophy as the lyric on the rainbow, the hypothesis conveyed by this term enables us to identify some of the most prominent features of the poetry of 1802. One of these is a strikingly altered presentation of mind; for mind, or at least some vital component of it, is to be regarded as essentially self-enclosed and self-contained, responsive to its natural environment but not shaped by it. One way of explaining the autonomously determined self is by viewing it simply as a part of man's natural being, its self-contained beginnings coinciding with the beginnings of human life itself. There is, however, a second explanation that frequently attaches itself to the notion of autonomy from nature that places the origins of mind beyond nature in some form of transcendence with which the mind's self-enclosed characteristics are continuous. Speculative hints of transcendental alternatives to the more naturalistic account of man's self-autonomy lie very close to the surface of Wordsworth's poetry of 1802 and help to explain why the middle phase is essentially transitional, its major assumptions so easily displaced in the transcendental developments that succeed it. Despite these subliminal tensions and waverings, the major orientation of 1802 remains sufficiently naturalistic in its ontology to indicate that even these self-contained aspects of man are grounded in the conditions of his natural existence. Certainly *My heart leaps up* suggests no history of prenatal origins to account for the continuity of affective reaction occasioned by the rainbow, nor is the piety that flows from these recurrent moments of feeling directed toward any objects apart from those of the natural world. Indeed, the very notion of a psychophysical parallelism of the heart and the rainbow, man and nature, suggests a community of purpose that binds man and nature together within a common natural order almost as closely as they had been bound by the more direct epistemological interaction of the empirical phase.

Reducing the role of nature from a formative and determining influence upon the mind's characteristics to an occasioning stimulus that activates characteristics already present as original components of the mind necessitates a drastically revised theory of human behavior by Wordsworth to accompany these important epistemological changes. Within the limited scope of the poems of 1802, few in number as they are and concentrating as they do upon the poet's immediate reactions to nature, Wordsworth provides nothing as detailed or as extended as the illustrations of and rules for conduct that appear in the poems of the earlier phase. Enough is suggested and implied, however, in the poems of 1802 to encourage, at least, some tentative speculations upon the new ethical attitudes that arise as a corollary to Wordsworth's other philosophic changes. One feature, notably omitted here is the use of growth and development as key principles in establishing what is most significant and valuable in the human character. The natural piety celebrated in *My heart leaps up* is an expression of changeless, internal continuity dating back to life's beginnings and not the result of the cumulative, shaping effects of man's natural environment; and though the habit of natural piety is present in maturity, its presence serves to illustrate the common identity underlying life's stages rather than to differentiate among them. What the habit of natural piety rests upon finally, the confirming evidence of life's internal continuity, is, of course, the persistence throughout life, which the poem claims, of stages of feeling, indistinguishable in intensity, even in maturity, from our earliest and most heightened emotions. In this, too, Wordsworth implicitly turns away from the postulates upon which he had previously constructed his moral theories, since earlier the intensity of childhood feelings had been regarded as morally limiting, the condition of heightened inner awareness restricting the child to a set of purely self-interested concerns. Only when intensity declines, according to this earlier view, its absence defined in 1798 as tranquility, can the mind develop those meditative capabilities that Wordsworth then saw as the sole basis of the morally generous life.

What emerges—even from the relatively unamplified speculations of the middle phase—is a thorough reshaping of Wordsworth's moral thought: the replacement of a rationally grounded ethic educed from the developmental hypothesis by a clearly emotive theory of ethics with unmistakably regressive implications. "Morality," to use Hume's famous dictum, had become for Wordsworth in 1802 a matter "more properly felt than judg'd of." [7] Assurances of his moral and spiritual well-being were to be sought by Wordsworth in those moments of awareness that testified to his continued possession of the spontaneous instincts of childhood, those first and best emotions upon which the habit of natural piety was based. These views frequently have a further corollary (a corollary that Wordsworth apparently himself adopts in *Resolution and Independence*) in which self-interested behavior is a result of acquired dispositions that arise only when the influence of custom comes to exceed that of originally planted feelings in determining the direction of our moral acts. [8] Hence the tendency of such an emotive ethic is not merely to substitute feeling for reason as the basis for right conduct but to reverse the chronology of development, making the individual's distance from childhood a measure of his declining moral power.

To the Cuckoo repeats the affirmations of *My heart leaps up*, omitting, however, the specifically ethical application of them that the poem on the rainbow offers. But the structure of experience both externally and internally, man's relations with nature and with his own past self, corresponds to the pattern of *My heart leaps up* and enables Wordsworth to reach the same implicitly value-laden judgment that revivifying contact with one's childhood being is not only desirable but also attainable. The depth of contact claimed in *To the Cuckoo*—perhaps a measure of the depth of Wordsworth's own regressive impulse—even exceeds that of *My heart leaps up*: where the latter simply pointed to the continuance into adult life of states of feeling experienced in and associated with childhood, the agent of natural renewal in *To the Cuckoo* actually calls forth in all their totality moments of the past to be relived not as memory but as present fact. So powerful are the ties that bind past and present, the ties that constitute the individual's self-identity, that the poet, listening to the bird's song, finds that he can essentially re-create the visionary apprehensions of his childhood and "beget / That golden time again" (27–28).

In its emphasis upon childhood as the location of primary human values and in its structural pattern of a nature-inspired quest for these through retrospection (here, as in the lyric on the rainbow, a quest successfully completed), *To the Cuckoo* exemplifies the poetic principle that gives the lyrics of 1802 their special character. But at a secondary and more philosophically speculative level, *To the Cuckoo* brings into clearer focus the metaphysical uncertainties and divisions of the middle phase. Without repudiating the dominant naturalism of the period, *To the Cuckoo* indirectly but discernibly raises the possibilities of grounds other than man's natural endowments to account for the special quality of the childhood experience that the cuckoo's song resurrects. Both the fullness of recovery of the past, the sense of its being literally begotten anew, and the perceptual distinctiveness of that past from the present, the unsubstantiality that the objects of sense seemed at that earlier time to express and now express again, contribute suggestive overtones to the poem of a dimension of experience that extends beyond the limits of the natural self. The act of recovery, by its completeness, suggests the presence of powers in ourselves different from, and superior to, the normal workings of memory, and the spiritual condition recaptured with its forms of visionary awareness seems to involve nothing less than a transformation in the poet's ontological status, a passage from nature to transcendence. Much in the direction of the poem, its reaching toward the transcendent, may be attributed to implications generated by the poem's major natural symbol, or at least by those aspects of the symbol Wordsworth chooses to stress. With its "twofold shout" sounding "At once far off, and near" (8), the cuckoo, from the time of its first appearance, expressed a seeming dualism within itself that is readily and expectedly translated into the ontological dualism of sensory and spiritual toward which the poem points. To sensory nature, the presumed object of the bird's nearer song, the cuckoo sings only of cyclical renewal, the awakening birth "Of sunshine and of flowers" (10). To the listening poet, the more distant song with its intimations of the visionary bears its message for him alone, inviting him to repossess those regions of spirit that the bird in this guise seems to represent. Coming as it does from no identifiable visual source, the cuckoo's remoter voice calls forth possibilities of origins of its song in a reality that lies beyond sense, possibilities that the innocent ear of childhood had shaped into fact, interpreting that reality as an order of being corresponding in essence to the consciousness of spirit that the child feels he has recognized within himself. And listening again in maturity, the poet seems once more in contact with the song's transcendent source, a reality that in this moment of heightened awareness seems to invest the concrete world with its own quality of spirit, so that

> the earth we pace
> Again appears to be
> An unsubstantial, faery place;
> That is fit home for Thee.
> (29–32)

In its closing emphasis upon the visionary, *To the Cuckoo* demonstrates obvious affinities with the *Immortality Ode,* the "wandering voice" of the bird, as A. C. Bradley long ago noted, suggestively furnishing like the "visionary gleam" of the ode an "expression through sense of something beyond sense." [9] But the degree of resemblance between the two poems should not be overstated; *To the Cuckoo*'s transcendental conclusions are far more problematical and its philosophic commitment far less assured. Not only does the cuckoo as symbol preserve an ambiguous duality, but even as an emblem of transcendence its authority and appropriateness are qualified by our knowledge that its visionary aspect, its distant song, derives from a sleight of hand practiced by nature upon the fancies of childhood and the nostalgic longings of a spiritually diminished maturity. These limitations upon the poem's major symbol, though not impeding its function as a catalyst to imaginative release, do seriously reduce its claims as a sufficient basis from which to develop considered philosophic convictions. Less a statement of belief than of desire, *To the Cuckoo*'s strongest affinities lie not with the carefully articulated transcendentalism of the *Immortality Ode* but with the poems of 1802 and their still incompletely determined metaphysical speculations. But in adopting even so tentative an approach to the transcendent here, Wordsworth expresses his growing doubts as to the adequacy of nature alone, the self-enclosed universe, to provide the ultimate substratum of his transformed poetic world.

Though the retrospective lyrics of 1802 contain a significant set of common denominators—their concentration on nature's relatively impermanent and usually minutely particularized forms, especially those identified with natural renewal; their heightened evaluation of childhood's experiences of intensity; and their deep concern with self-identity and the means of reproducing in later life the consciousness of intensity originating in childhood—these lyrics display far less agreement about the philosophic meanings of the issues they examine and the experiences they describe. Whether some self-uniting bond of personal identity runs through life's temporal course is a question to which Wordsworth's lyric testimony gives no consistent response. Whether his quest for the originating causes of his redefined scheme of values can be confined within the limits of the natural order is another matter upon which he speaks with a hesitancy unvoiced in the major poems of the preceding period. There is a significant unifying element in the poems of 1802, but it is primarily an experiential unity derived from the shared character of their initiating perceptions. But philosophically the poems of 1802 tell of uncertainty and self-division, the instability of those newly established ordering principles by which Wordsworth sought to organize the materials of immediate experience within a framework of purpose and meaning.

These philosophic waverings are symptomatic of a still more profound and crucial instability indicated by the poems of 1802, an instability embodied in percept as well as concept, in the very nature of the objects and events selected by Wordsworth for interpretation. Whereas the poetry of the earlier period had utilized the observed constancy of landscape and an apparently similar changelessness experienced in the perceiving self as the primary empirical data for its philosophic argument, the poems of 1802 are empirically rooted in the consciousness of what, without and within, is itself evanescent and unstable, and it is this that must be utilized as the basis of their formulations. Even those works that most exultantly affirm the poet's feelings of continuity that he possesses between the spontaneity and vivid splendors of childhood and adult emotions and perceptions make their claims within a context of instability shaped by our knowledge that the testifying experiences that produce this awareness come only intermittently. There are long periods, we know from the outset, when the voice of the cuckoo must be silent and the earth no longer "appears to be / An unsubstantial, faery place" but the world given man in his ordinary perceptions. And in the lyric on the rainbow Wordsworth's faith in the principle of continuity is wholly dependent upon the most fitful, transitory, and insubstantial of nature's appearances, so that what is sustained from day to day is not the poet's reenactment of moments of childhood intensity, for these are occasioned only by the comings of the rainbow, but rather a faith in life's unity abstracted from such moments that enables him to carry on his usual activities with "natural piety." Thus, although Wordsworth professes confidence in a unity that runs unbroken through the whole of his experience, the basis of this confidence is, paradoxically, the irregular both in nature and his own being, the fluctuating emotions that respond to the brief and spasmodic appearances of the rainbow with an intensity remote from his customary feelings.

Such considerations are, of course, essentially unvoiced in the major lyrics of the spring of 1802. Concentrating as they do upon the episode of renewal, the natural event and its immediate effect on the poet, these poems provide neither the narrative detail for a full cyclical history nor the speculative range that would allow Wordsworth to elaborate the larger philosophic context of these episodes. Even when this history and this context remain outside the expressed meaning of these lyric celebrations of renewal, they continue to exist—at least by implication—as logically necessary extensions of that meaning: however profound or exhilarating the episode of renewal, we recognize that its aftermath must be an episode of loss; and whatever assurances are offered concerning the self's continuity through time, these assurances derive from the character of a world governed finally not by a principle of permanence but one of process, the alternating rhythms of renewal and decline in both nature and the self.

At one point, however, in the poetry of 1802, these predominantly implicit considerations become explicit. In *Resolution and Independence*, though the perception of natural renewal still engenders the poem's responses, the episode of renewal is treated not as a self-contained event falling within the boundaries of lyric utterance but is instead absorbed into a larger narrative and meditative structure as simply one element in that full sequence of events which in their entirety as a completed cycle serve as the basis for philosophic judgment. But in elaborating upon the meanings of the major lyrics of 1802, in implanting the moment of renewal within a broader temporal scheme of change and process, Wordsworth in *Resolution and Independence* also indicates the inadequacy of such a scheme—a monistic naturalism based solely upon laws of cyclical change—to satisfy personal needs already exhibited in the poetry of the earlier period, needs that require for satisfaction not the consciousness of renewal but the promise of permanence. Nowhere, then, does the transitional character of the poetry of 1802, its position in Wordsworth's intellectual history as a bridge between two opposing ontologies of permanence, become more apparent than in *Resolution and Independence*. Grounded in the views of the middle phase and summarizing and developing them with an unequalled fullness and complexity, the poem, nonetheless, has as its major aims the exposure of the limitations of naturalism and the projection of a tentative alternative, the renunciation of nature for the transcendental conclusions reached through Christian faith.

In *Resolution and Independence,* just as in *Tintern Abbey,* the observed characteristics of nature that the poem first describes serve as its primary vehicle of meditation, the basis for Wordsworth's reflections not only upon the operations of nature but upon the behavior of man as well. But where Wordsworth in *Tintern Abbey* had viewed nature with a painter's eye, a silent and static harmony arrived at by a careful blending of the scene's larger and more prominent features, *Resolution and Independence,* its focus on what is less imposing and closer at hand, presents a setting whose defining attributes are animation and vitality. Even its har-

mony is animate rather than static, deriving not from silence
but from a skillful orchestration of nature's voices: a range
of tones—the "sweet voice" of the Stock-dove, the chattering
of the Magpie, and the answer of the Jay—joined together in
a single melody against a background of "the pleasant noise
of waters." And this atmosphere of awakened vitality is further reinforced by the visual images of the second stanza as
earth, sky and nature's sentient life all respond to and, in
their turn, express the morning's mood of joy. In fact, setting
is most fully defined not by bringing together any harmonious ordering of detail but by focusing upon a brilliantly
animate particular, whose activity epitomizes nature's irre-
pressible vitality on such occasions of renewal:

> on the moors
> The hare is running races in her mirth;
> And with her feet she from the plashy earth
> Raises a mist; that, glittering in the sun,
> Runs with her all the way, wherever she doth run.
>
> (10–14)

Wordsworth's departures from the symbolic setting of
Tintern Abbey go well beyond these contrasts of silence and
song, stasis and movement. In *Tintern Abbey*, the poet had
returned to earlier scenes confident, after a five years' absence, that they had suffered no alteration, that the enduring
and stable forms of nature could revive and restore the faded
images of memory with no essential modifications. The bril-
liant prospect that the traveler of *Resolution and Independence* comes upon is, however, admittedly impermanent,
transitory, the product of a "morning's birth." The rain-
brightened grass and the mist trailing the hare exist in their
splendor only for a moment, their radiance subject to dissolution by the rising sun. Moreover, it is nature in another
mood, nature as storm, that has, in part, generated this set-

ting, and traces of the previous night still remain in the morning's most dazzling effects. The antithesis of nature as storm and nature as sunshine does not force upon Wordsworth the bleak choices of the *Elegiac Stanzas;* but the first two lines of *Resolution and Independence* do reveal this second face of nature, and in the word *floods* there is perhaps even a hint of nature's potential ominousness. The major emphasis of *Resolution and Independence* is not, however, upon nature as a set of opposing states but upon a process in which sunshine follows storm, and, implicitly, storm waits to begin the cycle anew. And all of nature, presumably, even man himself insofar as he is a creature of nature, is under governance of this process; and it is from its effects that Wordsworth weaves the themes of the first half of the poem.

With the entrance of the traveler in stanza III, Wordsworth turns from the details of his natural setting to the human significance of the world view toward which these details point. The immediate relation of man to nature is that of *My heart leaps up:* renewal in nature occasioning a similar consciousness of renewal in the poet himself. But the larger context of process in which the joyous scene has been placed is given human equivalents as well. The evening storm has had its personal counterpart for Wordsworth in an earlier mood that has been momentarily banished by his present happiness: "My old remembrances went from me wholly; / And all the ways of men, so vain and melancholy" (20–21). And just as the mist and sparkling grass intimate the cyclical brevity of nature's moment of renewal, Wordsworth similarly characterizes his own sense of joy in terms of the alternating rhythms of revival and loss, first in recognizing the morning's essential transience, its delights those of a "pleasant season" (19), and later in chastizing himself for behaving "As if life's business were a summer mood" (37). More conclusive proof, however, of man's necessary submission to the laws seen earlier governing nature, eternal process working itself out as eternal change, comes with the poet's sudden and apparently unmotivated fall from joy to despair. *Two April Mornings* had recorded a similar movement from happiness to sorrow on a gay spring morning, but there the cause had clearly been the workings of memory, which force man, in accordance with the laws of association, to draw from seemingly insignificant natural detail the buried sorrows of the past. In *Resolution and Independence,* however, there is no such psychologically familiar cause specified for Wordsworth's abrupt transition; instead, it seems a simple necessity—a kind of fortune's wheel—that determines the poet's moods:

> But, as it sometimes chanceth, from the might
> Of joy in minds that can no further go,
> As high as we have mounted in delight
> In our dejection do we sink as low;
> To me that morning did it happen so.
>
> (22–26)

So strong a consciousness of instability induces other forebodings about life's expectations as well. In the initial stages, however, of its act of self-analysis, *Resolution and Independence* seems to confirm once more the hopeful disclosures of the poem on the rainbow. For the poet's sense of renewal as he moves across the moor indicates not only his direct affinities with his natural surroundings but also the important strand of continuity that runs through his entire personal history, linking past to present. In answering the joys of nature, the poet finds his responses a re-creation of the emotional fullness of the child: "I heard the woods and distant waters roar; / Or heard them not, as happy as a boy" (17–18). Childhood here is conceived of not as the visionary past founded upon transcendence, first hinted at in *To the Cuckoo* and then given its detailed exposition in the *Immortality Ode,* but rather as a vivid state of natural feeling, almost rapturous in its intensity, a condition exemplified by "glad animal movements" that awaken in man the unself-conscious pleasures he shares with the warbling skylark and the "playful hare." However exhilarating its direct effects may be, such felt intensity is not to be understood as an end in itself, a sensation of pleasure to be sought for its own sake. Here as in *My heart leaps up*, the primary importance of retaining these first emotions lies in their connection with value, the assurance their continued presence provides that our actions are motivated by impulses more spontaneous and generous than "the ways of men, so vain and melancholy" (21).

Restricted in focus to the experience of renewal alone, *My heart leaps up* is understandably optimistic that the experienced self-continuity the poem discloses shall carry forward into the poet's later future, that the stages of life (no longer childhood, youth, and maturity but childhood, maturity, and old age) shall be bound together by a unity of feeling whose persistence guarantees a continuity in the moral life and its habits of natural piety as well. Though Wordsworth admits the possibility that these wishes may not be granted, a possibility expressed by the forbidding alternative he parenthetically puts forward in the event of any failure of emotional continuity—the prayerful wish "Or let me die" (6)—the poem's general tone is undeniably expectant and assured. *Resolution and Independence,* dealing in a larger segment of experience, the full cycle of renewal and loss, seemingly abandons these earlier prospects of future happiness, the hope of the poem on the rainbow, "So be it when I shall grow old," as a longing that seems incapable of fulfillment. The intensity of childhood emotion may continue into maturity, but to project feelings so unstable and impermanent into a still more distant future, to deem them powerful enough to withstand the eroding pressures of time, has become for the poet, so sensitive to his recent consciousness of flux, a judgment he is unwilling to risk. Although he can still speak of himself as a "happy Child of earth," old age is understood to mean the loss of spontaneity and joy, the coming of "Solitude, pain of heart, distress, and poverty" (35).

There is, however, an alternative to this prospect, a means to escape from the threat of process. Unlike the hare, man has the choice of living according to nature and its laws or of creating and following a specifically human set of laws designed to resist the hardships that nature can impose upon its creatures. He can—with the assistance of reason—ignore the urgings of the heart, base his actions upon the principles of self-interest, and thereby gain some measure of security against the pain and poverty that the poet, following nature, foresees as his own future. The condemnation that Wordsworth in stanza III had directed at man's vanity becomes, in stanza VI, self-condemnation of his own innocence in trusting simply to "genial faith," a folly that may cost him not merely the luxuries of the vain but "all needful things" that he will require in later years. The child's innocence is only possible, after all, because the adult provides for him; but when an adult attempts to carry the child's attitudes into later life without such provision, he betrays his obligation to himself. The stanza ends with a pessimistic questioning of the once confidently held view that stability and enduring happiness, the life of natural piety, can be attained through behavior unmotivated by self-interest.

> But how can He expect that others should
> Build for him, sow for him, and at his call
> Love him, who for himself will take no heed at all?
> (40–42)

Even as he defines his predicament, Wordsworth recognizes that there is no turning away from it, for the ways of men are not only "vain" but "melancholy." To adopt the ethics of egoism has as its consequence the withering away of joy and a descent into that permanent grayness that colors the majority of lives. Abandonment of the child's response to the world means for Wordsworth the rejection of nature and more importantly the rejection of his birthright as a poet. The poet as Wordsworth defines him in the "Preface" to the *Lyrical Ballads* is "a man pleased with his own passions and volitions, and who rejoices more than other men in the spirit of life that is in him; delighting to contemplate similar volitions and passions as manifested in the goings-on of the Universe, and habitually impelled to create them where he does not find them." [10] It is only through possession of a sense of joy in "the spirit of life" within man, a retention of the spontaneity of childhood, that poetry is possible. If, in *The Prelude,* Wordsworth had described the child as poet by pointing to the infant's creative sensibility as the "first / Poetic spirit of our human life" (II, 275–76), here, conversely, he sees the poet as child trusting simply to feeling unimpaired by reflection to guide him through life. Chatterton and Burns are children not only because they have retained the child's power of joy but because they were innocents mistakenly relying on the benevolence of nature and the trustworthiness of their own instincts to provide for their well-being. Yet as innocent, the poet, it would seem, achieves a happiness denied to other men: "By our own spirits are we deified" (47). W. W. Robson has contended that this line "comes in oddly" and asks "just what, for all its familiarity, it means." [11] What it means, I think, can be glossed from the meaning of *We Are Seven,* where the "animal vivacity" of the child manages to immunize her from the fact of the human condition, the knowledge of sorrow and the knowledge of death. Such immunity is not permanent, and experience will, of course, bring with it a knowledge of the sorrows of human life. The poet, however, by retaining the child's animal vivacity in later years also manages to retain the child's immunity from sorrow; and in a sense, man may become like a god, both in exhilaration of spirit and freedom from pain. The line carries with it though its own implicit irony, for the poets chosen—Chatterton and Burns—also reveal, in the highest degree, the brevity of human happiness and the extent of human suffering. In truth, the forces that govern the lives of those who would be the happiest of men are the same forces already seen in nature and Wordsworth's own states of mind; and Wordsworth describes the workings of the universal processes with epigrammatic clarity in the closing couplet of stanza VI: "We Poets in our youth begin in gladness; / But thereof come in the end despondency and madness" (48–49). But this act of definition is also an act of identification. By using the pronoun "We," Wordsworth confesses the full extent of his commitment to the way of the poet, accepting both its joy and its fate. The alternative—a life guided by self-interest, which might rescue him from that fate—has never been a genuine alternative after all.

In one sense, this implied gesture of commitment at the structural midpoint of *Resolution and Independence* marks the culminating moment in Wordsworth's advocacy of the values of the middle phase. Truly rendering for the first time the workings of process from which these values emanate, Wordsworth in his extended meditation can acknowledge pains as well as pleasures and assess future liabilities as well as present happiness. Chosen realistically from the spectrum of legitimately admissible modes of behavior, that is, those available to man as a being in nature, the values of the middle phase, an ethic and aesthetic based upon preservation of a childlike spontaneity of feeling, are determined not nostalgically but reflectively by Wordsworth as the only means by which man can maintain a genuinely poetic and moral existence. But if this first portion of *Resolution and Independence* provides Wordsworth's fullest and most reasoned argument in behalf of the views of 1802, it also, in its presentation of their inadequacies, gives impetus to the search for more stable metaphysical foundations of human behavior that occupies the poem's second half.

The first indication that the judgment of stanzas I–VII does not exhaust the poem's metaphysical or moral options is given in stanza VIII where Wordsworth interrupts his personal meditation to observe new and significantly transformed details of setting. The sense of life that had earlier pervaded the moor and occasioned the poet's own impulse of happiness is now seen to be apparently nothing more than an accident of rain and dawn; and now as the rising sun continues in its transit to become "the eye of heaven," the moor seems to assume its essential form as a "lonely place." Nature, as this altered perception suggests, has become less humane and hospitable, less congruent in its workings with man's own behavior. The most compelling aspect of this new setting, however, is its remarkable human inhabitant: "I saw a Man before me unawares: / The oldest man he seemed that ever wore grey hairs" (55–56). To the poet, the figure's impressiveness arises less from his appearance or isolation than from his unexpected relevance to the disturbing conjectures that the poem has just expressed. It was as though the poet's recently voiced apprehensions that his own future will be a time of "Solitude, pain of heart, distress, and poverty" (35) have become incarnate through the presence of this old man, who stands before the narrator like one summoned to authenticate these forebodings about the destructive powers of the processes of nature and its necessary consequences for the destiny of man. In his initial effects, the Leech-gatherer seems almost a kind of döppelganger, though acting, in this case, not as a present but as a future apparition of the self. Poorly clad, bowed by pain, and, in his loneliness, obviously uncared for and unloved, the old man presents himself to Wordsworth as a revelation of the poet's own fate, the product of a "genial faith" that had trusted that "all needful things would come unsought" (38).

Yet the results of the encounter that the poet is directed to are far different than those he had anticipated, for what the history he learns of discloses is the possibility for man of a spiritual existence alien to and transcending the processes of nature, a source of permanence in the midst of flux. Physically, of course, the Leech-gatherer has not escaped these processes, and his body, bent by age and sickness, attests to nature's power to inflict suffering on man. Moreover, dependent upon nature to provide for him in his old age, he finds that nature has, in fact, multiplied his difficulties, since a once-plentiful supply of leeches has grown increasingly scarce. If the Leech-gatherer is just such a victim of natural decay as Wordsworth had foreseen as his own future, it becomes clear during the poet's questioning that the old man is not, after all, a kind of döppelganger figure giving substance to and confirming Wordsworth's earlier premonitions. The "yet-vivid eyes" and "stately speech" of the Leech-gatherer disclose that there has been no decay of the inner life to correspond to that of the outer life, that despondency of spirit is not the necessary consequence of physical decline. Both of the poet's questions—" 'What occupation do you there pursue?' " (88) and " 'How is it that you live, and what is it you do?' " (119)—reflect his earlier anxiety for the fortunes of those who do not conduct their lives in accordance with the principles of self-interest. The real source of this anxiety was not simply concern for his future economic well-being but his assumption that age and poverty must necessarily bring with them despair, so that either alternative, the life governed by self-interest or the life lived according to nature, must ultimately conclude in melancholy. Although the Leech-gatherer's poverty is sufficient proof that he has not followed self-interest, and although he himself tells of na-

ture's unconcern for his welfare, nevertheless, the old man
has managed to retain his cheerfulness and defy that drift to
melancholy which Wordsworth regarded as inevitable in the
course of human experience. Moreover, such cheerfulness
seems to rest upon a base more stable and, in the end, perhaps more suited to the needs and conditions of adult life
than those recurrent episodes of recapturing the spontaneous
emotions of childhood, upon which Wordsworth earlier had
rested his own hopes for happiness. The Leech-gatherer's
account of himself is a tale of privation and "Employment
hazardous and wearisome!" (101). But he tells it with

> Choice word and measured phrase, above the reach
> Of ordinary men; a stately speech;
> Such as grave Livers do in Scotland use,
> Religious men, who give to God and man their dues.
>
> (95–98)

Dignified by piety, the old man not only transcends his
suffering but finds himself "with God's good help" (104) provided for, thus dispelling Wordsworth's fears that by turning
away from self-interest to follow a mode of life that gives to
man his due, he would excessively burden those upon whom
he had called to "Build for him, sow for him, and at his call
/ Love him" (41–42) and, thereby, sacrifice all hope of securing life's material necessities. An exchange that had originated in Wordsworth's apprehensions of the old man's sufferings has become instead a triumphant affirmation of God's
ability to sustain his creatures against the processes of nature
and change and a rebuke to the poet himself, delivered to
give him "human strength, by apt admonishment" (112).
Wordsworth's admonishment, derived not from nature but
from the faith of a pious man, comes about because he has
unnecessarily limited the possible guides available to man
in assuming that man must either follow self-interest or fol-

low nature. What the Leech-gatherer represents is a third way, resting neither upon man's fluctuating emotions nor the selfish inclinations of his ego but upon the fixed and abiding principles of revelation. By turning to God for guidance, man is granted access to a form of the ethical life that satisfies not only the claims of others but also the deepest claims of the self and that not only enhances man's present welfare but also opens up the prospect to him of eternal happiness.

Since the conclusion of *Resolution and Independence* involves the abandonment of an exclusively naturalistic interpretation of man and a new awareness of man's dual participation in the world of process and the world of permanence, it might well be described as Wordsworth's first genuinely Christian poem.[12] There is one important qualification to this; *Resolution and Independence* is not, in any real sense, a poem of conversion. The religious experience includes neither direct contact with nor direct knowledge of God, and the inner voice remains silent. In calling upon God in the closing lines to be "my help and stay secure" (139), Wordsworth underlines the principal lesson he has learned from the Leech-gatherer: how God can aid and comfort his creatures, the benefits that accrue to faith. Such commitment is, at best, a pragmatic commitment, and it is not until the 1804 stanzas of the *Immortality Ode* that Wordsworth truly substitutes fact for wish and supplies the experiential foundation upon which to erect his transcendental scheme of belief.

---

1. A number of recent interpretations have argued against viewing the passages as pessimistic departures from Wordsworth's general philosophy of man and nature. E. D. Hirsch considers *The Two April Mornings* a poem "which refers to death and change in human life, yet its spirit is affirmative" (p. 84). For Hirsch, counterbalancing Matthew's loss and consoling him for it are the permanent and recurrent forms of nature and the permanent and recurrent forms of human life that the poem describes. Anne Kostelanetz, with a similar emphasis on the recurrent in nature, sees the meaning of these works determined basically by the narrator's point of view. This, she

claims, produces a "structural irony of the poems which works against the authority of Matthew's statements." See "Wordsworth's 'Conversations': A Reading of 'The Two April Mornings' and 'The Fountain,'" *ELH* 33 (1966): 43.

2. David Ferry characteristically treats the poem as an example of Wordsworth's rebellion against human self-consciousness in which Matthew is "offered a choice between the living and the dead, and he chooses the dead" (p. 64). Anne Kostelanetz employs a more generalized variant of this critical position in explaining Matthew's choice. Matthew, by remaining faithful to the memory of his dead child, satisfies "his human need for particularity, definition and order," but in so doing he "has rejected the very essence of nature—the eternal cycle of joy and vitality, the constant possibility of spontaneous delight in the beauty of being" (p. 47). Closer to the mood of the poem and more plausible, I feel, is the suggestion that John Danby offers as one of several possibilities: "The words might mean, 'I did not wish her mine, to undergo all the risk of loss again'" (*The Simple Wordsworth: Studies in the Poems 1797–1807* [New York, 1961], pp. 86–87).

3. Though *A slumber did my spirit seal* reflects the basic concerns of the Goslar lyrics with the pains of loss, initiation from innocence into experience, and the conflict of natural time and human time, I have postponed discussion of it until chapter 7, where it can be considered in the context of Wordsworth's changing views on death and immortality.

4. Ferry, p. 76.

5. The special character of the poetry of 1802 has received considerable attention in two recent books devoted almost exclusively to the work of that year. In *Wordsworth and Coleridge: A study of their Literary Relations in 1801–1802* (Oxford, 1970) William Heath carefully examines the biographical background of the poems of 1802; and Jared R. Curtis in *Wordsworth's Experiments with Tradition: The Lyric Poems of 1802* (Ithaca, N.Y., 1971) deals primarily with voice, form, and the literary antecedents of these lyrics.

6. Alfred North Whitehead, *Science and the Modern World* (New York, 1953), p. 87.

7. David Hume, *A Treatise of Human Nature*, ed. L. A. Selby-Bigge (Oxford, 1888), p. 470. No direct antecedents are, of course, needed to account for this shift to emotivism, since Wordsworth's ethical speculations in 1802 are so few in number, so limited in scope, and so free of abstract theorizing. The ethical position I am outlining is based upon elements I feel to be implicit in the poems rather than from abstract and extended philosophic arguments of the kind familiar to us from *The Prelude* and *The Excursion*. Without raising any claims for influence, I might add, however, that the theorizing of such writers as Shaftesbury, Hutcheson, and Hume upon the importance of the emotions in conduct did much to create the intellectual climate that sanctioned ethical beliefs like those adopted by Wordsworth in 1802.

8. Just as Hartley and Priestley found in the alleged amorality of children empirical evidence to support their claim that virtue is acquired, so too do the leading emotivists, Shaftesbury and Hutcheson, turn to the behavior of children, at their seemingly more generous moments, to demonstrate the contrary proposition that the disposition to benevolence results from faculties

that man possesses at birth. Arguing in behalf of the moral sense, Francis Hutcheson writes, "The *Universality* of this *moral Sense,* and that it is antecedent to *Instruction,* may appear from observing the Sentiments of *Children,* upon hearing the Storys with which they are commonly intertain'd as soon as they understand Language. They always passionately interest themselves on that side where *Kindness and Humanity* are found; and detest the *Cruel,* the *Covetous,* the *Selfish* or the *Treacherous.* How strongly do we see their Passions of *Joy, Sorrow, Love,* and *Indignation* mov'd by these *moral Representations,* even tho there has been no pains taken to give them Ideas of a DEITY, of *Laws,* of a *future State,* or of the more intricate Tendency of the *universal Good* to that of each *Individual" (An Enquiry into the Original of our Ideas of Beauty and Virtue* [London, 1726], pp. 214–15). Similarly, Shaftesbury speaks of our "Sense of right and wrong" as "a first principle in our constitution and make" and adds the corollary that only "contrary habit or custom (a second nature)" can displace this "original and pure" faculty and "by frequent checks and control, can operate upon it, so as either to diminish it in part or destroy it in the whole" (*Characteristics of Men, Manners, Opinions, Times, etc.,* ed. John M. Robertson [London, 1900], 1: 260.

9. A. C. Bradley, *Oxford Lectures on Poetry* (London, 1909), p. 132.

10. *PW,* II, 393.

11. W. W. Robson, "Resolution and Independence" in *Interpretations,* ed. John Wain (London, 1955), p. 121.

12. Albert S. Gérard, whose interpretation of *Resolution and Independence* is in many ways similar to my own, also concludes that the poem points significantly to the qualified adoption by Wordsworth of belief in a new principle, transcendent and Christian: "There can be little doubt that the poem intends to describe the workings of a transcendent power which Wordsworth was only beginning to recognize, somewhat obliquely and with considerable caution, as the grace of God" (pp. 134–35).

7

The Final Phase:
The *Immortality Ode* and
Transcendence

The end of the middle phase must be regarded as essentially the terminating point of Wordsworthian naturalism, the last stage in an effort to maintain an ontology rooted in an empirical perception of this world and this world alone. In this final attempt to rest his hopes for human happiness upon some form of sympathetic identification linking nature and the self, some indwelling feature of the world design that required no appeal to transcendent or supernatural authority, Wordsworth showed himself willing to reduce considerably his claims for the powers of nature and the possibilities of the self in the interests of preserving what can only be called a secular position. Even these diminished claims appear in the enacted self-dramatizations of 1802 as difficult to sustain for the most part and at times, indeed, illusory, so that as we observe this desperate rear-guard action carried on by Wordsworth in the service of naturalism, we also find significant anticipations of the beliefs to which he would finally submit.

By 1804 the disposition of this inner conflict is clear, and what had earlier been detected only as longing becomes plainly discernible as a firm commitment to a metaphysics of transcendence with distinctively Christian implications that were to become more explicit and dominant in the years to come. How Wordsworth arrived at this commitment, the actual stages of philosophic debate or psychological conflict during the two-year period from 1802 to 1804, can, of course, never be determined with certainty, since he leaves us no recorded testimony, neither through correspondence nor con-' versation, of an intellectual conversion whose importance to him is equaled only by that restoration and conversion to nature described in the closing books of *The Prelude*. But Wordsworth does leave us with one major imaginative recapitulation of the process by which his beliefs underwent their final transformation: the *Immortality Ode,* a work that, though having its base in the naturalistically oriented conceptions of 1802, does not have its meaning completed until 1804 when Wordsworth adopted a transcendental faith. Read as we conventionally read it, in its finished and unitary form, the poem can be seen to function as a bridge between two very different conceptual worlds, an imaginative rendering of the means Wordsworth chose to lead himself out of the impasse to which he believed naturalism had brought him. To utilize the *Ode* properly in our present account of Wordsworth's philosophic history, we must necessarily look upon the arguments of chronologically divided parts as distinct and discrete units of meaning, each of them shaped by the differing context from which each had originally evolved.

Begun, as we know, on March 27, 1802, and separated by a matter of days or, at most, a very few weeks from the retrospective lyrics written in the spring of that year, the *Immortality Ode* in its earliest form clearly belongs within the poetic milieu of 1802. Indeed, looked at not from our present perspective as the introduction to an unfolding whole but from the point of view of 1802 where it must have seemed to Wordsworth, though not a finished utterance, nevertheless a well-developed fragment, the 1802 section of the *Ode,* its first four stanzas, might easily be classified as another and fuller version of the retrospective lyrics of that spring. These stanzas, in fact, offer a crucial amalgam of the primary themes of 1802, the continued flux of the poet's own inner being, the springtime world of natural process, the location in past experience of his most meaningful modes of feeling. Their dominant values, too, are those of the works that surround these stanzas: intensity, identity, and renewal. But where the *Immortality Ode* provides a more complex formulation of the themes and values of the poetry of the spring of 1802 is in its attempt to hold in near simultaneity the contradictions of Wordsworth's experience of recurrence and loss, to present within the compass of a single psychological event his dual consciousness of renewed intensity and vanished splendor. Yet its very fidelity to Wordsworth's own psychological experience leads almost inevitably to the inconclusiveness with which this segment of the *Ode* closes. Given his unitary and naturalistic conception of mind, Wordsworth seems to have no means available to him by which he can assess the values or determine the causes of these opposing facts of consciousness.

Wordsworth's naturalistic orientation did, however, furnish him with a way, at least, of presenting these contradictions. Since he had habitually tended to regard mind as a function of sense, conflicting testimony about the nature of self-identity could be interpreted through a dualism within sense-experience itself, opposing reports on the character of experience from the two primary modes of perception, sight and hearing. And this principle of opposition forms the pattern of organization not only for the stanzas of 1802 but also, the implications of this conflict vastly extended, for the finished poem of 1804.

The *Immortality Ode* begins with a statement of total and radical loss. A "celestial light" that had once "Apparelled" all visual objects has now gone completely from them; and through the operations of the mechanism of association, every visual impression the speaker now has becomes itself a painful reiteration of diminished splendor, every "common sight" a reminder that

> Turn wheresoe'er I may,
> By night or day,
> The things which I have seen I now can see no more.
>
> (7–9)

The values of this heightened consciousness now lost are not merely those of simple aesthetic awareness, and in the second stanza Wordsworth differentiates between beauty and glory in a way that almost verges upon the distinction between the transcendent and the natural made in the later portions of the *Ode,* where differences are suggested both in kind and in import. Natural beauty seems a relatively isolated occurrence, lacking the universality of that other attribute of his early life which in every visual appearance had come to him with "The glory and the freshness of a dream" (5). Instead, beauty is confined solely to certain particulars of nature, the intermittent visits of the rainbow, the ephemeral loveliness of the rose, or certain scenes in which every element seems in harmony—the grandeur of the moon, solitary in the heavens, or the fairness of "Waters on a starry night" (14). Even in his perception of beauty, pleasure is muted by regret, the act of apprehension at the same time an act of remembrance informing the viewer of the departure from these objects of a splendor wholly unlike that which he now perceives.

Wordsworth's sense of irrevocable separation from his past forms only one component of his attitudes in the spring of 1802. The feelings described in stanzas three and four, where Wordsworth can respond in childlike fullness to the pleasure and animation of the Maytime scene, stand in sharp contradiction to his initial melancholy self-portrait, now viewed only as a momentary lapse from spiritual vigor:

> To me alone there came a thought of grief:
> A timely utterance gave that thought relief,
> And I again am strong.
>
> (22–24)

The literal origins of the "timely utterance" must, I suspect, remain obscure, but the phrase itself serves as a useful focal point for what is to come in the following stanzas. Despite his fixed and burdensome knowledge of loss, Wordsworth still retains eddying currents of powerful feeling whose movements are determined by temporal events. Moreover, the phrase suggests a new system of imagery as the source of restoration, auditory rather than visual impressions.[1] Setting now takes on specific interest as a festive spring morning in which "all the earth is gay" (29); and that gaiety is presented almost wholly through the medium of those happy sounds that urge the poet toward self-renewal: the joyous tones of the birds, the trumpeting of the cataracts, the answering voices of the echoes, and the happy shout of the Shepherd-boy. And as he recognizes the pervasiveness of this animating power, the jubilee of earth responsively answered by the laughter of the heavens, Wordsworth too finds himself impelled by its influence, transformed from adult observer to youthful participant in this moment of rejuvenescence:

> My heart is at your festival,
> My head hath its coronal,
> The fulness of your bliss, I feel—I feel it all.
>
> (39–41)

Significantly, he reiterates his sense of oneness with his surroundings by affirming communion with its voices: "I hear, I hear, with joy I hear!" (50). What Wordsworth claims for himself here is not simply a strength that thwarts melancholy, a capacity for vital response to the energies of spring. His joy, felt with a fullnesss identical in kind and equal in intensity to that of the Shepherd-boy, the children culling flowers, or even the infant who "leaps up on his Mother's arm" (49), indicates a point of contact at which the stages of life touch and provides a guarantee that the processes of change have not severed the poet from his own past. Apparent radical loss is now disclaimed, for there is no hint that the vitality and intensity associated here with a mighty world of ear have in any way declined since childhood. But the objectification of the contradictions of Wordsworth's experience through contrasting modes of perception contains within it the implicit judgment that success in the quest for personal identity can be, at best, temporary. Heavily pictorial, like most of us, in his thinking about the content of consciousness, Wordsworth tends to regard the auditory faculty from which he gleans his evidences of continuity as the less prominent of our two principal sources of significant experience, its data forcing itself upon our attention with less frequency and less forcefulness than that of our visual impressions. Ultimately, ways of hearing must once more yield to ways of seeing and its attendant melancholy. Even with triumph apparently within grasp, Wordsworth again picks up the poem's earlier thread of imagery. Objects of sight—a tree, a field, a flower—interrupt his auditory communion with his surroundings by silent rebuttal and visually renew his dormant awareness that, whatever he may retain, he has suffered a loss of inestimable value:

> —But there's a Tree, of many, one,
> A single Field which I have looked upon,
> Both of them speak of something that is gone:
>> The Pansy at my feet
>> Doth the same tale repeat:
> Whither is fled the visionary gleam?
> Where is it now, the glory and the dream?
>
> (51–57)

These stanzas of the *Ode* offer, at least in one sense, a final judgment on the apparent contradictions of *My heart leaps up* and *To a Butterfly*. By bringing opposing evidences as to the nature of identity within a single perspective, Wordsworth is able to infer not contradiction but complexity, a dualism within the senses themselves that provides continuity and yet fosters change. Moreover, Wordsworth is also able to measure the degree of continuity and the magnitude of change and, thus, to assess the significance of each. It is evident in the assignment of spiritual priorities that what is lost far outweighs what is retained. Although in the first two stanzas Wordsworth can generalize upon loss from all visual experience, the knowledge of continuity is limited by his responsiveness to certain seasonal stimuli whose inconstancy suggests that such knowledge is a far less stable element in his adult life than his persistent consciousness of loss. And even in stanzas three and four, where fullness of response apparently insures self-identity, awareness of change once more intrudes, determining the inconclusive fragment's final emphasis and pointing toward the direction in which resolution must lie. What the 1802 segment plainly demands is not a reassertion of life's wholeness like that expressed in the triumphant paradox of the child as father of the man but an explanation of loss, a way of accounting for the momentous falling-off in a power ambiguously defined as vision. Yet it is a task to which Wordsworth's naturalistic theory of mind seems painfully inadequate: the cognate faculties of sight and hearing offer only a technique of representation and not a means of solution. Full resolution of the difficulties of 1802 would seem to require a conception of mind more complex in scope, the adoption of an epistemological dualism that allows Wordsworth to make necessary and essential distinctions in the mind's ways of knowing. Such a distinction implies, in turn, a corresponding distinction among the objects of knowledge, the adoption of a metaphysical dualism of transcendent and sensory orders of reality as the needed complement to an epistemological dualism of transcendental and sensory modes of cognition. But the condition of philosophic change is conscious acknowledgement of the insufficiency of old ways of thinking, an admission that Wordsworth in early April of 1802 seemed not yet ready to make. The poem, thus, was to stand in fragmentary form until new beliefs accommodated themselves to its urgent questionings.

By the early months of 1804, Wordsworth gives clear indication that he has abandoned the strict philosophic naturalism of earlier years, and a new context for the concluding portion of the *Ode* can be seen taking shape. The spiritual supremacy he bestows upon the child of Book V of *The Prelude,* whose "Dumb yearnings" and "hidden appetites" (V, 530) struggle against a yoke of submission to custom and "reconcilement with our stinted powers" (V, 541), the destined restraints of the "meagre vassalage" (V, 542) of adulthood, is a significant instance of how far Wordsworth has departed from the developmental theories stated in *Tintern Abbey* or even the hypothesis of spiritual continuity set forth in the lyric on the rainbow. Again in the portentously somber *Ode to Duty,* where the dictates of immutable law countermand more familiar impulses from "the genial sense of youth," a commitment to dualism, at least in its ethical form, seems inescapable. More conclusive and perhaps more immediately relevant to the problems of the *Ode* is the famous moment of visionary illumination that follows the account of the crossing of Simplon Pass. From this momentary usurpation of the normal processes of knowledge—the interchange between sense and its objects— Wordsworth affirms the existence of a second order of experience, a suprasensuous reality whose contents can be read by a special human faculty correspondingly liberated from sense that Wordsworth uneasily terms "Imagination." What flashes before him here is not a knowledge of essences, his earlier insight, in *Tintern Abbey,* into a vital core of being infused within the natural order as "the life of things." Instead, he now recognizes the existence of an "invisible world," whose operations, although concurrent with those of the sensory world, are altogether distinct in nature from them. Moreover, this essentially dualistic division implies an inevitably hierarchical arrangement. Unchanging and imperishable, the transcendent world informs the spirit that flux and transience maintain only an illusory bondage over us, that "Our destiny, our nature, and our home, / Is with infinitude, and only there" (*Prelude,* VI, 538–39).

No longer confined by the purely naturalistic milieu of his earlier thought, Wordsworth could now return to the fragment of 1802 and find in the aura that had once invested all visual objects a spiritual dimension that heretofore could not be articulated and yet was deeply implicit in the poem's initial phase. With this broadened framework, Wordsworth stood ready to resolve the troubled discourse of 1802. He need not interpret conflicting reports on the continuity of self as contradictory but could instead view them as evidence that a consciousness of loss and a consciousness of recurrence may occur simultaneously yet separately if they occur within disparate planes of experience, that the problem of identity applies to both natural man and spiritual man. With spirit as the paramount element in his dualism, Wordsworth could readily transform the dominant concern of the 1802 verses, the fact of perceptual loss, into a statement of spiritual deprivation, though the experience of continuity remained a purely sensory event and inadequate compensation for a knowledge of alienation from his being's real destiny.

Yet this by no means completes Wordsworth's scheme for the finished *Ode.* For in 1804 he chose to complicate the work further by extending its concerns to still another theme, one that Wordsworth finally came to look upon as the poem's principal source of interest. By concentrating his quest for identity within the realm of the ideal and changeless, Wordsworth was also assuming the existence of a component of self whose being must extend beyond life's temporal boundaries. Hence any claim for continuity in man's spiritual nature was also inevitably a claim for immortality. The manifest connection of these ideas is parenthetically hinted at even in Book V of *The Prelude,* where Wordsworth, distinguishing between the special and regal spiritual powers of childhood and the "stinted powers" of later years, almost irrelevantly obtrudes his unwillingness to follow the implications of his argument any further: "I guess not what this tells of Being past, / Nor what it augurs of the life to come" (V, 534–35). Eventually, of course, Wordsworth was unable to maintain such restraint, and in the years to come he was to attempt guesses, to seek auguries, and to convert those judgments, now withheld, into dogma. By 1810, in the first essay of *Upon Epitaphs,* a similar distinction between reports from "the outward senses" and prior "communications with our internal Being" forms the experiential basis for Wordsworth's conviction of immortality:

> It is to me inconceivable, that the sympathies of love towards each other, which grow with our growth, could ever attain any new strength, or even preserve the old, after we had received from the outward senses the impression of death, and were in the habit of having that impression daily renewed and its accompanying feeling brought home to ourselves, and to those we love; if the same were not counteracted by those communications with our internal Being, which are anterior to all these experiences, and with which revelation coincides, and has through that coincidence alone (for otherwise it could not possess it) a power to affect us.[2]

Although less overt and dogmatic than he was later to be in *Upon Epitaphs,* Wordsworth, apparently unhampered by reservations in the *Ode,* similarly derives a faith in immortality as the logical corollary of the fact of dualism. The "dream-like vividness and splendour which invest objects of sight in childhood" are not explained as phenomena of the "outward senses" but rather as faded emblems of "those communications with our internal Being, which are anterior to all these experiences"; and this, in turn, Wordsworth finds to be "presumptive evidence of a prior state of existence" that forms "more than an element in our instincts of immortality." [3] Evidence that Wordsworth conceived this to be the poem's primary emphasis has been carefully and convincingly assembled by Thomas M. Raysor: the clear references to immortality both in lines later excised from the original and in the final text itself; the awkwardly elaborate but plainly denotative title; the explicit directions for reading the poem contained in the letter to Mrs. Clarkson and again in the Fenwick note; and finally Wordsworth's special classification of the *Ode* in the arrangment of his collected works, where, set uniquely apart, it follows "Poems referring to the Period of Old Age" and "Epitaphs and Elegiac Pieces" to conclude the shorter poems, so that, as Raysor remarks, "one passes from the poetry of old age to the poetry of death and finally to the poetry of life after death, as in Tennyson's poems one comes at the end to 'Crossing the Bar.' " [4] Readers, of course, have been reluctant to accept Wordsworth's thematic assessment of the *Ode* at face value, and the complex task assigned the poem does, in fact, disguise its drift. Preliminary matters that seem more closely related to Wordsworth's usual concerns must be attended to, his divided awareness of loss and continuity given form, interpreted, and transposed into a more significant intuition to make possible the poem's broader metaphysical categories. Only then—with this elaborate foundation that so deeply engages our attention finally laid—can Wordsworth address himself to the concluding matter of immortality.

Wordsworth, however, did address himself to this matter;

and to understand why it should prove so critical an issue, we must turn once again to his period of optimistic naturalism and to the troublesome enigma that the question of immortality raised in the midst of his most hopeful beliefs. Raysor, who has most fully pursued the relationship between Wordsworth's views on immortality and its treatment in the *Ode,* holds that the poem's judgment on the subject is conventionally Wordsworthian, that it is unlikely "that Wordsworth at any time gave up completely the concept of a finite personal soul after death, or accepted the idea of the annihilation of personal identity and self-consciousness by absorption into the infinite." [5] But the poems on death prior to the *Ode,* without ever assertively disputing the concept of personal survival after death, surely convey a deep disquietude about it. In neither the "Matthew" poems nor the "Lucy" poems, where the problem of death is paramount, is the seemingly irreducible fact of man's limited mortality in any way assuaged by the profession of Christian faith and the consolation of belief in the hereafter that Wordsworth characteristically appended to his elegiac verse from 1804 onward. Instead, the bereaved possesses only the bleak and hopeless remembrance of "what has been / And never more will be" (*Three years she grew in sun and shower,* 41–42).

As yet unhabituated to piety, Wordsworth could find little in his basic beliefs during these early years upon which to ground any hope of immortality in the conventional sense, the retention of one's finite identity beyond death. His universe, molded and impelled by immanent power and goodness but seemingly devoid of the marks of transcendence, could support what was, at best, only a vague and impersonal notion of immortality that involved dissolution of the conscious self and its absorption into a world of insensate being. Yet it is precisely at this point that his metaphysic of nature seems inadequate to or even subversive of the human needs objectified in his empiricist epistemology. For an Epictetus or Spinoza, interpreting reason as the sole human good and nature as the expression and embodiment of the workings of the cosmic logos, death itself may be a release from the trammels of sense, a final liberation from human bondage, and, indeed, even a contribution to the rationality of the whole. But man's uniqueness and special glory, for Wordsworth, reside in what most clearly differentiates man from the nonhuman world, his sensory alertness and receptivity to external impulse and his power to construct from his impressions the edifice of the moral self. However profound or serene the joys promised man by his final act of participation in the life of things, they scarcely mitigate death's penalty, the sacrifice of those faculties of sense and consciousness by which he has gained what he cannot help but feel constitutes the only truly human source of happiness.

So deep a conflict inevitably induces tensions of the kind that typify the "Lucy" poems. An unvoiced yet implicit note of protest and reproach tempers Wordsworth's aesthetic judgments; the processes of nature remain agents of pleasure, but that they are humane in any familiar sense he discredits as illusion. Man and nature here stand in apparent opposition, contesting rivals for Lucy in *Three years she grew in sun and shower;* and if nature finally claims the bride he has already so richly endowed, the tones of celebration are deeply muted by her human lover's concluding elegy with its bitter intimations that this personification of nature is only an elaborate and evasive metaphor for death, that Lucy's nuptials are, in reality, a yielding up of those attributes that give us our human identity, and that the wedding garment is, in fact, the shroud. A less figurative statement of this same conflict appears in the second stanza of *A slumber did my spirit seal.* Nature still carries the impress of sublimity and even hints at possession of a vital beauty in the closing line that subtly passes from barrenness to blossoming. The starkness of this account, nonetheless, suggests nature's essential remoteness from the richness of human desires and activities. Death may, of course, be interpreted as relinquishment of an individuating "motion" and "force" in order to share in the larger rhythms of nature's movements and the enduring strength of nature's energies. But there is also a loss here for which nature provides no equivalents. In death, Lucy "neither hears nor sees" (6); and the intense and varied life of the senses—man's only known access to pleasure or knowledge or power—is finally and fully arrested.

Wordsworth's tendency to define death in terms of the pathos of sensory deprivation also appears in one of the least familiar of the "Matthew" poems, *Address to the Scholars of the Village School of* ———, and again induces many of these same tensions. Matthew, characteristically zealous in his devotion to nature, "loved the breathing air" and "loved the sun" (22–23); but, like Lucy, he in death has had his ties with the rich world of perceptual awareness severed, so that if the sun

> rise
> Or set, to him where now he lies,
> Brings not a moment's care.
> (23–25)

Although the mourner quickly dismisses this as "idle words," the gesture of dismissal in itself constitutes Wordsworth's recognition of the darkness of these speculations. Moreover, in a manuscript copy of the same work, presumably written in 1800, this qualification has been deleted, deepening the note of desolation and final hopelessness. There is to be no future renewal of human awareness, no release from death, only eternal bondage for Matthew as

> A prisoner of the silent ground.
> He loved the breathing air,
> He loved the sun—he does not know

Whether the sun be up or no,
He lies forever there.[6]

Confronted by death, Wordsworth's consolations in 1798
and 1800 are wholly secular, remembrance and resignation.
But when finally published in 1842, the lament for Matthew
includes an addition of sixteen lines entitled "By the Side
of the Grave Some Years After." Although the first twelve
lines seem merely a reavowal of earlier consolations, the final
stanza injects the previously absent note of Christian hope—
"the promise from the Cross" that shines upon the "happy
grave"—and, in so doing, renders even more conspicuous
the troubled mood of the original.

Other works prior to 1804 also touch upon death, but in
none of them does Wordsworth imply any conviction of
hopes beyond the grave. When the subject appears in the
dramatic narratives, its treatment is unspeculative, incidental, for the most part, to Wordsworth's primary purpose of
delineating the passions of domestic sorrow. Here death and
grief are wholly secularized, the emblem of loss not yet the
cross with its pledge of resurrection but the twisted thorn,
the abandoned sheepfold, the ruined cottage. Orthodox consolations are alluded to in *The Brothers* by the village priest,
whose justification of the town's unmarked burial site is,
in part, that "for our immortal part! *we* want / No symbols,
Sir, to tell us that plain tale" (180–81). This remark, however, seems determined by the poem's dramatic conventions
rather than by any thematic relevance, since Leonard, the
surviving brother, abandons his original purpose of homecoming and instead returns uncomforted to the sea and to
the bleak exile that will claim his remaining years.

Perhaps the one clear instance where Wordsworth, speaking in his own voice, looks hopefully upon death is the
curious fragment of the spring of 1802, in which, wholly
tranquil amidst the peace of his hushed chamber, he asks:

> Oh who would be afraid of life,
> The passion the sorrow and the strife,
>   When he may be
>   Shelter'd so easily?
> May lie in peace on his bed
> Happy as they who are dead.

Following this uncharacteristic Wordsworthian yearning to experience death's dark and silent pleasures is the second fragment's second section entitled "Half an hour afterwards," which reverses his earlier judgment and recognizes that to die is not to purify life of encumbrance and distraction and thereby to intensify its richness but to repose in nullity, to "become a sod" deprived of those sensory faculties that constitute our sole access to happiness:

> I have thoughts that are fed by the sun.
>   The things which I see
>   Are welcome to me,
>   Welcome every one:
> I do not wish to lie
>   Dead, dead,
> Dead without any company;
>   Here alone on my bed,
> With thoughts that are fed by the Sun,
>   And hopes that are welcome every one,
>   Happy am I.[7]

Of the works written prior to composition of the final portion of the *Immortality Ode,* only one, *We Are Seven,* is commonly held to prefigure the themes of the *Ode* and to hint obliquely at Wordsworth's later intuitions concerning death and immortality. Yet it is a mistake, I feel, to look upon *We Are Seven* as the great *Ode* transposed into a minor key. The significance of their relationship resides in the contrast posed rather than in any shared resemblance. And it is to underscore this contrast that Wordsworth directs attention to the earlier poem in the Fenwick note to the *Immortality Ode:* "Nothing was more difficult for me in childhood than to admit the notion of death as a state applicable to my own being. I have said elsewhere—

> 'A simple child,
> That lightly draws its breath,
> And feels its life in every limb,
> What should it know of death!'—

But it was not so much from [feelings] of animal vivacity that *my* difficulty came as from a sense of the indomitableness of the spirit within me." [8] Later in the same note, Wordsworth explains that this sense of spiritual indomitableness—carefully distinguished from animal vivacity with its feeling of corporeal life pulsing "in every limb"—was taken "as presumptive evidence of a prior state of existence" in the *Ode.*[9] *We Are Seven,* however, is radically empirical in its theory of knowledge and presents a child dependent for her concepts upon the strength of received impressions and therefore incapable of grasping so alien an abstraction as death. Nor is it simply the notion of death as termination of consciousness that she refuses to admit. Though acknowledging that her brother and sister are no longer present, that both are gone away, she remains unmoved by her preceptor's insistence that her dead brother and sister are in heaven, that their release from pain somehow involves their translation into some form of purely spiritual existence that can sustain itself after death or, presumably, before birth, apart from the envelope of sense and corporeal awareness that constitute the child's sole knowledge of being. Confined within the narrow sphere of immediate physical reality, she grasps at no trees to preserve her hold upon material fact, recognizes no high and compelling instincts that compete for sovereignty with her intensely felt mortal nature, and surely proffers no clear intimations of immortality to buttress her pious listener's faith. To rightly understand *We Are Seven,* we must view it in conjunction with *Anecdote for Fathers,* a companion-piece that immediately preceded it in *Lyrical Ballads,* recognizing both to be not soundings of the deep and inexpressible intuitions of childhood but disclosures of ignorance, dramatizations of the meagerness of the child's intellectual resources through which Wordsworth seeks to rebut an educational theory that would attempt to educate the child beyond his years by instilling adult concepts or evoking adult judgments in an as yet unformed mind. Both poems are essentially mildly comic dialogues whose subjects are incidental to their form, the intrusion of adult concerns into the mind of a child—limited both by narrowness of experience and imperfect conceptual powers—to whom such concerns must be necessarily meaningless. That death should be numbered among those concerns upon which "outward sense" has not yet spoken and from which the child is therefore debarred is perhaps the fullest measure of Wordsworth's commitment to empiricism in 1798 and of the distance to be traveled before he could reach beyond experience for a solution to the problem of death in the concluding stanzas of the *Immortality Ode.*

Thus, in returning to the *Ode* in 1804, Wordsworth addressed himself to two primary tasks: resolution of the perplexities of human identity by interpreting his two-fold awareness of continuity and loss as tangible proof of a dualism within the self and, *mutatis mutandis,* within the very nature of reality; and satisfaction of his deeply rooted desire that human self-consciousness transcend life's purely physical boundaries. But fulfillment of the first of these tasks is, in effect, fulfillment of both. By establishing a dualism, one of whose components is an eternal and changeless spiritual order, a goal toward which man's illimitable spiritual powers may successfully reach, Wordsworth can clearly overcome the menace of death.

It is in stanza V that Wordsworth, drawing upon the Platonic myth of preexistence to answer the concluding questions of 1802, first affirms the existence of such an order, a purely spiritual realm from which we derive our true source of being and with which we retain lingering but fading connections even after assuming our mortal natures. The machinery of Platonism is not, as it is sometimes claimed, a way of metaphorically asserting the mind's dominion over nature or of explaining nature's banished splendor as an attribute of the projective powers of imagination, an overflowing of creative energies "whose fountains are within." Indeed, Wordsworth consistently emphasizes the passivity of our perceptions of the light that flows out upon us from divinity, apparently as an additional guarantee of its literal reality. Upon our entry into life, we remain suffused by divinity; but even as human development begins to draw us away from infancy and the security of its enclosure in divinity, we may still, for a time, preserve our unmediated apprehension of the realm of pure spirit: the "growing boy" still "Beholds the light, and whence it flows, / He sees it in his joy" (70–71). In youth, this immediate awareness is finally relinquished, but divine light yet lingers as a reflected presence in nature. It is this period, when the child still perceives the "visionary gleam" but without knowledge of its source or its implications, to which the opening stanzas of 1802 must specifically refer. Again Wordsworth is careful to make clear the splendor perceived is not a splendor with which the child has been endowed, that it belongs to the external objects of perception rather than to the internal modes of perceiving:

> The Youth, who daily farther from the east
> Must travel, still is Nature's Priest,

And by the vision splendid
Is on his way attended.

(72–75)

In both syntax and meaning, the closing lines too reiterate
the individual's essential passivity in his relationship to
vision, which he continues to behold in the reflected splendor
that accompanies him on his journey until "At length the
Man perceives it die away, / And fade into the light of common day" (76–77).

His unwillingness to appropriate this power of illumination to the human mind, a refusal actually to translate the
potential dualism of the opening stanzas into something
analogous to the Coleridgean categories of the imagination,
should indicate the direction Wordsworth intended the completed poem to take. The implications latent in the earlier
sections have become finally "a point whereon to rest his
machine" from which Wordsworth can develop a Christian
dualism of heaven and earth, soul and body, immortality
and mortality. To give meaning to both the soul-concept
and the intimations of immortality derived from it, Wordsworth first needed to establish the existence of a reality that
is ideal, eternal, and the true dwelling place of the human
spirit. Thus, in the fifth stanza, what he emphasizes is not
his loss but the source of the now departed vision, its objective character and external location. Moreover, despite pagan
associations for which Wordsworth dutifully apologized, the
myth of preexistence, as he uses it, seems pointedly Christian
in its language, referring literally to the "Soul," to "God,"
and to "Heaven." If the journey of mortal life seemingly
withdraws man from God's presence and diminishes his
power of spiritual awareness, divinity itself remains fixed
and stable, eternally radiant, and a potential source of hope
and comfort for the poet even amidst the darkness of human
change.

In stanzas VI and VII, Wordsworth fully completes his metaphysical dualism and hierarchically organizes it by defining its second element, the realm of sensory phenomena. Nature with "no unworthy aim" offers man "pleasures of her own," but these pleasures induce forgetfulness and distract man from remembrance of the deeper "glories" of "that imperial palace whence he came" (85). Human life too has its values and interests that lure man from the visionary. It is the child whose links with divinity seem most secure; yet parental affection quickly attaches him to his earthly home, and the drama of adult life unfolds its attractions and absorbs him into its preoccupations. Nor does the child himself resist these pressures but, instead, struggles eagerly to free himself from vision. But as he observes this premature and voluntary submission to the yoke of life, Wordsworth recognizes that even here the child carries on his communion with splendor, still remains poised between his divine origins and his human future, knowing both simultaneously since intuition has not yet been banished by the alien mode of sense.

Having set forth the terms of his metaphysical dualism in stanzas V–VII, Wordsworth is free to consider more fully in the stanzas that follow their epistemological equivalents, the dualism within man of soul and body, intuition and sense, that furnishes him with access to and knowledge of both spiritual and natural orders. But his treatment of these matters is also an attempt to recast the difficulties of 1802 within a framework of thought extensive enough to clarify them. In what is perhaps the most significant of the changes of 1804—one that reduces the risk that his introduction of new subjects and systems to a work originating in a purely perceptual puzzle might be judged unconvincing or arbitrary —Wordsworth in stanzas VIII and IX turns again to his earlier distinction between the visual and auditory. But these basic materials of 1802 undergo in 1804 a substantial shift in function, transposed from literal facts of perception into broad epistemological metaphors. Ways of seeing have now come to stand for man's divine endowments, spiritual faculties carried into this life that enable him briefly to maintain communication with a more perfect order of being than nature; and the power of hearing becomes a symbol that governs the whole range of man's natural attributes, sense organs, and reflective faculties by which he comes to know and understand the natural and human worlds to which his activities must eventually be confined.

This symbolic fastening of the poem's earlier concerns to later speculations is made explicit in the opening lines of stanza VIII, where Wordsworth binds soul and sight in apposition, apostrophizing the child first as "Thou, whose exterior semblance doth belie / Thy Soul's immensity;" (109–10) and again as "thou Eye among the blind" (112). Moreover, the child seems in his essential nature immune to those auditory distractions that dominate "Our noisy years"; instead, "deaf and silent," he reads "the eternal deep, / Haunted forever by the eternal mind" (113–14). Finally through his capacity to see beyond sense into eternity, the child becomes a repository of those necessary truths—necessary both as self-evident and immutable in character and as the underlying ground of all meaning and value in human existence—that adult man, his power of spiritual vision obscured, vainly seeks, "In darkness lost, the darkness of the grave" (118). Wordsworth has, in effect, recapitulated the poem's original issues and resolved its initial questionings, but his answers carry little comfort. Lost in our failure of vision is a consciousness of identity with a self that had once held communion with the eternal; retained as our sole source of knowledge of the continuity of self is a form of auditory awareness, bounded by birth and death, whose din, shutting out the silence of the eternal, affirms only our mortality.

It is to this problem—the nature of man's final destiny—

that the apotheosis of the child in stanza VII is, I believe, actually directed. For the sole concept treated, the single truth specified in this account of the child's spiritual insight, is the dominating fact of immortality that over him "Broods like the Day, a Master o'er a Slave, / A Presence which is not to be put by" (120–21). But possession of this truth is for Wordsworth the necessary basis of our happiness and, in an important sense, ample recompense for whatever losses in immediate spiritual awareness we may have undergone. In *Upon Epitaphs,* which echoes the *Ode* at a number of points, Wordsworth remarks "that, if the impression and sense of death were not thus counterbalanced, such a hollowness would pervade the whole system of things, such a want of correspondence and consistency, a disproportion so astounding betwixt means and ends, that there could be no repose, no joy." [10] His knowledge of immortality, however, does more than simply shield man from despair; it provides a principle of interpretation, an argument from design for an existence that must otherwise be judged purposeless.

The importance for Wordsworth of his assurance of immortality explains and, to some extent, justifies what seems the poem's most disturbing contradiction: the abrupt transition from the closing lines of stanza VIII, rightly called "the darkest point in the *Ode* and the only unqualified assertion of life's diminishment," [11] to the statement of recovery, made in apparent disregard of the poem's harsher realities, in the lines that immediately follow. In this transition from denial to certainty, Wordsworth has actually shifted attention from concern with a state of being and mode of knowing admittedly lost beyond recovery, at least for this life, to consideration of the objects of knowledge, the central truths, then apprehended. These truths though initially given man through intuition are capable of reformulation into the concepts of discursive thought. If praise is to be given "that in our embers / Is something that doth live"

(130–31), it is not because some spiritual component of the self has actually survived the numbing passage from childhood to adulthood. Neither inner nor outer experience— neither "High instincts" nor "Fallings from us, vanishings"— any longer directly challenge the authority of natural man and his environment. But validated at least as recollected fact, these experiences and the central and imperishable truth disclosed by them offer natural man a principle that orders the otherwise random events of his existence with intelligibility and purpose and thus forms "the fountain light of all our day," "a master light of all our seeing" (152–53). And by reclaiming this principle from the losses of childhood, Wordsworth is able to bring the separate elements of his dualism into a single coherent pattern, to assimilate the order of sense within the order of spirit so that "Our noisy years seem moments in the being / Of the eternal Silence" (155–56). A similar reconciliation is also attempted within the poem's structure of imagery. Still careful to distinguish between a unity of self and a unity of knowledge by isolating the adult observer from the enthusiasms of the sportive children even though both share common surroundings and jointly survey "that immortal sea / Which brought us hither" (164–65), Wordsworth, nonetheless, claims in the culminating metaphor of stanza IX that sight and hearing are, in fact, related, that they are simply separate ways of apprehending a single object of experience, separate ways of knowing the varied manifestations of divinity:

> Hence in a season of calm weather
> Though inland far we be,
> Our Souls have sight of that immortal sea
> Which brought us hither,
> Can in a moment travel thither,
> And see the Children sport upon the shore,
> And hear the mighty waters rolling evermore.
> (162–68)

At this point we may again ask whether Wordsworth, urgently driven to reconcile divisions, has not breached the poem's imagistic logic and, consequently, its logic of ideas in the attempt. In what sense can we appropriate to the adult, so that he too "may have sight of that immortal sea," the visual powers of the child who moves among us as an "Eye among the blind"? And in what sense can we attribute to auditory faculties, seemingly limited by the bounds of sense, a capacity to "hear the mighty waters rolling evermore," when we know full well the child must remain "deaf and silent"—undisturbed by the intrusions of "our noisy years"—during his moments of spiritual perception, his readings of "the eternal deep"? If there is no fully satisfactory resolution of these contradictions, there is, I believe, a reasonably coherent explanation of why they arose. For Wordsworth plainly intended the dualism at which these middle stanzas arrive to be only a tentative statement of the nature of things. What he must ultimately strive toward is a new principle of unity. He must disclose a single ground of being, in essence spiritual, that underlies the opposing elements of the poem's dualism, a single design, the purposes of divinity, that governs the operations of both spiritual and natural orders. But given the character of the poem's epistemology, its acute polarization of sensory and spiritual knowledge, there seems little likelihood that the adult mind, confined as it is within the limits of sense, can cross this barrier and perceive a unity determined by the primacy of spirit. In addition to sense and spirit, however, Wordsworth provides what is really a third mode of cognition spoken of in stanza X as "thought," that power by which we abstract, remember, reflect, and judge. Although Wordsworth classifies thought naturalistically as a unique capacity developed by man during his earthly existence to render sensory phenomena intelligible, it actually functions in the poem as a kind of middle term linking spirit and nature, a way of converting our first intuitions into more conventional objects of knowledge. In doing this, Wordsworth is following the common practice of most of those who deal with special forms of spiritual experience; for if the deep truth is imageless, if our moments of illumination cannot be literally reconstructed during their prosaic aftermath, nevertheless, the knowledge then gained can again be grasped conceptually, can, as I suggested earlier, be reformulated in accordance with the categories of discursive thought. However remote those moments in which we experience the direct presence of vision, the mind has still indelibly recorded them as spiritual fact and abstracted from their contents the central truths of God, of heaven, of immortality. And by integrating these truths with the truths of sense, we may come finally to understand life's pattern in its totality, to recognize the destiny made possible for man by the reality of spirit. Because thought defies the categories of dualism and seems to provide us with freedom to traffic in both sense and spirit, Wordsworth sees in it a principle that assures us of an ultimate unity of self, looks upon it as a faculty by which we may comprehend the ultimate unity of all being. Having formulated this *tertium quid,* neither sense nor spirit, Wordsworth, though retaining the vocabulary of dualism, has, in effect, passed beyond it. Thus, in the metaphor of reconciliation that concludes stanza IX, he feels himself free, despite all that has gone before and despite any apparent contradiction, to claim both that some function of soul carries over into adult life and that some element within natural man can apprehend the eternal; or returning to the poem's symbolic structure, we may both see "that immortal sea / Which brought us hither" and "hear the mighty waters rolling evermore."

His meditation completed and his anxieties dispelled, Wordsworth is able to turn once more to the poem's natural setting, to assume his place again within the landscape of 1802. But he returns having acquired a new conception of natural man that enables him to modify considerably his earlier response to "the gladness of the May." Since thought must ostensibly be classified as a part of the order of nature, its origin and development taking place wholly within our life on earth, Wordsworth has provided himself with a new and useful dichotomy between thought and sense that he can apply to natural man and that then makes possible a new relationship with his physical environment by allowing him to interpret its activities in accordance with the truths of the life of the spirit. With an obvious glance backward at stanza IV, when momentary recovery of the child's intensity of awareness and fullness of emotion had drawn Wordsworth into a purely sensory participation with the joyful but unconscious life about him, Wordsworth in stanza X again speaks of participation in his surroundings. But this time distinctions between man and nature are more carefully maintained, participation is to be more restrained, more mature, more essentially human. Only "in thought," Wordsworth says, will we

> join your throng,
> Ye that pipe and ye that play,
> Ye that through your hearts to-day
> Feel the gladness of the May!
>
> (172–75)

Insofar as human thought and the unconscious processes of nature belong to a single order of being, Wordsworth can still claim a kind of participation in the morning's activities. But his pose is basically that of the contemplative and detached observer, well aware that his dignity, his happiness, his true nature reside in his slowly acquired intellectual powers, those specifically human attributes that set man apart, as different in kind, from the instinctual life of nature.

Contained within this tacit admission of the essential separateness of man and nature, which for Wordsworth marks a crucial break with his own past, is a corollary judgment, especially relevant to our purposes. For Wordsworth, in choosing thought as a new basis for his relationship with nature, has effectively abandoned his quest for self-identity, at least, in its original form. The intensity of response that in stanza IV hopefully indicated a direct and unchanging connection with his childhood self is no longer pertinent to the poem's major concerns, because it is not to the spontaneity of childhood, its precognitive perceptions and responses, that man is now to look for assurance of his well-being. And turning to the poem's other major form of perception, Wordsworth neither seeks to recover nor, indeed, even to grieve for those irrevocably lost pleasures of sight known during "the hour / Of splendour in the grass, of glory in the flower" (178–79). Instead, in the closing lines of stanza X, using a tripartite division somewhat akin to that of *My heart leaps up,* Wordsworth affirms a new principle of continuity, resting not upon some stable element within the flux of self but upon the abiding presence of divinity through all the phases of man's life. In childhood, of course, it is divinity directly intuited that lends authority to this conviction and brings into being that first and most deeply binding sense of "the ineradicable kinship of the soul with the life of God"[12] which Wordsworth speaks of as the "primal sympathy." Even when divinity no longer forms part of the immediate content of our experience, it provides an ordering framework that renders purposeful the harsh processes of our decline, that fosters in maturity "the soothing thoughts that spring / Out of human suffering" (184–85) and beyond that —confronted by the unbending fact of physical dissolution— a "faith that looks through death, / In years that bring the philosophic mind" (186–87).

Having effected this necessary inner reconciliation, Wordsworth once more turns his attention outward to those particulars with which the poem began and denies that his increase in spiritual knowledge has in any way impaired his familiar relationship with nature or led to "any severing of our loves" (189). But it becomes apparent in the lines that follow that, having surrendered delight for submission to a "more habitual sway," Wordsworth now looks to nature for an image of order and expression of law or for a potential allegory of destinies higher than nature's own. This last emerges in the poem's concluding natural observation, an account of the sun's transit that by explicitly mirroring life's pattern quickly restores us to the poem's meditative center and reasserts man's fundamental separateness from, and superiority to, the order of nature. As an analogue to Wordsworth's own experience, the sun's movements initially suggest only the finite limits of a life begun in "innocent brightness" but concluded amidst the darkening shadows of stern actualities, among clouds that "take a sober colouring from an eye / That hath kept watch o'er man's mortality" (198–99). Yet this closing sunset also serves as a kind of period to the day's concrete, temporal events, and "Another race hath been" (200) that, as Professor Raysor suggests, probably means "the race of the sun from dawn to sunset." [13] But, Wordsworth adds, this day has been much unlike other days, its complex meditation having bestowed upon him a special grace, the knowledge of a kingdom beyond nature and of his own freedom from mortality, those other palms just won by him through the assumption of faith.

With the closing lines, Wordsworth brings the poem almost full circle to address gratefully those elements in nature and in man whose collaboration had stimulated uncertainty and occasioned those necessary questionings that concluded in his new spiritual acquisitions:

Thanks to the human heart by which we live,
Thanks to its tenderness, its joys, and fears,
To me the meanest flower that blows can give
Thoughts that do often lie too deep for tears.
                    (201–4)

In a sense, these lines summarize the day's events. For it had
been the promptings of the heart, its anguished need to at-
tune itself once more to the unconscious energies of nature
and thereby to recapture the freedom and spontaneity of
childhood, that had impelled Wordsworth into participation
in the morning's activities. But it was the heart too—dissatisfied by confinement within nature's narrow limits and fear-
ful of what this augured for its human future—that had remained intractable against the encroachment of sense and
had turned Wordsworth, even at the height of involvement
in the present, to remembrance of his vanished past, to the
Pansy (and it seems reasonable in this connection to equate
the Pansy of stanza IV with "the meanest flower" of the closing lines) and its urgent queries. It is upon these, the stirrings of the human heart and the crucial responses of nature,
that Wordsworth has founded his meditation and garnered
for himself those "thoughts that do often lie too deep for
tears" (204), the knowledge of a fixed and changeless order
beyond nature and of the indestructibility of his own spiritual being. And surely there is nothing here for tears.

In assessing the *Ode*'s place in Wordsworth's spiritual
history, we must recognize that its significance for its author,
the reason for its position outside the general categories he
devised for classifying his shorter poems, is not simply that
it declares his faith in immortality. Other poems touch upon
the same subject and indicate the same convictions; but the
Ode alone remains *sui generis,* set apart in magnificent isola-

tion to conclude triumphantly the collected poetry. By examining its complex genesis, its varied contexts, and the elaborate transformations that occur within them, we can discern in the *Ode* not just an affirmation of a life hereafter but, more important, a document of inner revelation and personal conversion, a spiritual record of the mind's advance from doubt to certainty. With the completion of the *Ode,* the pragmatically inspired hope of *Resolution and Independence* that human life stands under the direction of divine providence had been intuitively validated by the direct testimony of the poet's own spiritual experience. Like Bunyan's *Grace Abounding* or Edward's *Personal Narrative,* Wordsworth's great *Ode* is, in essence, a study in conversion, its May morning giving a local habitation and a fixed moment to that experience by which divine truth permanently instilled itself as a living presence within the poet's heart.

If the idea of conversion figures prominently in this discussion of the *Immortality Ode,* it is primarily because the changed state of belief that the poem announces was to prove so enduring. Some form of transcendental faith, either a relatively undogmatic philosophic version of it, as in *Ode to Duty,* or increasingly with the passage of years, a more restrictively Christian expression of transcendence, became from 1804 onward, throughout the remainder of Wordsworth's poetic career, the governing principle in all of his metaphysical speculation.

How immediate and extensive these changes in philosophic orientation are is partially obscured for us by Wordsworth's decision in 1804 to turn his attention again to the introspective history of *The Prelude* and to complete that indispensable preliminary to a still greater undertaking, *The Recluse.* In choosing to return to *The Prelude,* Wordsworth found himself, of necessity, forced to pay heed to the premises with which the poem had originated in 1798 and 1799, the intertwined conceptions of the mind's growth in power and achievement and of nature's beneficent influence upon those who remain receptive to it. And much in these later books does remain consistent with these premises and faithful to the history of his own development as Wordsworth in 1798 had understood it. In the books on Cambridge and London and particularly in those that describe the aftermath of his spiritually debilitating involvement with revolutionary France and philosophic radicalism, the sustaining and improving powers of nature are celebrated almost as exuberantly as they are in the poem's earliest written portions. And in Book VIII, *The Prelude*'s retrospective summary of events prior to his departure for France, the history of Wordsworth's growth is faithfully recapitulated in the same sequence of developmental stages and conditions he had employed in describing that process of growth in 1798 and 1799.

Yet the final effect of the completed *Prelude,* despite these gestures toward its original conception, is not one of philosophic unity.[14] With very few exceptions, episodes of framing or fashioning, the environmental determining of the individual's development, disappear from the poem's epistemological argument after Book II, and mind rather than external impulse assumes the dominant role as shaping agent in the act of perception. The "spots of time," a pair of episodes composed by Wordsworth at the same time as the other childhood incidents described in Book I but not incorporated into the poem's total structure until 1805, probably offer (because of the gap between composition and inclusion) the clearest illustration of the extent to which Wordsworth had reversed his epistemological position during these years. For in their first appearance in the V manuscript, the "spots of time" form part of a series of events describing the sway held by nature over the child's mind, how nature, utilizing the child's preoccupation with other concerns, had managed to impregnate and affix itself to the youthful poet's consciousness in accordance with nature's own formative ends. Or to use the interpretative statement furnished by Wordsworth in the lines that in the V manuscript immediately follow the "spots of time," such incidents show

> How nature by collateral interest
> And by extrinsic passion peopled first
> My mind with forms or beautiful or grand.[15]

When Wordsworth reviewed these events again in 1804 or 1805, having moved them out of their chronological sequence in Book I to the later portion of the poem describing the restoration of imagination following his crisis of rationalism, their continuing significance to him is accounted for on grounds to which he could scarcely have appealed in 1798. Instead of stressing the operations of the external world, nature's "peopling" of a mind presumably receptive to its activities, Wordsworth in his later commentary upon these episodes attributes their enduring importance and renovating power to the feeling induced by them

> that the mind
> Is lord and master, and the outward sense
> Is but the obedient servant of her will.
> (XI, 271–73)

Because these later books tend to minimize the dependence of the mind upon nature, the moments of self-reflection that occur in them speak to us primarily of a consciousness of spiritual autonomy undisturbed by the press of external events; or in moments of deeper revelation, they disclose not merely an independence of the world of sense but the spirit's knowledge of unity with a reality transcending sense. Beginning with Book III, the poem's major occurrences are interpreted less and less frequently as demonstrations of nature's indwelling powers, like the episodes of the stolen boat or the plundered nest, than as manifestations of personal resources, the awesomeness of "the might of Souls, / And what they do within themselves" (III, 178–79), and as revelations emanating from the self-contained life, from "Points" that lie hidden "within our souls, / Where all stand single" (III, 186–87). Thus, Wordsworth's discovery upon returning to Hawkshead that his inner life has been unimpaired during his aimless first year at Cambridge calls forth not the expected statement of obligation or thanksgiving to nature—of the kind offered in *Tintern Abbey*—but claims for the spirit's essential inviolability against the retarding influences of the everyday world. He speaks here of his inward being not in a context of growth and decline or through figures expressing causal determination but in terms of a spiritual life, changeless and "undecaying," that may sleep or wake, be veiled or be "Naked as in the presence of her God" (IV, 142). What his revival at Hawkshead offers Wordsworth is another lesson in "the might of Souls," revealing to him

> How Life pervades the undecaying mind,
> How the immortal Soul with God-like power
> Informs, creates, and thaws the deepest sleep
> That time can lay upon her.
> (IV, 155–58)

The far more important account of spiritual faltering and recovery that dominates the later books concludes in a similar discovery of the soul's changeless powers that, even when obscured or dormant, are recognized as constant and imperishable agents of the poet's viewless, inward life. There had been, he tells us, an interval of temporary "eclipse" (XI, 96) during his alliance with rationalism, and this was followed by an unsuccessful and unsatisfying experiment with nature in which, "craving combinations of new forms, / New pleasure" (XI, 192–93), the eye "rejoiced / To lay the inner faculties asleep" (XI, 194–95). But as these metaphors of eclipse and slumber suggest, the soul's powers remain fundamentally unaffected during these events by the life of outward circumstance. The changes produced by revolution, reason, or pursuit of the picturesque are finally dismissed as accidental and transient, a veil of custom woven to conceal momentarily the essential self:

> I had felt
> Too forcibly, too early in my life,
> Visitings of imaginative power
> For this to last: I shook the habit off
> Entirely and for ever, and again
> In Nature's presence stood, as I stand now,
> A sensitive, and a creative Soul.
>   (XI,   251–57)

Unquestionably there is a major part assigned nature in Wordsworth's final restoration; but what this return of the soul to its former condition implies about nature's agency at this period in Wordsworth's thought is that nature now functions purely as a stimulus to the awakening of the soul's autonomous powers, prompting it to shake from itself—and by itself—the lethargy induced by spiritually numbing "habit." Nowhere, however, does he indicate that nature any longer possesses the influence he had ascribed to it in *The Prelude*'s opening books: that the "creative Soul" that stands "In Nature's presence" is itself the product of that presence's formative effects.

But if the soul that emerges here before nature, therapeutically assisted but in no sense formed by it, seems self-sustaining and hence autonomous, the concept of autonomy is meaningful only so far as it applies to the soul's relationship to the external and material world. For the principal revelation supplied by the poem's two major epiphanies, the moment of illumination in Book VI following the composition of the passage on the crossing of the Alps and the vision granted Wordsworth at the summit of Snowdon, denies to the soul any final autonomy by testifying to the existence of a transcendent reality with which the soul is indissolubly linked and upon which it is ultimately dependent both in this world and beyond it. The first of these revelations supplies the most direct experience of the transcendent, the prefigurative disclosure to the spiritual eye of an "invisible world" that is our true and destined home. But the meditation atop Snowdon, though mediated through the world of eye and ear, extends even further the points of contact between the life of the soul and the "invisible world." Unity with the transcendent as a permanent condition is not, as the earlier passage had indicated, just a future expectation of the soul but a present and continuing actuality of the life of "higher minds," persisting for them even as they carry on their daily commerce with the sensory world. The allegory of the mind's powers furnished by moon, mist, and "the homeless voice of waters" (XIII, 63) presents these powers as in the world but not of it, as emanations from the soul's hidden but ever-flowing source in the transcendent. Such a mind, Wordsworth tells us, carries the kingdom of spirit with it, being

> one that feeds upon infinity,
> That is exalted by an under-presence,
> The sense of God, or whatsoe'er is dim
> Or vast in its own being.
> (XIII, 70–73)

And drifting closer toward a conventionally transcendental epistemology, Wordsworth adds that, for such minds, perceiving and knowing are essentially extensions of the spiritual into the phenomenal, reflexive activities by which

> the highest bliss
> That can be known is theirs, the consciousness
> Of whom they are habitually infused
> Through every image, and through every thought,
> And all impressions.
>
> (XIII, 107–11)

With mind so thoroughly involved in the transcendent, there is clearly little of value nature can offer man in the philosophic scheme derived from the vision at Snowdon. It may provide a pictorial emblem of the unseen, as it does here; or it may act as a reflective medium enabling the soul to comprehend its own nature; or it may, in its most self-negating function, serve as a catalyst to the soul's release from the sensory into a more direct relationship with the transcendent. But nowhere in this closing revelation is it suggested that the impulses of nature can in any way exert that formative influence which in the opening books of *The Prelude* had been the crucial determinant in shaping the minds and characters of the best of men. Indeed, the effect of such influence upon the mind is now characterized as bondage, a restraining of the soul from knowledge of its source. In one of the most striking of the final book's departures from the poem's original empirical premises, Wordsworth speaks of the mind in its transactions with the objective world as being

> By sensible impressions not enthrall'd,
> But quicken'd, rouz'd, and made thereby more fit
> To hold communion with the invisible world.
>
> (XIII, 103–5)

The vision at Snowdon and the philosophic conclusions it leads to are plainly of crucial importance to *The Prelude*. The poem's culminating event and culminating argument, the Snowdon passages, we feel, are intended to disclose to us, firmly and finally, the true directional current that has carried the poem forward in its admittedly wandering course. From these lines we are to understand that *The Prelude*'s detailed personal narrative has been, in its essentials, a recounting of the self's strenuously preserved fidelity to its transcendent origins, its independence of, and superiority to, all external determinants, even nature itself. Though justification for so detailed an autobiographic accounting still remains, as it was in *Home at Grasmere,* the exemplary and instructive instance that the poet's life supplies, what we are now expected to learn from that example, the primary lesson that the life presented in *The Prelude* contains, is not how society may be reconstituted under the benevolent and shaping auspices of nature but how the soul comes finally to perceive its own sanctity and freedom,

> how the mind of man becomes
> A thousand times more beautiful than the earth
> On which he dwells, above this Frame of things
> (Which, 'mid all revolutions in the hopes
> And fears of men, doth still remain unchanged)
> In beauty exalted, as it is itself
> Of substance and of fabric more divine.
> (XIII, 446–52)

Whether these closing lines of *The Prelude* do accurately summarize, as Wordsworth so obviously wishes them to do, the basic argument elaborated by the poem's overall narrative and the commentary accompanying it is a matter open to dispute. With the largest segment of the poem having been written in 1804 and 1805, and with all of that segment (apart from a few scattered sections and passages that by their references to the empirical views of 1798 seem almost vestigial presences within the later books) having been formulated in accordance with the transcendental beliefs of 1804 and 1805, it might well seem that what *The Prelude,* with its recurrent cycle of impairment and restoration, is essentially about is how the autonomous self maintains its inviolability against the pressures of the world. But so simple a measure of meaning as length and bulk fails to do justice to the complexity of the poem as a whole. For the opening books, though they account for a relatively small portion of the entire work, contain episodes of immeasurable consequence for the history of the self, those moments of early and earliest life, some antedating even the dawn of rememberable time, when sensory phenomena engage the mind so powerfully that Wordsworth is willing to credit their workings not only with the largest share of influence in determining the self's future growth and behavior but, even beyond that, with a critical responsibility for the self's very emergence into human life and authentic being. And by attaching so much significance to episodes that show the self's creation and development to be dependent upon processes of external causation—episodes, it should be added, whose prominence is considerably magnified by the memorableness of the poetry they contain —Wordsworth fixes deeply within the scheme of *The Prelude* a pattern of empirical design that is not to be easily banished by the rhetorical assertions of spiritual autonomy and inviolability set forth as the poem's summarizing argument.

Yet the problem of philosophic unity in *The Prelude,* the question of whether the poem is essentially empirical or transcendental in conception or effect, is less relevant to our present purposes than the matter of how these disparate elements in *The Prelude* reflect the shifting course of Wordsworth's thought. Viewed as an event in the history of his thought, the revelation achieved at Snowdon is less a conclusion than a beginning, an extended exposition of the new, nonnaturalistic set of premises that philosophically was to govern Wordsworth's writing not only during the last phase of the golden decade but during the whole of his remaining career as well. For the transition from the later poetry of the golden decade to that written during its long, anticlimactic aftermath involves little in the way of fundamental alteration in the metaphysical and epistemological positions Wordsworth had assumed in 1804. The changes that do occur as we move into the final stages of Wordsworth's career are changes primarily in the means and manner by which these beliefs receive expression, changes both in the voice that articulates them and in the material that illustrates them. That characteristic which more than any other had supplied unity within the philosophic diversity of the poetry written between 1797 and 1805 was a consistent reliance upon the personal and experiential as the basis of authority for belief: the revelations of *Tintern Abbey, Resolution and Independence,* and the *Immortality Ode,* or those of *The Prelude* that had arisen from stealing a boat or ascending Snowdon were, however dissimilar their philosophical implications, essentially alike in being personal revelations, their several truths given credence by the validating authority of direct experience. Where personal revelation in 1798 had enabled Wordsworth to formulate a philosophic scheme uniquely his own, the major revelations of the winter and early spring of 1804, the months in which he described his reactions to the crossing of the Alps, presented his meditation on Snowdon, and wrote the last seven stanzas of the *Immortality Ode,* convey beliefs that already exist as the fundamental articles of established religious faith: the superiority of the human soul to its natural surroundings; the reality of a realm transcendent and eternal, an "invisible world" that is that soul's destined dwelling place; and the abiding fact of the imperishability of the individual consciousness, the immortality of the soul. Because of this, the revelatory episodes of 1804 seem less discovery than corroboration, providing Wordsworth with that necessary personal assurance to affirm for himself, as authentic truths of experience, those Christian principles that it seems clear at this time he wished to accept. Once these principles had been authenticated by personal revelation, however, the need for such revelation soon diminished; the widely shared creed that Wordsworth came finally, in 1804, to adopt and during the remainder of his poetic life to expound, possessed other sources of confirmation, more traditional and familiar, and, therefore, more likely to appeal to that audience Wordsworth sought to reach and instruct.

In availing himself of these alternative sources of confirmation of belief, as he did in the years following completion of *The Prelude,* Wordsworth, of course, submitted to a new control, one that was to have a deep and permanent effect upon his poetic future. But the changes that take place after 1805 and that determine the character of his poetry for all the long years thereafter result not from any dramatic shift in doctrine itself, a movement of the mind from disbelief or even doubt to orthodoxy, for the philosophic foundations of that orthodoxy had already been firmly established in the writings of 1804. It is rather the transfer of authority itself that stands as the crucial act, the determining influence upon Wordsworth's choice of subject and form, voice and diction, during that final and most extended phase of his career. From the hiding places of power, now closed or, perhaps, no longer sought after, Wordsworth turned for sanction for his poetic argument to publicly accredited sources of faith, the authorized creeds and settled traditions of Christian faith. But establishing this authority required that it be given forms of expression more conventional and impersonal than those developed before 1805. For the poetry of illumination and remembrance, Wordsworth substituted what is essentially a poetry of public statement, a received faith expounded through the narrative example and moral generalization that replaced the direct reports of vision. Where the moment of epiphany, intense and private, gave the life described in *The Prelude* its meaning and significance, *The Excursion, The Prelude's* epic counterpart of Wordsworth's later years, unsurprisingly utilized more detached and customary methods of exposition, the cautionary history of the Wanderer, the blank-verse sermons of the Pastor, and the illustrative tales of his departed parishioners forming the basis of the poem's moral argument.

The relationship of Wordsworth's poetic decline to the adoption of these more objective modes of poetic discourse cannot, of course, be determined with any exactness or certainty. Such a poetry of conventional form and public voice need not be without its own value and interest, and it must still remain puzzling to us that a poet possessing Wordsworth's gifts and resources could not achieve a greater success in this mode. Yet the fact of decline—indeed, collapse—seems an almost inescapable conclusion; and the poetry of Wordsworth's later career, as even those who must be numbered among his most sympathetic readers have generally acknowledged, is a poetry that rarely engages us. The answer to the problem of the failure of Wordsworth after 1805 may lie, however, not in the adequacy of his poetic powers to his newly adopted poetic mode but in the transfer of authority which required that he adopt that mode. This does not mean that Wordsworth's decline is a kind of parable for poets, illustrating the ill effects of choosing political conservatism or religious orthodoxy, for the decision for conservatism and orthodoxy was already implicit and rendered powerfully in the great revelatory poems and passages of 1804; it means rather that having passed through and having understood the philosophic situation in which man found himself in the post-Christian world, having learned that only personal revelation could authenticate our beliefs, and that the world view we have assumed—a world view conditioned by the perceptions and feelings of individual experience—must therefore be unshared, uniquely our own, Wordsworth could never extend to external authority that depth of conviction and firmness of assurance that poets who had come before him, untouched by the transforming power of modern life, were able so easily to do. It is as if the early poetry stood always in judgment upon the later, a subversive presence continually calling into question the genuineness of that assent which after 1805 Wordsworth would give only to an authority whose origins could be traced to the common beliefs and traditions of generations of men.

The ready moral to be drawn from the Wordsworthian decline is that the modern spirit with its trust in the independent and personal judgment cannot be forsaken without just such a price being exacted in spontaneity and joy and power as Wordsworth himself was compelled to pay. Yet even in this there is a saving integrity that does much to mitigate so costly a failure. For Wordsworth paid his price only because he refused to shield the optimistic faith that answered so well to his wishes, the teleological naturalism of *Tintern Abbey,* from critical scrutiny, because he proved willing to submit himself to the further demands of the modern spirit and to acknowledge even those darker facts of experience whose harsh truths were certain to disturb his first hopes and desires. If in the end there were to be compromises and defections, and Wordsworth was to turn elsewhere for faith when he could not accept as final that skepticism to which submission to experience eventually led (a demand of the modern spirit that would not be fully met in our poetry until this century), Wordsworth had, nonetheless, served that spirit well and faithfully, providing us in his subordination of system to experience, of desire to fact, with a crucial instance—perhaps our first example—of heroic sincerity, the openness and honesty which that spirit required be applied impartially to all creeds, even those of its own creation.

1. This shift from visual to auditory imagery is pointed out by Cleanth Brooks in his essay on the *Ode*, "Wordsworth and the Paradox of Imagination," in *The Well Wrought Urn* (New York, 1947), pp. 124–50. As Brooks notes, at the one point in these two stanzas in which a visual image is used, "I see / The heavens laugh with you in your jubilee," Wordsworth has not really deviated from the consistent pattern because "another strong auditory image intervenes again to make sound the dominant sense, not sight. One sees a smile, but laughter is vocal" (p. 135).

2. *Wordsworth's Literary Criticism,* ed. Nowell C. Smith (London, 1905), pp. 82–83.

3. *PW,* IV, 463–64.

4. Thomas M. Raysor, "The Themes of Immortality and Natural Piety in Wordsworth's Immortality Ode," *PMLA* 69 (1954): 867. Though some of the evidence cited by Raysor (the title, the placement of the poems in the collected works, the Clarkson letter, and the Fenwick note) are of a later date than the poem, they are, nonetheless, valid as external evidence because they reinforce rather than conflict with views already present in the poem in 1804.

5. Ibid., p. 862.

6. *PW,* IV, 452.

7. Ibid., pp. 365–66 (Appendix B, III, ii).

8. Ibid., p. 463.

9. Ibid., p. 464.

10. *Wordsworth's Literary Criticism,* p. 83.

11. Hirsch, p. 169.

12. Raysor, p. 870.

13. Ibid., p. 871.

14. An excellent discussion of the philosophic changes that occur in the books of *The Prelude* written in 1804 and 1805 appears in Edward E. Bostetter, *The Romantic Ventriloquists* (Seattle, 1963), pp. 42–52.

15. *Prelude,* I, 572–73 (MS. V).

Index

PERSONS

POEMS, PREFACES, AND ESSAYS